SUPER LIFE, SUPER HEALTH

Publisher's Note

This book is for information only. It does not constitute medical advice and should not be construed as such. We cannot guarantee the safety or effectiveness of any drug, treatment, or advice mentioned. Some of these tips may not be effective for everyone.

A good doctor is the best judge of what medical treatment may be needed for certain conditions and diseases. We recommend in all cases that you contact your personal doctor or health care provider before taking or discontinuing any medication, or before treating yourself in any way.

In everything you do, stay away from complaining
and arguing, so that no one can speak a word of
blame against you. You are to live clean, innocent
lives as children of God in a dark world full of
people who are crooked and stubborn. Shine out
among them like beacon lights, holding out to them
the Word of Life.

Phillipians 2:14-16 TLB

A glad heart makes a healthy body, but a crushed
spirit makes the bones dry.

Proverbs 17:22 BBE

CONTENTS

Super Health Secrets

Super Life Extenders

If only, when one heard
That Old Age was coming
One could bolt the door,
Answer "Not at home"
And refuse to meet him!

Anonymous Japanese poet (905)

SEARCH FOR ETERNAL YOUTH

Man is constantly searching for a way to bolt the door against old age. This poem, written in Japan in 905, shows that avoiding old age has been a common goal among people the world over for centuries. Many people in different parts of the world at different times in history made it their life's obsession. Though no one has succeeded in finding eternal youth, some did at least become well-known for their efforts.

❧ Ponce de Leon searched for years for the mysterious fountain of youth. He discovered Florida instead. With its sunny weather, beautiful beaches, and palm trees, perhaps Florida itself is a kind of fountain of youth. Many people today who retire to Florida do seem to recover their youthful energy and vigor. Ponce de Leon

1

died in Florida in 1521 from a poisoned-arrow wound. He was 61, which was extremely old by 16th century standards. Maybe old Ponce found the fountain of youth after all — and just didn't tell anyone.

❦ In 1808, Goethe wrote of a 14th century alchemist, Faust, who sold his soul to the devil in exchange for a youth-restoring potion. As you might expect of someone willing to sell his soul to the devil, Faust came to an unpleasant end.

❦ In 1890, Oscar Wilde wrote *The Picture of Dorian Gray*, a novel about a man with a picture of himself in his attic that grew old while he remained young. In the end, however, Dorian Gray lost his eternal youth and his life.

---

8 TIPS FOR A LONGER, HEALTHIER LIFE

According to the Oakland-Alameda Health Study, conducted in Oakland, Calif., there are eight things you can do to live a longer, healthier life.

❦ Eat breakfast every day
❦ Maintain a sensible weight for your height
❦ Stop smoking
❦ Exercise every day
❦ Eat a variety of fresh foods
❦ Learn how to handle stress
❦ Get six to eight hours of sleep a night
❦ Drink less than 2 ounces of alcohol a day

This study found that people who followed more than five of these recommendations typically lived 6.7 years longer than people who followed less than five.

Throughout history, man has been fascinated with remaining young and living longer. Books and poems written centuries apart contain the universal theme of fictional quests for eternal youth. In real life, doctors and scientists have searched throughout the ages for ways to help people live longer.

Today, people are living longer than ever before, thanks to medical advances like the invention of the smallpox vaccine and the discovery of penicillin and other antibiotics. The skill of plastic surgeons has even enabled many people to keep their youthful appearance long into old age.

The eternal search for eternal youth goes on. There's nothing wrong with wanting to remain young and healthy as long as possible. Although no one lives forever, the search for eternal youth has uncovered secrets you can use to help you live a longer, healthier life.

Education is the best provision for old age.

Aristotle (384 - 322 B.C.)

THE MYSTERY OF AGING

Education is probably not only the best provision for old age but the best insurance against old age. You can educate yourself about strategies for combating aging and its effects by taking advantage of the education and wisdom of others. Research scientists are continually searching for answers to the questions of aging.

The first question could be: What is aging? According to Denham Harmon, one of the leading experts in the field of anti-aging research, "Aging is the progressive accumulation of changes with time associated with or responsible for the ever-increasing likelihood of disease and death which accompanies advancing age."

In other words, your body gradually wears out. When you buy a new car, it has a lot of pep and all the nice gadgets work correctly. However, after thousands of miles and years of use, things begin to wear out. Belts break, fenders rust, brake pads wear thin, and the knobs fall off your radio. Some things can be replaced or repaired, and some you can just live without.

Your body is similar. You might break a bone and have it set. You can't see as well as you once did, and so you get eyeglasses. Your hearing may start to go, but you decide that you can live with a little hearing loss. All that noise distracted you anyway. Like the knobs on your radio, you might consider it optional equipment, not worth the effort to repair or replace.

Sometimes major problems require major repairs, like triple bypass surgery to repair a faulty heart. Modern medicine has even made it possible to get new parts, like transplanted organs or prosthetic limbs. Long John Silver's wooden peg leg has been replaced by state-of-the-art plastic and metal creations.

All these medical innovations have helped extend man's life expectancy greatly. A child born in 1900 could expect to live about 47.5 years. A child born in 1993 can expect to live 75.5 years, an increase of about 28 years ... you can accomplish a lot in 28 years.

Because people are living longer, the population of older people is growing rapidly. In the United States, the percentage of people over 65 has tripled, from 4.1 percent in 1900 to 12.7 percent in 1994. Today there are about 33 million people age 65 or older living in the United States, but by the year 2030, there will be about 70 million.

But merely living longer isn't good enough, and it shouldn't be. People want to live longer, healthier lives. Who wants to live longer if it means just existing, unable to enjoy life?

Number of Persons Over Age 65: 1900 to 2030

1900	3.1 million	1994	33.2 million
1920	4.9 million	2000	35.3 million
1940	9.0 million	2010	40.1 million
1960	16.7 million	2020	53.3 million
1980	25.7 million	2030	70.2 million

Based on data from the U.S. Bureau of the Census

Fortunately, modern research has provided the information you need to fight aging and enjoy the benefits of a super life-span and super health.

Though theories on aging abound, most scientists agree that there is not just one cause but rather a combination of factors. However, the free radical theory is currently the leading theory of aging. Although the free radical theory is not the only one, because it is the most accepted, many sections of this book will deal with how to fight free radical damage.

FREE RADICAL THEORY OF AGING

"Too many free radicals, that's your problem."

"Free radicals, Sir?"

"Yes. They're toxins that destroy the body and brain caused by eating too much red meat and white bread and too many dry Martinis."

"Then I shall cut out the bread, Sir."

James Bond in Never Say Never Again (Ian Fleming 1983)

You know your body wears out over time, but why? Exactly what drives this process that slowly robs you of your health and vigor? Your body ages because your cells become damaged, and your body can't repair them fast enough. There are many different reasons for this damage, and scientists don't agree on which one is the main cause. But most agree on this: The long-term effect of this wear and tear on the cells in your tissues is the main factor in aging. This gradual damage reduces the number of brain cells you have, allows some of the cells in your body to become cancerous, destroys the part of your cells that produces energy, limits blood flow by clogging your arteries, and weakens your heart.

In the mid 1950s, Denham Harmon was toiling in a science lab at the University of Nebraska. His hard work paid off when he proposed the free radical theory of aging. His name is famous in the research world, and the free radical theory is more widely accepted today than any other in the scientific and medical communities.

Take a deep breath. Feel refreshed? As you breathe, you take in invigorating oxygen. Without oxygen, you will die, but as your body processes oxygen, it also produces chemicals called free radicals. These free radicals are molecules that are unstable because they lack an electron. They travel through your body like a band of pickpockets, trying to steal electrons from healthy cells. When they succeed, they leave the cell irreversibly damaged. One damaged cell will not usually cause your body much distress. But over time, lots of these pickpocket molecules can cause so much damage that your body becomes weak and more likely to fall prey to cancer and heart disease. This cell damage is called oxidation, and it is similar to the oxidation of metal that produces rust.

Don't feel betrayed by your body because it creates these roving thieves. Luckily, your body also produces antioxidants, which neutralize free radicals. Antioxidants fight oxidation by combining with free radicals to form a harmless substance or by contributing an electron to the free radical, making it stable. However, when free radical levels get too high, these protective processes can't keep up. Cigarette smoke, pollution, radiation, stress, excessive sun exposure, and other factors can increase your level of free radicals, causing you to use up your store of antioxidants more quickly. In addition, as you get older, your body's production of antioxidants slows down, allowing free radicals to damage more and more of your cells.

MAJOR ANTIOXIDANTS

❦ Vitamin E	❦ Vitamin C
❦ Selenium	❦ Beta-carotene
❦ Vitamin A	❦ Zinc
❦ Gingko	❦ Ginseng
❦ Melatonin	❦ Pycnogenol
❦ Glutathione	❦ Coenzyme Q-10
❦ Chromium	

How can you stop free radicals from slowly taking over your body, overpowering and outnumbering your antioxidant protectors? You can help your body manufacture antioxidants, like glutathione, and you can get other antioxidants, like vitamins E and C, from your diet. The following chapters will show you how.

Are antioxidants really that important? Only if you want to live a longer, healthier life. Researchers are continually finding new evidence of the benefits of antioxidants. They can, for example:

Prevent heart disease. Your heart pumps oxygen-rich blood to every part of your body, from your toes to your scalp. How can antioxidants help keep your heart pumping smoothly for years? Atherosclerosis, or hardening of the arteries, begins when too much LDL (bad) cholesterol in your blood causes a build-up of fatty plaque on your artery walls. This plaque makes your arteries narrower, causing your heart to work much harder to pump blood throughout your body. The harder your heart works, the faster it wears out. Research shows that exposure to free radicals oxidizes LDL cholesterol and makes it even more damaging to your arteries.

In laboratories, antioxidant vitamins E, C, and beta-carotene have been shown to help prevent the oxidation of LDL. Animals deprived of these vitamins often develop fatty deposits in their

BEST FOOD SOURCES OF ANTIOXIDANTS

Vitamin C:

Citrus fruits, broccoli, strawberries, turnip greens, cantaloupe, brussels sprouts

Vitamin E:

Whole wheat, oats, yeast, brown rice, wheat germ

Beta-carotene:

Carrots, broccoli, sweet potatoes, cantaloupe, apricots, spinach

Selenium:

Whole grains, brown rice, fish, liver, legumes (beans, peas, and soy products)

arteries. Many studies have shown that people who eat diets rich in antioxidants have a lower risk of heart disease.

Lower cancer risk. What's the last word you want to hear from your doctor? If you're like most people, it's cancer — the most feared disease of all. Billions of dollars in research have been spent trying to wipe out this killer in the United States. Though great strides have been made in the treatment of cancer, the number of new cases continues to rise every year. How can you stop this killer from adding you to the statistics? Numerous studies have shown that a high level of antioxidants is associated with a low risk of developing most, if not all, types of cancer.

Antioxidants can help prevent a serious disease like cancer by protecting your DNA. DNA contains all the genetic information necessary for life and is present in every cell of your body. DNA has a lot of surface area and offers a large target for free radicals. By the time you are 70, the DNA in each of your cells has sustained hundreds of thousands of direct hits from free radicals. Most of the time, your DNA has the ability to repair itself, and this free-radical damage may not be too serious. But the odds are fairly good that in at least one of your trillions of cells, free radicals will cause damage in your DNA that won't be repaired. The result is a mutant cell, and it only takes one mutant cell to cause cancer.

To protect your body from cancer, make sure you have plenty of antioxidants guarding your cells. Remember ... an ounce of prevention is worth a pound of cure.

Help keep bones strong. Can an orange help fend off joint pain as you get older? Osteoarthritis, the most common form of arthritis, strikes many people as they age, making life painful and restricting activities. In a recent study, people with osteoarthritis of the knee who ate foods high in vitamin C experienced less pain, and their osteoarthritis didn't get worse. Vitamin E and beta carotene, also antioxidants, seem to have the same protective effect, but more research is needed.

Protect your vision. Ever see a rabbit wearing eyeglasses? Yes, it's an old joke, but if everyone would eat more of the green, leafy vegetables that rabbits love to steal from gardens,

THE FLIES HAVE IT

While theories like this often look good on paper, the true test comes in the laboratory. One of the first to hint at the power of free radicals to promote aging came in 1985. Rajindar S. Sohal, Ph.D., conducted an experiment using flies. One group of flies was kept in a container large enough for them to fly around like they normally would. The other group was kept in such small containers that their flight was restricted. The flies in the big container lived a normal life span of about 28 days, while the flies in the smaller containers lived 65 days. Dr. Sohal attributed the difference to the fact that movement causes more intake of oxygen. The flies that couldn't move consumed less oxygen, which resulted in fewer free radicals. That slowed the aging process and allowed the flies who couldn't fly to live longer. Luckily, there are other ways to fight free radicals than lying still all the time.

perhaps fewer people would lose their sight as they age. Age-related macular degeneration is the leading cause of blindness in people over age 65. One study found that people who ate lots of dark green, leafy vegetables, which contain carotenoids, were almost half as likely to develop macular degeneration. Carotenoids make up the yellow coloring of the macula, or central retina. Researchers speculate that carotenoids protect the macula by absorbing light that could set off free radical damage in your eye. Another study found that antioxidant supplements help stop vision loss in people with macular degeneration.

Improve mental function. If you worry about growing senile in your old age, be sure you get plenty of antioxidants. The loss of a certain amount of mental abilities with advancing age was once considered unavoidable. Not according to at least one scientific experiment. The experiment compared old and young gerbils and found that the old gerbils had more difficulty running a maze than the young ones. However, when the old gerbils received antioxidant injections, their maze-running abilities returned to the level of their more youthful companions.

Protect your immune system. Dangerous germs lurk everywhere in your environment. Fortunately, your body contains an army of killer cells whose specific job is to attack and destroy foreign substances like bacteria. This is how your immune system protects you from disease and infection. Free-radical damage, however, can reduce the number of fighting cells in your

CROSS-LINKING: ANOTHER THEORY ON AGING

The free radical theory is the big kid on the aging theory block, but it is by no means the only one. There are several other theories, and although none are as widely accepted as the free radical theory, one other major theory does deserves mention.

The cross-linking or glucose theory. You know too much sugar can cause cavities in your teeth. If it can eat holes in tooth enamel, which is the hardest substance in the human body, just imagine what it might be doing to your cells.

Glucose, a form of sugar, is actually essential to life. It is your body's main fuel, but too much of a good thing can hurt you. Besides causing you to gain extra pounds, glucose may, over time, damage certain proteins in your body, like collagen. Collagen helps form bones, teeth, skin, and tendons. These damaged proteins may become cross-linked to each other and cause tissues to become stiff. This may contribute to hardening of the arteries, cataracts, nerve damage, and kidney problems.

Although cross-linking usually occurs as you get older, it also happens to younger people with diabetes. In fact, diabetes is sometimes considered an accelerated model of aging.

immune system. This makes you more likely to get sick. Antioxidants can help keep your immune system working at full force.

Keep your skin young, too? If antioxidants can battle free radicals in your body, can antioxidants on your skin protect it from the damage that sun, weather, and time can cause? Many cosmetic companies think so. You can now buy moisturizers and other skin-care products that contain antioxidants like vitamins E, A, and C. Though it would take years to determine if antioxidants on your skin can keep it young, research shows that sunscreen does help stop skin damage. If you're going to put something on your skin every day in an effort to keep it young and dewy, use sunscreen. If your sunscreen has antioxidants in it, you may just double your skin-protection quotient.

Since antioxidants are such incredible disease-fighting powerhouses, should you take megadoses? No ... more is not necessarily always better. For example, zinc is an essential mineral that improves your senses of taste, smell, and sight and boosts your immune system. However, if you take too much zinc, it can block your absorption of copper and cause your level of harmful LDL cholesterol to rise.

You may think that good old vitamin C could never hurt you. But did you know that high levels of iron in your body can cause vitamin C to become a "pro"oxidant instead of an "anti"oxidant, making it harmful to your body instead of helpful?

It's simple. Pick your parents very carefully.

Dick Clark,
when asked about his secret for staying young

THE GENETIC CONNECTION

Obviously, you can't pick your parents, otherwise Ozzie and Harriet would have had thousands of children. However, who your parents are can have a huge impact on how long you live. Diseases that can cut your life short, like heart disease, Alzheimer's, and most types of cancer, have a strong genetic connection.

Long before scientists knew what genes were, people knew that certain diseases ran in families. Children can inherit the tendency to develop deadly diseases from their parents just as they can inherit blue eyes or red hair.

Scientists now know that traits children inherit from their parents are controlled by genes. You have thousands of pairs of genes in your body. Genes come in pairs because you inherit one from your father and one from your mother. Some genes are dominant and some are recessive. If you inherit just one dominant gene from a parent, you will have the trait that gene controls.

For example, some people can roll up their tongues like a tube, and some people can't. The gene for that ability is dominant, so if you inherit that gene from your mother, but not your father, you will still be able to roll your tongue. If a gene is

PUTTING GENES TO THE TEST

Did you know that genetic testing can identify many genes responsible for diseases? Tests are now available for genes that cause or contribute to Alzheimer's; osteoporosis; Huntington's disease; and breast, ovarian, and colon cancers, as well as many other less common conditions.

Would you want to know if you were going to inherit a deadly disease? According to a survey, 49 percent of the people polled would want to be tested, while 51 percent would not. What are the benefits of genetic testing? Some tests, like the one for Huntington's disease, can tell you for sure if you will get the disease. Most tests, however, can only tell you if you are more likely to get the disease than most people. If you can take steps to reduce your risk, this information may be life-saving, but for some people, the stress of knowing they are likely to get a serious disease can do more harm than good.

Another factor to consider before having genetic testing is how it might affect your health insurance. Would your rates go up if your insurance company becomes aware that you are at risk for a particular disease?

Genetic testing for healthy people is very controversial. If scientists learn how to safely alter dangerous genes, genetic testing may become a routine exam done at birth. Until then, the decision to test or not to test is up to you.

recessive, you must inherit that gene from both your parents to inherit the trait.

Push your hair back from your forehead and look at your hairline. Does it grow straight across, or does it point down into a "widow's peak?" If your hair grows straight across, you inherited that gene from both parents because the widow's peak gene is dominant, and the straight across gene is recessive. In other words, if you had a widow's peak gene, it would bully the recessive gene into not showing up.

Since genes can affect your health in the same way they affect your appearance, genetic research may one day unlock the secret to a healthy, longer life.

Headlines recently have been filled with news about genes. "Scientists isolate gene that controls obesity," or "New test identifies gene for Alzheimer's Disease." This may sound very hopeful, and it is. But simple it isn't. If you've ever had a diagnostic test done on your car, you know that the mechanic hooks it up to a computer, and you get a five-foot-long printout of every part of your car that could possibly be malfunctioning. The mechanic identifies the problem and fixes it.

Unfortunately, our bodies aren't quite as simple as a car (and cars are pretty complex these days.) You can't just go get a diagnostic test, find out everything that's wrong with you, and get those things fixed.

Very few diseases are controlled by just one dominant gene. Huntington's disease is one exception. If you have the gene, you have the illness, as well as the potential to pass it on to your children. A few other diseases are controlled by a pair of recessive genes, like cystic fibrosis. You have to inherit the gene from both your parents in order to have the disease.

Most diseases, like heart disease and cancer, are controlled by several pairs of genes. For example, the likelihood that you will develop heart disease is influenced by genes that control cholesterol.

Scientists recently discovered a gene they call apo A-1. In some people, this gene seems to cause high concentrations of HDL (good) cholesterol. Since a high level of HDL cholesterol is associated with a lower risk of heart disease, people with this apo A-1 gene tend to live longer than average. Genes like this are sometimes referred to as "Methuselah genes." They just might help some people live well into their golden years.

The genes that control metabolism also affect your heart. You all know some lucky person who seems to be able to eat and eat and never gain a pound. Now that's genetics in action, but genes do not determine for certain who will get heart disease and who won't. Lifestyle factors can make a difference as well. Diet, exercise, and how you handle stress all play a role in keeping your heart, and the rest of your body, in good health.

You can't change your genes, but understanding genetics can help you live longer. If you know that heart disease runs in your family, you have an extra incentive to keep your heart healthy by changing your diet and lifestyle.

"If I could save time in a bottle ..."

Jim Croce

ANTI-AGING SUPPLEMENTS

People searching for eternal youth are looking for just that — time in a bottle of supplements. Shelves in health food stores, drugstores, and supermarkets are crammed with a confusing array of pills, powders, creams, and elixirs claiming to restore your lost youth and extend your life.

Do you need to take supplements? If so, with so many choices, how do you decide what to buy? Can a pill, or a variety of pills, help you live a longer, healthier life? How do you know what a particular vitamin, mineral, or herb can do for you?

The answers are in this book. You'll find the latest information about anti-aging dietary substances and strategies. You'll also learn the most natural ways to get these dietary substances. Read the cautions and consumer advice sections carefully before you decide to use a particular dietary substance. If the benefits don't outweigh the risks, it should get a thumbs down.

Supplements, however, cannot replace a well-balanced diet. Most experts agree that the best anti-aging strategy is to eat the right foods. Foods contain many nutrients that scientists cannot isolate and put in a pill.

Remember when your mother forced you to eat broccoli because it was good for you? Mom always knows best. People who secretly fed their broccoli to the dog under the table as children probably won't eat it as adults — just ask former U.S. president George Bush. Even though research provides over-whelming evidence that people who eat lots of fruits and vegetables have a lower risk of the diseases associated with aging, most people still don't eat enough of them.

The United States government recommends that you eat at least five servings of fruits and vegetables every day, but only about 9 percent of Americans actually eat that much.

Even though getting your nutrients from food is best, some studies have found that supplements did decrease the risk of certain diseases. For example, in one study, people who took vit-amin E supplements had fewer deaths from heart disease.

On the other hand, one important study on beta-carotene in Finland found that smokers who took beta-carotene supple-ments actually had a greater risk of lung cancer. Of course, stud-ies can be flawed. Most of the people in the Finnish study were men who had smoked over a pack a day for almost 40 years. Perhaps it was too late for a mere supplement to help them, but that doesn't necessarily mean supplements won't help you.

READING SUPPLEMENT LABELS

If you go to a health food store and look at the labels on the supplement bottles, you won't find much information except ingredients. That's because these substances are considered dietary supplements. According to law in the United States, no claims for medicinal use can be made on the label.

VITAMINS AND MINERALS

A wise man should consider that health is the greatest of human blessings, and learn how by his own thought to derive benefit from his illnesses.

Hippocrates (460 - 377 B.C.)

Hippocrates is the father of modern medicine. In fact, the oath that medical students take prior to officially becoming doctors is called the Hippocratic oath. His advice to derive benefit from your illnesses was taken to heart by many researchers, including the discoverers of vitamins and minerals. Because of this discovery, you can benefit greatly from the illnesses of people from the past.

The ancient Chinese were the first to identify and record the symptoms of a vitamin deficiency disease. Beriberi is a thiamin deficiency disease that causes pain, weakness, nausea, vomiting, constipation, and mental disturbances. In extreme cases, it can be fatal. Over 4,000 years ago, about the same time the milling process for rice was used, Chinese people experienced an increase in the incidence of beriberi. Thiamin is found in the husks or bran of rice. When the Chinese began to mill their rice, they were removing their supply of thiamin, causing large numbers of people to suffer beriberi. It was not until 1900 that the connection between rice hulls and beriberi was proven. Today, thiamin is added to milled rice products, a process called enriching the rice.

In 1753, a British Naval doctor found that limes, lemons, and fresh green produce taken on long ocean voyages could prevent scurvy. Scurvy is a vitamin C deficiency disease that causes fatigue, bleeding gums, loose teeth, bruising, and hemorrhaging, which can be fatal. Although Americans of the 18th century began to call British sailors "limeys" because of the fruit they carried with them on voyages, this fruit may have helped make the British navy the strongest in the world at the time.

Unfortunately, a 1912 expedition to the South Pole did not follow the example the British navy set over a century before. They did not take foods with vitamin C on their expedition, and every member died of scurvy.

Today we know much more about vitamins and minerals than the unfortunate people who died from scurvy or beriberi. However, with so much information, it's easy to become confused. Simply reading labels in the store may leave you with more questions than answers.

What are vitamins? Vitamins are a group of compounds vital to life. Vitamin deficiencies can make you sick.

Vitamins are either water-soluble or fat-soluble. Water-soluble means they dissolve easily in water. These vitamins are stored in your body for just a few days before they are washed away. Your supply of water-soluble vitamins needs to be replenished every day. They include vitamin C and the B-complex vitamins.

UNDERSTANDING FOOD LABELS

It's best to get the nutrients you need from food, but how do you know if you're getting enough? The U.S. government has established levels of certain nutrients that it recommends you get every day. The government requires that food be labeled with information to help you determine if you are getting these recommended levels.

When looking at a food label, the first item you should look at is the serving size, because all other information is based on that. The levels of nutrients are listed on a percent daily value, based on a 2,000 calorie a day diet. This will help you determine about how much of each nutrient you take in from the food you eat. If you eat enough to add up to 100 percent, you have met the U.S. Recommended Dietary Allowance (RDA) for that nutrient. If you decide you need more than you are getting from your diet, you may decide to take a supplement.

It is important to take into consideration the amount of nutrients you get from your food and add that to the amount you get from your supplement. You want to get enough, but not too much.

How To Read A Supplement Label*

BRAND NAME Tablets USP ◄——

USP means that product meets U.S. Pharmacopeia standards for quality, strength, purity, packaging, and labeling.

Serving Size is the manufacturer's suggested serving. It can be stated per tablet, capsule, soft-gel, packet, or teaspoonful.

Amount Per Serving identifies the nutrients contained in the supplement, followed by the quantity present in each serving.

International Unit (I.U.) is a unit of measurement for vitamins A, D, and E.

Milligrams (mg) and micrograms (mcg) are units of measurement for B complex and C vitamins and minerals.

Nutrition Facts
Serving Size 1 tablet

Amount Per Serving	Daily Value
Vitamin A 5000 I.U.	100%
50% as Beta-Carotene	
Vitamin C 60mg	100%
Vitamin D 400 I.U.	100%
Vitamin E 30 I.U.	100%
Thiamine 1.5 mg	100%
Riboflavin 1.7 mg	100%
Niacin 20 mg	100%
Vitamin B6 2 mg	100%
Folate 0.4 mg	100%
Vitamin B12 6 mcg	100%
Calcium 120 mg	10%
Iron 15 mg	100%
Iodine 150 mg	100%
Magnesium 100 mg	25%
Zinc 15 mg	100%
Boron 5 mg	*
Copper 2 mg	100%

*Daily Value not established

Daily Value (DV) is a label reference term to indicate the percent of the recommended daily amount of each nutrient that serving provides.

A complete list of all ingredients used in the product appears outside the Nutrition Facts box. The nutrients are listed in decreasing order by weight.

INGREDIENTS: vitamin A acetate, beta-carotene, lactose, magnesium stearate, talc, starch, ascorbic acid, ergocalciferol, d-alpha tocopherol acetate, thiamine hydrochloride, riboflavin, niacinamide, pyridoxine hydrochloride, folic acid, vitamin B12, calcium gluconate, ferrous sulfate, sodium iodide, magnesium sulfate, zinc chloride, sodium metaborate, copper.

Directions: Take one tablet daily with a meal.

STORAGE: Keep tightly closed in a dry place; do not expose to excessive heat.

Storage information for the product.

KEEP OUT OF THE REACH OF CHILDREN

All dietary supplements (especially those containing iron) should be kept out of the reach of children.

This is the manufacturer's batch number for the product.

LOT # 87QF

EXPIRATION DATE: May 2005

This is the expiration date for the product. It should be used before this date to assure full potency.

Manufacturer or distributor's name, address, and zip code

*This is a sample supplement label and is not intended to describe a particular product.

Copied from *The USP Guide to Vitamins and Minerals*,
©1996 The USP Convention, Inc. Permission granted.

Fat-soluble vitamins, on the other hand, are stored in your body's fat supply and in certain organs, like your liver. Vitamins A, D, E, and K are fat soluble. Because they are stored for longer periods of time, it is easier to accumulate toxic amounts.

What are minerals? Minerals are naturally occurring chemical elements your body uses to help perform certain chemical reactions. You need minerals to build strong bones and blood and maintain healthy nerves. If you become deficient in important minerals, you can become sick.

Minerals are divided into two groups: major minerals and trace minerals. Your body needs larger amounts of major minerals than trace minerals, although trace minerals can be just as important for good health. Calcium, chloride, phosphorus, potassium, sodium, sulfur, and magnesium are major minerals. Iodine, iron, zinc, selenium, fluoride, chromium, copper, molybdenum, and manganese are trace minerals.

How much do you need? Although scientists seem to agree that vitamins and minerals are necessary for life, not all scientists agree on how much of each one you need. In an effort to help people decide how much of certain nutrients they need, the Food and Nutrition Board of the National Academy of Sciences has set RDAs for vitamins, minerals, and other dietary substances. In the book published by the National Academy of Sciences describing these allowances, they define RDAs as "the levels of intake of essential nutrients that, on the basis of scientific knowledge, are judged by the Food and Nutrition Board to be adequate to meet the known nutrient needs of practically all healthy persons." RDAs are established for different age groups, males and females, and for pregnant or breast-feeding women.

RECOMMENDED DIETARY ALLOWANCES (RDAs)

Nutrient	Age	Amount
Vitamin A	Males 50-70	900 mcg RAE
	Males 70+	900 mcg RAE
	Females 50-70	700 mcg RAE
	Females 70+	700 mcg RAE

RDAs *(continued)*

Nutrient	Age	Amount
Vitamin D	Males 50-70	10 mcg
	Males 70+	15 mcg
	Females 50-70	10 mcg
	Females 70+	15 mcg
Vitamin E	Males 50-70	15 mg
	Males 70+	15 mg
	Females 50-70	15 mg
	Females 70+	15 mg
Vitamin K	Males 50-70	120 mcg
	Males 70+	120 mcg
	Females 50-70	90 mcg
	Females 70+	90 mcg
Vitamin C	Males 50-70	90 mg
	Males 70+	90 mg
	Females 50-70	75 mg
	Females 70+	75 mg
Thiamin	Males 50-70	1.2 mg
	Males 70+	1.2 mg
	Females 50-70	1.1 mg
	Females 70+	1.1 mg
Riboflavin	Males 50-70	1.3 mg
	Males 70+	1.3 mg
	Females 50-70	1.1 mg
	Females 70+	1.1 mg
Niacin	Males 50-70	16 mg
	Males 70+	16 mg
	Females 50-70	14 mg
	Females 70+	14 mg
Vitamin B6	Males 50-70	1.7 mg

RDAs *(continued)*

Nutrient	Age	Amount
	Males 70+	1.7 mg
	Females 50-70	1.5 mg
	Females 70+	1.5 mg
Folate	Males 50-70	400 mcg
	Males 70+	400 mcg
	Females 50-70	400 mcg
	Females 70+	400 mcg
Vitamin B12	Males 50-70	2.4 mcg
	Males 70+	2.4 mcg
	Females 50-70	2.4 mcg
	Females 70+	2.4 mcg
Calcium	Males 50-70	1200 mg
	Males 70+	1200 mg
	Females 50-70	1200 mg
	Females 70+	1200 mg
Phosphorus	Males 50-70	700 mg
	Males 70+	700 mg
	Females 50-70	700 mg
	Females 70+	700 mg
Magnesium	Males 50-70	420 mg
	Males 70+	420 mg
	Females 50-70	320 mg
	Females 70+	320 mg
Iron	Males 50-70	8 mg
	Males 70+	8 mg
	Females 50-70	8 mg
	Females 70+	8 mg
Zinc	Males 50-70	11 mg
	Males 70+	11 mg

RDAs *(continued)*

Nutrient	Age	Amount
	Females 50-70	8 mg
	Females 70+	8 mg
Iodine	Males 50-70	150 mcg
	Males 70+	150 mcg
	Females 50-70	150 mcg
	Females 70+	150 mcg
Selenium	Males 50-70	55 mcg
	Males 70+	55 mcg
	Females 50-70	55 mcg
	Females 70+	55 mcg

The preceding chart is based on the RDAs for healthy adults. So, should you just follow this chart? Unfortunately, it's not quite that simple. Getting your RDAs is a good start to healthy living, but, according to the definition, these amounts are adequate for *practically* all *healthy* persons. The RDAs help you meet your nutritional needs and prevent vitamin and mineral deficiencies, but if you want to slow down the aging process, you may need more of certain substances. And, don't forget, your needs may not be the same as your next-door neighbor's. If you are ill or injured, you may need more of certain vitamins or minerals to help you heal. A pregnant woman needs more vitamins and minerals to help nourish her growing baby.

Use this chart as a starting off point. Then refer to the following chapters of this book to help you determine your needs.

Should you buy natural or synthetic vitamins? Does the word "natural" on a label mean there's a better product inside? When it comes to vitamins, not usually. Natural simply means that the vitamin was made from natural substances. For example, natural vitamin C may be made from rose hips, and natural vitamin E may come from vegetable oil. Synthetic vitamins are made in a laboratory. A vitamin is a vitamin no matter what the source, and some vitamins that are labeled "natural" may be mostly synthetic anyway. They could just be mixed with natural substances. According to research, the only vitamin that may be better in its natural form is vitamin E because it is absorbed by your body better than the synthetic form. If a vitamin costs more because it is labeled "natural," it's probably not worth the extra expense.

Are vitamins and minerals ever harmful? According to an old Hindu proverb, "Even a nectar is a poison if taken in excess." That can certainly be the case with vitamins and minerals. For example, vitamin A is vital for the health of your eyes and the growth of skin, bones, and reproductive organs. In large doses, however, vitamin A can cause headache, vomiting, peeling of your skin, anorexia, and swelling of your bones.

Be sure to read the cautions in each chapter of this book to avoid turning your anti-aging nectar into a life-threatening poison.

HERBS

"... and the fruit thereof shall be for meat, and the leaf thereof for medicine."

Ezekiel 47:12

Herbs can add flavor and zip to your cooking. Some herbs may also add a little zip to your life. Man discovered the healing power of herbs before he learned to write. Chinese texts dating back to 2800 B.C. contained information about herbal medicine. Although today you look to your doctor and pharmacist for drugs to heal you, for centuries people merely looked in their fields and gardens.

Many of today's drugs were originally created from plants. Aspirin, for example, was first extracted from the bark of a willow tree. Digitalis, long used in the treatment of heart failure, came from the dried leaf of the foxglove plant. In fact, many newer drugs still come from plants. One fairly new anti-cancer drug, paclitaxel, is made from the bark of the Pacific Yew tree.

HERBS COME IN MANY FORMS

If you don't have your own herb garden, you can still take advantage of healing herbs by buying them at your local health food store. Herbs come in different forms, and this can be confusing. Here's a quick list for a little guidance:

❦ **Liquid extracts or tinctures.** Considered by some experts to be the most reliable way to take herbs, they are sold in eyedropper bottles. The active ingredient is extracted in a solution of alcohol and water.

❦ **Herb powders in capsules.** Capsules are convenient, but they can become outdated in a short time, about a year for some.

❦ **Dried herbs.** You can buy loose, dried leaves that you can chop up and make into a tea. These also lose their effectiveness rather quickly, so buy only small amounts.

❦ **Teas.** You can purchase herbal tea ready to brew. Cover the pot and let it steep for about 15 minutes. The tea should have a strong odor.

❦ **Syrups and elixirs.** These are herbal extracts mixed into a sweet liquid base. Some people prefer the sweet taste, but others may find them too sweet. Syrups and elixirs also tend to be more expensive than other forms of herbs.

If so many drugs have plant origins, why don't doctors prescribe herbs? Actually, some doctors will suggest herbal remedies for their patients whenever possible, but they cannot be prescribed because they are not patentable. The law in the United States requires that a drug must be proven to be safe and effective before it can be sold to the public. This law is to protect you from ineffective drugs and from drugs that could hurt you.

The testing process to prove a drug's safety and effectiveness is very expensive. Pharmaceutical companies can only recover the huge expense of developing these drugs if they are able to patent them. This means they will be the only company allowed to sell that particular drug for a period of several years. This gives them time to earn back their investments. Since most plant remedies have been around for centuries, they cannot be patented. Drug companies have no interest in conducting expensive tests to prove the safety of most herbal products. It simply isn't cost efficient. However, that may be changing.

A patent was recently issued for a pharmaceutical version of mistletoe to be used in the treatment of AIDS. This was the first such patent issued for an herbal product. If more herbal preparations can be patented, it could change the industry. As things stand now, it is difficult to know if the herbal product you buy is safe because there are no rigorous tests and quality control procedures for herbs as there are for drugs.

How do you know if an herbal product is safe and effective, and how do you know what a particular herb can do for you? You can ask your doctor, but since herbal medicine is not taught in medical school, he may not be able to help. You can read labels at the health food store, but since they qualify as food supplements, manufacturers cannot make medical claims on

HERBS THAT MAY CAUSE SERIOUS SIDE EFFECTS

- ❦ **Chaparral.** Used as a cure for acne and for stopping the aging process, this supplement can cause liver disease.
- ❦ **Comfrey.** Speeds healing and prevents bruises and swelling from injuries when used in a paste. Don't take it by mouth because it contains alkaloids that might cause cancer.
- ❦ **Ephedrine.** Raises blood pressure and heart rate.
- ❦ **Germander.** Germander is used to fight obesity, but it may cause hepatitis, an inflammation of the liver.
- ❦ **Licorice.** Licorice candy may be dandy, but too much of it can raise your blood pressure to dangerous heights.
- ❦ **Pokeroot.** Extremely toxic.
- ❦ **Sassafras.** Contains safrole, which has been proven to cause cancer.
- ❦ **Mistletoe.** Although a pharmaceutical version of mistletoe has been patented, home use is not recommended. The berries are poisonous, and the leaves may cause dangerous blood pressure problems.

TOP ANTI-AGING HERBS

❦ **Echinacea.** Reduces inflammation, fights diseases like cancer through its ability to enhance your immune system, treats skin conditions, promotes growth of new tissues

❦ **Garlic.** One of the richest sources of antioxidant protection, lengthens cell life, fights infections, battles cancer, lowers blood pressure, protects your heart

❦ **Ginger.** Prevents blood clots, eases arthritis, clobbers cholesterol, soothes your stomach

❦ **Gingko.** Improves circulation, boosts brain power, lowers cholesterol, protects against heart disease

❦ **Ginseng.** Lowers cholesterol, boosts immunity, improves sexual function, combats fatigue, helps prevent cancer

❦ **Flaxseed.** Helps keep blood thin, lowers cholesterol, protects against cancer

the labels. One useful piece of information that should be on the label is whether the herb has been standardized. This means that the manufacturer has measured the active ingredients. Herbs that are not standardized may not contain enough of the active ingredient to be effective.

Learn as much as you can before taking any herb. Even though herbs are not strictly regulated like drugs, some products have been used for centuries with no reports of side effects. On the other hand, some herbs are harmful.

For more extensive information on herbs, see herbal expert Dr. Varro Tyler's book *The Honest Herbal.*

SUPER
NUTRITION
STRATEGIES

You know that taking care of your heart will help you live a long, healthy life. So you don't smoke, and you watch your cholesterol level. But did you know that a deficiency of vitamin B6 can raise your risk of heart disease as much as smoking or high cholesterol? Evidence also indicates that about 40 percent of heart attacks and strokes suffered by American men may be caused by a deficiency of folic acid, another important B vitamin.

B VITAMINS

When scientists first discovered the mysterious food factors they called vitamins, they began by naming the first one fat-soluble A and the second one water-soluble B (and then C, D, and so on). Later, researchers found that vitamin B wasn't just one simple vitamin. There's a whole complex of substances, like an apartment complex, under the vitamin B roof. Each unit in building B has a lot of common features, but unit 6 has its own unique properties.

Although the B vitamins are separate substances, they often work together. It is very unusual to have a deficiency of just one B vitamin. For example, your body requires folic acid in order to absorb the other B vitamins. A deficiency of folic acid could quickly lead to deficiencies in the other B vitamins as well. It is important that you get a balanced intake of B vitamins because each contributes in its own way to your good health. Look at this quick rundown of the different B vitamins, and you'll see how they function together and perform many of the same duties in your body to help keep you young.

Thiamin (B1). The leader of the pack is thiamin, the first B vitamin to be discovered and named. A deficiency of thiamin is responsible for beriberi, a disease that can cause symptoms ranging from weakness to mental disturbances. Thiamin is essential for turning protein, fat, and carbohydrates into energy. It's also needed to make copies of DNA whenever cells divide, helping assure proper growth and maintenance of healthy skin. Thiamin is also necessary for nerve signals to travel, carrying important information to your brain from different parts of your body.

Niacin (B3). A deficiency of niacin can cause pellagra, which means "rough skin." Symptoms include red scaly skin; swollen, red tongue; diarrhea; and mental disturbances. Niacin is required for turning protein into energy and for making DNA, fatty acids, and cholesterol. Your body can manufacture niacin from tryptophan, which is an amino acid (a component of protein). In fact, niacin deficiencies can often be corrected just by increasing the amount of protein in your diet.

Riboflavin (B2). Do you want healthy, younger-looking skin? Without adequate riboflavin, your skin may become dry, itchy, and flaky. Riboflavin is essential for healthy skin, eyes, and blood. It is needed to break down fat for energy in your body and for the synthesis of red blood cells, glycogen (a storage form of glucose), and corticosteroids (steroid hormones secreted by the adrenal gland). It also helps convert tryptophan to niacin.

Pantothenic acid (B5). Have you been ill recently, or just emotionally upset? If so, make sure you get enough pantothenic acid. Vitamin B5 has been called the "anti-stress" vitamin. It is needed to keep your adrenal gland healthy and functioning properly, which is critical during times of stress. It also helps stimulate antibody production, which can help you fight off illness, and is necessary in the production of red blood cells, brain chemicals, and cholesterol.

Folic acid. Folic acid has become a bit of a celebrity in the vitamin world lately. Evidence that it helps fight heart disease has been published not only in medical journals but in national magazines and newspapers as well. Another big health news story was the decision of the U.S. government to begin fortifying foods with folic acid to help prevent birth defects. What other jobs does this media darling perform to make it so popular? It helps make protein and red blood cells, it is vital for cell division, and it removes fat stored in your liver.

Cobalamin (B12). Vitamin B12 works along with folic acid to make red blood cells. A deficiency of B12 can cause pernicious anemia, an energy-sapping disease that is difficult to diagnose. Vitamin B12 protects nerves from damage by helping to produce their protective coverings (sheaths). A deficiency of B12 can eventually lead to severe nerve damage, even paralysis.

Biotin. Bacteria in your body are a bad thing, right? Not necessarily. Some "good" bacteria in your intestines are responsible for producing biotin, but your supply of these bacteria can be depleted by taking antibiotics. You don't want to come up short on biotin because it plays an important role in energy metabolism, growth, and the production of fatty acids and

B-VITAMIN TIDBITS

❦ Drinking large amounts of coffee or tea (even decaffeinated) can hinder your body's ability to absorb thiamin.

❦ Cooking, especially in water, lowers the content of many B vitamins.

❦ Antibiotics, alcohol, and oral contraceptives may interfere with your body's ability to absorb riboflavin.

❦ Raw fish contains a substance that destroys thiamin, so if you enjoy sushi, you may want to boost your thiamin intake.

❦ Biotin is sometimes suggested as a cure for baldness, but it will only reverse hair loss caused by a skin condition.

digestive enzymes. Biotin, which displays insulin-like activity in lowering blood sugar, is also found in certain foods.

Pyridoxine (B6). Vitamin B6 is one of the busiest vitamins in your body. It helps your body use protein, fatty acids, and glycogen efficiently, and it helps produce brain chemicals and the hemoglobin portion of your red blood cells. A deficiency of B6 can cause skin problems like dermatitis (itchy, red skin) and acne. A deficiency can also cause mouth sores, nerve damage, and even seizures.

8 WAYS B VITAMINS FIGHT AGING

Heart helper. If you want to live a long, healthy life, you must keep your heart healthy. The U.S. government recognizes the heart-healing potential of B vitamins and recently approved a plan to fortify grain products with folic acid. Experts estimate that 50,000 fewer Americans would die from heart attacks each year and many serious birth defects would be prevented as a result of folic acid fortification.

The fortification plan has been put into effect, but it remains to be seen if it will bring about the dramatic reduction in heart disease deaths as predicted.

Why is folic acid so important to your heart health? It's because of an amino acid in your blood called homocysteine. Researchers began to make the connection between homocysteine and heart disease when it was observed that people with very high homocysteine levels (due to a genetic disorder) often died from severe heart disease in their teens and 20s.

Doctors have been baffled for years by certain heart disease deaths. You know ... the person who eats right, doesn't smoke, gets plenty of exercise, appears to have no heart disease symptoms, and yet keels over at 45. Medical researchers were excited to discover that homocysteine might provide a possible explanation for those mysterious deaths. Even more exciting is the fact that those deaths may be preventable.

That's where folic acid comes in, along with its B-vitamin brothers, B6 and B12. This trio of vitamins works in your blood to convert homocysteine to a less dangerous substance.

Why is homocysteine so dangerous? In normal amounts, it isn't, but an excess can damage your arteries, causing a buildup of plaque that can lead to heart disease and stroke.

Homocysteine is made from another amino acid, methionine, during the process of metabolizing protein. Afterward, it should be turned back into methionine. The catch is that it needs B vitamins, especially folic acid, to be converted back to its original form. If you don't have enough B vitamins to do the job, homocysteine can build up to dangerous levels.

Because homocysteine is a by-product of protein metabolism, people who eat high protein diets should take special care to get enough B vitamins.

Strikes down strokes. High homocysteine levels are the life-shortening culprits in more than just heart disease. The damage that too much homocysteine does to blood vessel walls can cause buildups that may form blood clots. If one of those blood clots breaks loose, it could travel to your brain, causing a stroke.

Better brain function. According to Leo Rosenberg, "First you forget names, then you forget faces, then you forget to pull your zipper up, then you forget to pull your zipper down."

The ability to laugh at yourself is a wonderful trait. However, that may be hard to do when your previously sharp-as-a-tack mind refuses to tell you where you left your car keys or, worse, you forget something really important, like where you live or what your name is. Sometimes this loss of mental ability is considered just a normal and unavoidable part of aging, but researchers are finding that proper nutrition can help prevent loss of brain function. Several different B vitamins can help keep your mind and your wit as razor sharp as they were in your youth.

❧ **Vitamin B12.** Older people who have low levels of B12 often have symptoms resembling Alzheimer's or other forms of mental disturbances. People can have memory problems due to low levels of B12 long before they are deficient enough to suffer pernicious anemia. One study found that among people who already had pernicious anemia, 71 percent had short-term memory loss. Treatment with vitamin B12 restored the memories of most of the study participants within 10 to 27 days.

❦ **Thiamin.** The severe memory loss that often accompanies beriberi is appropriately called "beriberi amnesia." This memory loss is reversible when thiamin is given. Thiamin levels tend to be very low in people with mental illness. In fact, some psychiatrists treat many of their patients with thiamin supplements, as well as other B vitamins.

❦ **Vitamin B6.** Vitamin B6 is necessary for the production of serotonin and other neurotransmitters in the brain. Serotonin is known as a "feel good" chemical, and low levels of serotonin have been associated with depression.

❦ **Folic acid.** A deficiency of folic acid may cause mental and emotional problems, including depression and schizophrenia.

Controls cholesterol. Did you know that doctors sometimes prescribe niacin to help lower cholesterol? Niacin effectively reduces both LDL (bad) cholesterol and triglyceride levels in your blood and raises your HDL (good) cholesterol. However, high doses of niacin may cause side effects like flushing, rash, and abdominal pain. Doctors have found that lower doses (1.5 to 3 grams daily) can be effective without the side effects of higher doses. Of course, even these lower doses are prescription strength, and you shouldn't take niacin to lower your cholesterol without your doctor's consent. You may never need a prescription drug for high cholesterol if you get plenty of niacin in your diet.

Helps beat bone pain. People with arthritis who are prescribed the drug methotrexate may have insult added to injury when they have to deal with side effects. However, researchers recently discovered that most of these side effects occur because the drug causes a deficiency of folic acid. Adding extra folic acid to your diet could help you avoid the pain of arthritis, as well as the side effects of your arthritis drug.

Carpal tunnel syndrome is usually thought of as a bone ailment, but the pain is actually caused by a pinched nerve. The nerve passes through a tunnel created by the carpal bones in your wrist. Carpal tunnel syndrome is more common in women than men, and often begins to affect them around menopause. Over a hundred thousand operations are performed each year

B VITAMIN RDAs FOR OVER 50

Thiamin (B1)	Men 1.2 mg
	Women 1.1 mg
Riboflavin (B2)	Men 1.3 mg
	Women 1.1 mg
Niacin (B3)	Men 16 mg
	Women 14 mg
Pyridoxine (B6)	Men 1.7 mg
	Women 1.5 mg
Folate	Men 400 mcg
	Women 400 mcg
Cobalamin (B12)	Men 2.4 mcg
	Women 2.4 mcg

to correct carpal tunnel syndrome, but there may be an easier solution. According to the latest research, merely increasing your intake of vitamin B6 may enable you to wave goodbye to wrist pain forever.

Keeps skin healthy. Having a youthful glow to your skin might help you look younger, and looking younger *can* help you feel younger. The cells of your skin are being replaced rapidly (though perhaps not quite as rapidly as when you were 18). B vitamins are vital to this cell division, so getting plenty of B vitamins is an easy way to enjoy healthy, younger-looking skin.

Increases resistance to disease. Because B vitamins are involved in the process of creating white blood cells that fight disease, they play an important role in disease resistance.

Beefs up physical fitness. B vitamins are involved in processing proteins and rebuilding muscles. If you want to reap the anti-aging benefits of an exercise program, B vitamins can help make your exercise more productive and efficient.

YOUR ACTION PLAN

HOW MUCH IS ENOUGH?

The Recommended Dietary Allowances (RDAs) for the B vitamins shown on page 39 are for healthy adults over 50. There is no RDA for biotin or pantothenic acid, but the Food and Nutrition Board's estimated adequate and safe intake is 30 micrograms (mcg) for biotin and 5 milligrams (mg) for pantothenic acid.

HOW TO GET MORE B VITAMINS NATURALLY

Eating a varied and balanced diet is the best way to boost your B-vitamin intake naturally. Consult the following charts for good sources of each B vitamin.

Riboflavin

Food	Serving size	Riboflavin (mg)
Milk	1 cup	.34
Cottage cheese	1 cup	.37
Yogurt	1 cup	.53
Spinach	1/2 cup, cooked	.21
Beef liver	3 ounces, fried	3.5
Mushrooms	1/2 cup, cooked	.23

Niacin

Food	Serving size	Niacin (mg)
Mushrooms	1/2 cup, cooked	7
Tuna	3 ounces	11.3
Pork chop	3 ounces, broiled	4.4
Chicken breast	3 ounces, cooked	11.7
Baked potato	one small	3.3

Thiamin

Food	Serving size	Thiamin (mg)
Pork chop	3 ounces, broiled	.87
Black beans	1/2 cup cooked	.21
Watermelon	one medium wedge	.20
Whole wheat bread	one slice	.11
Sunflower seeds	2 tablespoons	.41
Green peas	1/2 cup, cooked	.23

Folate

Food	Serving size	Folate (mcg)
Liver	3 ounces, fried	187
Asparagus	1/2 cup, cooked	131
Spinach	1 cup, raw	108
Cantaloupe	one small wedge	15
Pinto beans	1/2 cup, cooked	147
Beets	1/2 cup, cooked	45

Vitamin B12

Food	Serving size	Vitamin B12 (mcg)
Cottage cheese	1 cup	1.3
Sirloin steak	3 ounces, cooked	2.4
Chicken liver	3 ounces, cooked	16.5
Tuna	3 ounces	1.8
Sardines	3 ounces	7.6

Vitamin B6

Food	Serving size	Vitamin B6 (mg)
Chicken breast	3 ounces, cooked	.51
Navy beans	1/2 cup, cooked	.15
Spinach	1/2 cup, cooked	.22
Baked potato	one small	.70
Beef liver	3 ounces, fried	1.2
Banana	one medium	.66

DO YOU NEED SUPPLEMENTS?

You should get as many nutrients as you can from the food you eat, but if you're going to take a supplement, a B-complex is important. Certain people may need supplements more than others. For example:

❦ Elderly people often have deficiencies of B12, folate, and B6.

❦ Vegetarians may need additional B vitamins, particularly vitamin B12, since it isn't found in plant sources.

❦ Illness or stress can increase your need for B vitamins.

THE WISE B-VITAMIN CONSUMER

Because B vitamins work together, you probably shouldn't take just one B vitamin. Instead, look for a supplement that contains a balanced amount of all the B vitamins.

B-VITAMIN CAUTIONS

Because they are water-soluble, most B vitamins are considered safe, even in large doses. The excess passes harmlessly out in your urine. However, there are a few exceptions.

❦ Too much niacin (over 100 mg) can cause an allergic-like reaction. If taken in very large doses (over 3,000 mg), niacin may cause liver enzyme changes that could be harmful. Take it with meals and avoid hot liquids and alcohol after taking it.

❦ Vitamin B6 can be toxic in daily doses of 200 mg or more, causing bone pain and muscle weakness. Very large doses can cause permanent nerve damage.

❦ Too much folic acid can mask the symptoms of anemia caused by a vitamin B12 deficiency.

You can deprive your body of calcium for years without suffering a single symptom. Only later in life do you suddenly discover that you've robbed the calcium savings account stashed in your bones. You must take in calcium every day, throughout the day. If you don't, then someday, your bones will begin to shatter.

CALCIUM

Here's a health brain teaser: What do fragile bones, high blood pressure, cancer (especially of the breast and colon), and senility have in common?

If you answered "they're diseases associated with aging," you're right — partially. All of these health problems are also linked to not getting enough calcium.

We can blame our high need for calcium on our Stone Age ancestors. Scientists believe that during the Paleolithic era some 10,000 to 35,000 years ago, our forebears took in a large amount of calcium, mostly from plant sources. They took in so much calcium, in fact, that the human body developed ways genetically to slow down the mineral's absorption so our ancestors wouldn't get too much. On the other hand, humans were able to survive periods when little calcium-rich food was available, thanks to the parathyroid gland's ability to pull calcium out of bones when needed.

While human lifestyles and life spans have changed dramatically since the Stone Age, our bodies haven't. Researchers say we're only consuming about a fifth as much calcium as our ancient counterparts — yet our bodies still make it hard to absorb what we do take in.

When we don't get enough calcium, our bodies react as though they are going through a bleak Stone Age winter — they start pulling calcium out of our bones.

The result? You may suffer not only from weakened bones, but from a host of other health problems. Calcium plays a role in many life-giving processes, from maintaining normal blood pressure and helping your blood clot properly to enabling muscles, including the heart, to contract. Calcium also is needed for the secretion of hormones, digestive juices, and brain cell messengers.

Recently, scientists have discovered even more evidence that getting enough calcium is an important way to make sure you stay healthy and stronger ... longer.

6 WAYS CALCIUM FIGHTS AGING

Keeps bones strong. What makes a person seem really old? It's more than gray hair and wrinkles— lots of middle aged folks have those attributes. But a person with stooped posture or a shuffling gait due to joint and bone problems appears fragile and elderly.

The cause? Far too often, it's osteoporosis, defined as porous bone. "When you have osteoporosis, your bones look like a sponge," says surgical floor nurse Suzanne Wilson.

Every year, over 1.3 million of these spongy bones break. If you are a woman, you are twice as likely to have an osteoporosis fracture than you are to have a heart attack and over five times more likely to suffer from a fracture than you are to have breast cancer.

Not only women suffer from osteoporosis, by the way. Twenty percent of the people with thinning bones are men.

The disease can silently steal skeleton strength for many years. So if you have osteoporosis, chances are you won't know it until you receive a frightening wake-up call — when your bones start to fracture. Your spinal column, hips, and wrists are the most likely to crack.

Just being careful doesn't protect you from the bone-snapping perils of the disease, either. You don't have to plunge down a staircase to end up with a fracture. A simple act like bending over to tie your shoelace can be enough to cause a "crush" or spinal compression fracture. These small breaks can add up — causing loss of height and the curved back known as a "dowager's hump."

Bones weakened by osteoporosis can actually shatter into so many pieces they can never be put back together. That means you'll need an artificial joint — a difficult surgery when your bones are weak. "Having a good result from joint replacement surgery is more likely if you have healthy bones," says Dr. James Braden, an orthopedic surgeon in Thomaston, Ga. "Bones with osteoporosis sometimes won't hold onto the prosthesis."

Up to 20 percent of elderly people who fracture their hips die within a year after the incident. Those who live are often unable to get around without a walker or a wheelchair.

Despite these alarming statistics, there's good news: You can successfully fight osteoporosis, no matter what your age, thanks to the bone-strengthening abilities of calcium. Two recent studies concluded that a high calcium intake can reduce your risk of hip fracture by up to 60 percent.

Natural colon cancer fighter. Colon cancer kills over 50,000 Americans every year. The malignancy often runs in families, yet only a small fraction of cases can be blamed on heredity alone.

So what triggers the cancer? Your diet is a likely culprit. Everything from fat to fiber may play a role, but scientists are zeroing in on the possibility that calcium may be able to halt the development of colon cancer.

A recent study conducted at Loma Linda University concluded that taking in 1,200 milligrams (mg) a day of the mineral could reduce your risk of colon cancer. That's because calcium appears to slow down the rate of cell division in the colon — and cells that multiply too quickly and eventually divide out of control add up to cancer.

Beats breast cancer. Adding a glass or two of milk to your diet every day could lower your risk of breast cancer. At least that's the conclusion of Finnish researchers at the National Public Health Institute in Helsinki.

The scientists were taken by surprise when they stumbled across that fact after tracking the dietary habits of nearly 5,000 women and then following up 25 years later to see which women developed cancer.

The scientists combed their records to see if they could find specific risk factors or behaviors that might provide clues about why 88 of the women developed cancer and others didn't. They looked at all sorts of things — from numbers of childbirths and smoking to intake of protein, fat, and vitamins.

The only thing that stood out was milk. The researchers concluded that drinking milk regularly had a "significant" protective effect against breast cancer.

They theorized that the high calcium level of milk could possibly prevent malignancies by binding to fatty acids and bile acids. But, the scientists added, they believe there is some other still not understood component in milk that may contribute to its anti-breast cancer properties.

Weapon against high blood pressure. "Epidemiology" may be a mouthful to say, but it describes a very practical branch of science — the study of how our lives and daily habits, from personal hygiene to what foods we eat, determine who gets what ailment. In over 20 studies that track the foods people eat, epidemiologists have linked getting too little calcium with having high blood pressure.

In more than 80 studies done on humans and animals, scientists have given various amounts of calcium to their "guinea pigs" to see what would happen to blood pressure levels. Most of the time, the scientists report, blood pressure drops when calcium in the diet goes up.

Researchers are unsure how this blood pressure/calcium link operates. One clue is that folks who are sensitive to the blood-pressure-raising properties of salt — especially African-Americans and the elderly — also tend to have low levels of calcium. And scientists have discovered that these same salt-sensitive people have the best blood-pressure-lowering response to calcium supplements. Researchers think they may have an explanation: Taking in calcium helps flush out excess sodium from the body. That, in turn, could lower blood pressure in people sensitive to salt.

If you have high blood pressure, does this mean you can trade in your medication for calcium supplements?

No. In fact, recent studies have shown that, on average, calcium lowers the top (systolic) blood pressure reading only slightly and doesn't have much effect at all on the more important diastolic pressure (the bottom number that records the pressure in your veins and arteries between heartbeats).

Still, making sure you are getting enough calcium in your diet makes sense if you have high blood pressure — scientists agree that the mineral plays a complex role in maintaining healthy readings.

So while calcium isn't a "magic bullet" for high blood pressure, it is one more weapon in your arsenal against this silent killer.

It could be especially smart to add calcium to your diet by drinking milk if you have high blood pressure.

High blood pressure can lead to stroke. But scientists who studied 3,150 men between the ages of 55 and 68 for 22 years found that as milk intake went up, stroke rates plummeted. In fact, men who shied away from milk had twice the number of strokes as men who drank at least 16 ounces of calcium-packed milk every day.

Alzheimer's disease connection. If you've ever seen someone going through the mental deterioration of Alzheimer's, you know it's a horrible death sentence — and a tragedy for everyone who watches a loved one's mind and abilities slip away.

Alzheimer's is primarily a disease associated with aging. And the ability to absorb adequate amounts of calcium declines as you age. Could there be a connection? So far, the answer is "maybe."

Calcium serves as a kind of messenger within many cells, including nerve cells in the brain. In Alzheimer's disease, scientists have learned, calcium inside those brain cells is altered. So, while the medical jury is still out on just what role, if any, a lack of calcium may play in Alzheimer's, it does appear possible that a deficiency of the mineral could damage the brain.

Fends off food poisoning? For all those times you are unlucky enough to get hold of some tainted food, Dutch researchers at the Netherlands Institute for Dairy Research think they may

have found a way to give you an extra edge in fighting the salmonella bacteria that causes food poisoning.

The secret? Calcium-rich dairy products. Experiments in
animals have shown that milk and yogurt may dramatically
lessen the severity of food-borne stomach infections.

The scientists theorize that calcium in milk products stimulates the production of stomach acid. Those digestive juices
then destroy many of the salmonella germs that end up in your
stomach if you eat spoiled food.

Low-calcium milk doesn't have the same effect as regular
calcium-rich milk. And yogurt, the scientists found, packs a
one-two punch against stomach infections. That may be
because the fermented milk in yogurt takes twice as long to
empty from your stomach as regular milk — so salmonella
germs ingested at about the same time you eat yogurt have an
extra long exposure to bacteria-zapping acids.

YOUR ACTION PLAN

Almost all — 99 percent — of your body's calcium is stored
in your bones. But the mineral doesn't just stay there. Think of
your skeleton as a kind of bank where you keep your calcium
until your body needs to "withdraw" some to help with all the
physical processes that need the mineral. Clearly, if you take
more calcium out of your bone bank than you put in, you'll eventually end up overdrawing your calcium account. The penalty?
Weak bones.

The best way to make sure you have a strong calcium bank
is to take in plenty of calcium while you're young, when your
skeleton is still growing. But what if you skimped on calcium in
your younger days? Are you doomed to suffer brittle bones as
the consequence?

Fortunately, the answer is no. Throughout your life,
remodeling units on your skeleton can actually build new
bone over a period of three to four months. You just need to
make sure you are getting enough absorbable calcium in
your diet.

How much is enough?

Unfortunately, getting enough calcium isn't as simple as it sounds. Many people simply don't realize just how much calcium they need —and far too many overestimate just how much they take in every day.

For example, a recent study of 351 women ages 22 to 85 concluded that nearly a third of them thought they were getting plenty of calcium to protect their bones. In fact, they were only getting about half the amount they needed each day.

RECOMMENDED DAILY CALCIUM INTAKE

Age	Amount
9 to 18	1,300 mg
19 to 50	1,000 mg
over 50	1,200 mg

Let's say you have a half cup of calcium-loaded milk with your breakfast cereal. For lunch, you eat a healthy meal, a salad topped with some broccoli and an ounce of cheese (both good sources of calcium). Dinner is broiled chicken, salad, a potato, and another milk product — frozen yogurt — for dessert.

Your diet sounds healthy and calcium rich, right? Wrong. Your meals only gave you about 410 mg of calcium, not even half the RDA for young women and only about a fourth of what an older person should be consuming.

Why are so many of us shortchanging our calcium accounts? At least part of the reason may lie in our obsession with fighting the battle of the bulge. Too many diets rob us of calcium.

A lot of people cut out milk products to save calories and cholesterol. Instead, switch to low or nonfat dairy products. A cup of calcium-rich skim milk has no fat and only about 80 calories, perfect for dieters and people with high cholesterol.

There's another calcium-robbing aspect to dieting. A high-protein diet, which people frequently go on to lose weight, causes your body to excrete calcium. Even when you boost your calcium intake up to 1,400 mg, too much protein can cause you to lose an unhealthy amount of calcium.

How to get more calcium naturally

The very best way to get all the calcium you need is to make it an important part of your diet every day. It's a simple fact: Pills shouldn't replace healthy eating habits.

Dairy products top the list of foods containing lots of calcium that your body can easily absorb and use. Another bonus for milk drinkers: You'll also be taking in a host of other health-enhancing vitamins and minerals.

You can eat milk, too — in yogurt and low-fat ice cream. You can also add nonfat milk powder to just about any dish, from meatloaf and soups to puddings and cookies. Only five heaping tablespoons provide the same amount of calcium as a cup of fresh milk.

What can you do if milk upsets your stomach? First of all, even if you are lactose intolerant, you may be able to drink milk if you don't go overboard.

A recent study showed that people who thought consuming any milk would make their bellies ache had no problems if they stuck to only 8 ounces (one cup) at a time.

If milk definitely doesn't agree with you, other food sources are loaded with calcium, including dark green vegetables like kale, watercress, collards, beet greens, and broccoli.

Some vegetables, like spinach and Swiss chard, contain a large amount of calcium that, unfortunately, your body can't absorb. That's because the vegetables also contain chemicals that bind to the calcium and keep your body from using it.

The fiber in wheat bran reduces your ability to absorb calcium. And when you eat fiber-rich beans, only about half their calcium is available to your body.

Fish, such as canned salmon and sardines, that are prepared with their bones are another rich source of calcium. So are oysters. Canned tomatoes (which are kept firm by calcium salts), tofu processed with calcium salts, stone-ground flour, cornmeal, and blackstrap molasses are also calcium-rich foodstuffs.

And don't forget to check your grocer's shelves for products that are especially fortified with calcium — including orange juice and soy milk.

Food	Calcium (mg)
Yogurt (nonfat), 1 cup	450
Milk, skim (1 cup)	350
Orange juice fortified with calcium, 1 cup	330
Cheddar cheese (1 1/2 oz)	305
Swiss cheese (1 oz)	270
Total cereal (3/4 cup)	250
Ice cream, fat-free, 1 cup	200
Sardines (canned, 2 oz)	175
Kale (1/2 cup, cooked)	90
Soybeans (1/2 cup, cooked)	90
Almonds (2 tablespoons)	80
Orange, 1	50
Bread, whole wheat (2 slices)	45
Broccoli (1/2 cup, cooked)	35

Do you need supplements?

Despite your best efforts, you and your doctor may decide you need calcium supplements in order to get an adequate amount of the mineral — especially if you're having a difficult time absorbing it from your diet, or if you've already developed osteoporosis.

The wise calcium consumer

Not all calcium supplements are the same. On the label, you may see calcium carbonate, phosphate, citrate, lactate, or gluconate.

These supplements contain calcium along with another substance, like carbonate, and they don't contain equal amounts of calcium. Look on the label for "elemental" or "pure" calcium to figure out exactly how much usable calcium you are really getting.

For example, a 650 mg calcium carbonate tablet has 260 mg of elemental calcium. A 650 mg calcium lactate supplement only provides 84 mg of elemental calcium.

Calcium carbonate is also usually the least expensive form. Tricalcium phosphate also rates high in the amount of pure calcium it contains, but it costs more than the carbonate form.

If you have a problem digesting milk products, avoid calcium lactate. It could give you an upset stomach.

Beware of calcium supplements made from oyster shells — it isn't absorbed well from your digestive system. Likewise, steer clear of calcium made from crushed or powdered bone. Not only is it hard to absorb, but it's sometimes contaminated with toxic materials like lead.

Antacids, such as Tums, are rich sources of calcium. But their job is to reduce stomach acid — and by doing that, they may also keep you from absorbing all the calcium they contain. In addition, some researchers think antacids like Rolaids, that are made with aluminum or magnesium hydroxides, may actually speed up calcium loss.

HOW TO GET MORE OUT OF YOUR CALCIUM

You can eat calcium-rich foods, take supplements, and still not get the calcium your body needs to stay healthy — especially after age 70, when your body's calcium absorption really declines. But don't despair. That doesn't mean it's impossible. You simply need to know how to help your body absorb this health-building mineral.

Vitamin D. It seems that our moms were right all along — to stay healthy we should drink our milk and get some sunshine.

In order to absorb calcium, we need vitamin D. Where does it come from? Mostly milk (as well as some cereals and fatty fishes) and sunshine. Our skin contains a substance that, when exposed to the sun's ultraviolet-B light, turns into vitamin D.

That substance declines as we get older. In addition, people over 60 tend to go outside less, so they produce less vitamin D from sun exposure. The ability to absorb vitamin D from food also lessens with age.

Scientists in France who studied over 3,000 elderly women found that those who received supplements of vitamin D and calcium dramatically reduced their risks of hip and other fractures.

To make sure you are getting enough vitamin D to help you absorb bone-strengthening calcium, drink four glasses of milk a day, spend some time outdoors, and discuss the possibility of taking a vitamin D supplement with your doctor.

Caffeine. While caffeine is perking you up, it can also be robbing you of calcium — but only slightly. Researchers at Tufts University in Boston found that women who drank just two or three cups of coffee a day faced an increased risk of bone loss. The more coffee the women drank and the less calcium they consumed, the weaker their bones became.

But, the scientists found that caffeine doesn't have any adverse effects on women who get at least the RDA of calcium (1,200 mg). In fact, adding just a tablespoon or two of milk to your coffee can offset the calcium-depleting power of caffeine.

Salt. Why do people in one country seem to need far more calcium than those in another location? The answer could lie in how much salt they eat.

If you take in too much salt, your body gets rid of the excess. But at the same time, it pulls calcium out of your body and removes it via your urine, too. That could be particularly hard on your skeleton if you eat lots of salty food, but skimp on your calcium intake.

Here's what researchers at the University of Western Australia report: If a woman who eats a very salty diet (about 4,000 mg of sodium a day) would cut that intake of sodium by half, she would protect her bones as much as if she was taking an extra 1,000 mg of calcium daily.

Estrogen. When a woman goes through menopause, around age 50, her calcium requirements go up as her estrogen levels plummet. Estrogen replacement therapy has been shown to actually increase your body's ability to absorb calcium.

Unfortunately, new information about hormone replacement therapy (HRT) indicates greater health risks — breast cancer, heart disease, heart attacks, strokes, and blood clots — than previously believed. The Food and Drug Administration advises doctors to prescribe HRT only when benefits clearly outweigh the risks, just long enough for successful treatment, and at the lowest effective dose.

If you are considering taking estrogen, be sure you discuss all the risks and benefits with your doctor first.

CALCIUM CAUTIONS

If you opt to take calcium supplements, make sure you know how and when to take them safely.

Safest time to take. You'll get the most out of your calcium supplements if you take them two times a day with meals, and again at bedtime. However, you need to avoid taking calcium carbonate or calcium hydroxyapatite at the same time you eat iron-rich foods. The reason? Those forms of calcium interfere with iron absorption and can even lead to iron deficiencies.

People who have a shortage of stomach acid should always take their calcium supplements with meals.

Possible side effects. Although it's rare, you can have side effects from taking calcium supplements at normal dosages. Check with your health care professional if you experience drowsiness, stomach upset, or difficult urination.

People who take far too much calcium, several grams a day, risk serious problems — including kidney stones, severe constipation, and weakness. Extremely large overdoses can disrupt the acid/alkaline balance of your body and result in heartbeat irregularities and confusion.

Are you taking any medications? To avoid possible interactions, make sure your doctor knows that you are also taking calcium supplements.

For example, if you take calcium supplements along with tetracycline, you may decrease the effects of the antibiotic. Waiting to take your calcium one to three hours after taking tetracycline can solve that problem. Likewise, if you are taking dilantin for seizures, you risk lowering the effectiveness of your medication unless you wait one to three hours before taking calcium.

Some prescription medicines may also contain calcium as an ingredient. So to avoid taking too much of the mineral, make sure your doctor knows how much supplemental calcium you are taking.

The older you get, the higher your blood sugar goes. Chromium helps insulin move sugar out of your bloodstream, and that may help prevent diabetes, heart disease, low blood sugar, and other problems of aging. But wait, say some experts, chromium supplementation only helps people who are lacking in the mineral. Read on for both sides of this controversy.

CHROMIUM

An anti-aging powerhouse? Maybe so. A weight-loss wonder drug? Definitely not.

Unfortunately, these days most people connect chromium with losing weight and building muscle. That's what you see on the advertisements: "Melt away fat and build muscle, without diets or endless exercise!"

The latest twist is an artificial sweetener laced with chromium. The aspartame-chromium combo is supposed to give you twice the weight-busting bang for your buck. The new product refers to chromium as a "popular weight management nutrient," but don't believe it.

The weight-loss/fat-burner claims are based on lousy studies done more than a decade ago by a chemist who had worked for the U.S. Department of Agriculture. A California food supplement company used his former government status to help pitch chromium, often in pyramid marketing schemes. Since then, several researchers have called his results preposterous, if not downright dangerous.

GET THE FACTS ON CHROMIUM FOR DIABETICS

Chromium is one of the most popular supplements for diabetics. It is claimed to improve glucose tolerance and positively affect cholesterol. The American Diabetes Association, however, is not convinced chromium lives up to all the hype.

Insulin, remember, is the hormone that moves glucose, or sugar, out of your bloodstream and into your cells. That's important because sugar is to your cells what gasoline is to a car's engine. It's the fuel your cells burn for energy. Basically, chromium helps insulin do its work.

In a clinical study, 13 diabetics took 600 micrograms (mcg) of chromium chloride a day and saw their fasting blood sugar level drop about 100 points. Five of the 13 were able to reduce their insulin or medication as a result.

In 1996, Dr. Richard Anderson reported excellent results in a study in China of 180 people with type 2 (noninsulin dependent) diabetes. The volunteers who got the most chromium — 500 mcg twice a day — had near normal levels on a glycosylated hemoglobin test, a measure considered to be the "gold standard" of diabetes tests. The group's fasting blood sugar levels improved, too.

There is no recommended dietary allowance (RDA) for chromium and no reliable test for chromium deficiency. Nevertheless, the Institute of Medicine suggests men over 50 years old get 30 micrograms (mcg) of chromium a day and women over 50 get 20 mcg.

While many of the studies showed benefits of chromium supplements, others demonstrated little or no effect. Most tested people with poor eating habits, and it's generally agreed that the better your diet, the less likely chromium supplements will help you. In addition, most studies used over 400 mcg of chromium a day. At this time, there are no studies on the safety of long-term, high doses of this mineral.

In health food stores, you'll see chromium promoted as an alternative to anabolic steroids. But researchers carefully tested 35 healthy young men involved in strength-training programs and decided that chromium makes no difference in body weight, amount of body fat, or strength.

It's too bad that this essential nutrient has been hyped as a miracle drug for burning fat and building muscle. All the false claims have given chromium an undeserved bad reputation in the science and health-care community.

4 WAYS CHROMIUM FIGHTS AGING

Have you ever taken a trip to the doctor only to be told that your ailment was just a "normal part of getting older"? That's what doctors have thought for years about glucose tolerance and insulin efficiency. Both gradually decline as you age.

But what if those declines are diet-related instead of age-related? Could you hold off, or reverse, the effects of aging? Some researchers think so.

Protects your proteins. One aging theory says that you age because your main energy source — glucose — damages your body's proteins. It causes them to hook together. An example is collagen, a protein that makes up your skin, bones, ligaments, and cartilage. When your collagen proteins hook to each other, all of your tissues can get stiff. When you think of stiffness, you think of the achy joints of arthritis, but your heart muscle is a tissue that can get stiff, too.

Chromium helps move sugar out of the blood, so it protects your proteins from damage. The anti-aging possibilities are huge.

Rejuvenates your hypothalamus. Another theory on how chromium helps keep you young has to do with a cherry-sized region of your brain, the hypothalamus.

Located behind your eyes, the hypothalamus acts as a middleman between the higher regions of the brain and your nervous system. If you are frightened, nervous, or excited, the brain sends messages to the hypothalamus, which starts a series of activities such as faster heartbeat, widening of the pupils, and increased blood flow to the muscles.

But the hypothalamus does much, much more. It is involved in your body temperature, your need for sleep, your appetite for sex, and your moods and emotions. It gets messages from the rest of your body about sugar levels in the blood and your body's water content. If those are too low, the hypothalamus sends a signal that tells you it's time to get something to eat or drink.

Some of the jobs performed by the hypothalamus are controlled by blood sugar levels, so it makes sense that reducing the amount of sugar in your blood will keep the hypothalamus from overworking or from sending out incorrect signals.

Dr. M.F. McCarthy, a major chromium researcher, says chromium "may help to maintain the hypothalamus in a more functionally youthful state."

SYMPTOMS OF CHROMIUM DEFICIENCY

- ❦ anxiety
- ❦ fatigue
- ❦ hypoglycemia
- ❦ sugar intolerance
  (borderline diabetes)
- ❦ stunted growth
- ❦ high cholesterol
- ❦ low HDL cholesterol
- ❦ weight loss (rare)
- ❦ brain disorders (rare)

Offers heart disease protection. Do you remember what your body's main fuel source is? That's right — the sugar pumping through your bloodstream. And if you don't have enough chromium, your body will have trouble converting that blood sugar into energy.

If the body can't use its main fuel source effectively, it has to find another one, namely fat. The problem with the body using fat as its energy source is that some of the byproducts of the process are made into cholesterol. Possible result: heart disease.

In one study, a group of people with heart disease had an average chromium level 41 percent lower than a group of people without heart disease.

Several studies have shown how chromium reduces heart disease risk:

❧ In lab experiments, rats fed a high-sugar, chromium-deficient diet had a shocking buildup of fat in their arteries. When the rats got the same high-sugar diet with a chromium supplement, their cholesterol levels went down significantly, and they had less fat buildup in their arteries.

❧ Another project studied 72 men who had been taking beta blockers for an average of seven years. Unfortunately, beta blockers tend to reduce HDL cholesterol (the "good" cholesterol). Chromium, 600 mcg a day, boosted the men's HDL levels, so it may provide extra protection for people taking beta blockers.

❧ HDL levels jumped from an average of 34 mg/dl to an average of 44.1 mg/dl in a group of 76 men and women with heart disease when they took a chromium supplement. They took 250 mcg per day for several months.

What do those numbers mean to your health? The risk of heart disease goes down two to three points with every mg/dl increase in HDL cholesterol. The 10 mg/dl increase in HDL cholesterol could lead to a potential 30 percent decrease in heart disease risk.

Helps hypoglycemia. Taking chromium dramatically improved symptoms for a group of people with hypoglycemia. Their symptoms included severe shaking, blurred vision, sleepiness, and heavy sweating. The researchers asked the hypoglycemics to guess the part of the study when they had been taking chromium instead of a fake pill. The change was so pronounced that every person in the study guessed correctly.

YOUR ACTION PLAN

Chromium is everywhere. We pick it up in the air and the water supply and from canned foods, since chromium leaches out of stainless steel cans. Some researchers also believe we have a reservoir of extra chromium somewhere in the body, although they're not sure just where the stash is hidden away.

But even with chromium floating around in the air and the water, many experts believe it's not enough to meet our bodies' needs. Americans consume less chromium in their food than people living in Italy, Egypt, South America, and India, in part because of the refining process used for grains in the United States.

HOW MUCH IS ENOUGH?

There's no Recommended Dietary Allowance (RDA) for chromium, but the Estimated Safe and Adequate Daily Dietary Intake for healthy adults is 20 to 30 mcg per day. Dr. Richard Anderson, a chromium expert with the U.S. Department of Agriculture, says you can safely take 50 to 100 mcg per day.

HOW TO GET MORE CHROMIUM NATURALLY

Some good food sources of the nutrient are:

❦ asparagus	❦ fresh fruit, especially
❦ beef	apples with skin
❦ brewer's yeast	❦ mushrooms
❦ calves' liver	❦ nuts
❦ chicken	❦ potatoes with skin
❦ dairy products	❦ prunes
❦ eggs	❦ whole-grain products
❦ fish and seafood	

White rice and white bread are poor sources, since the milling of grains removes up to 83 percent of the chromium, and the enrichment process doesn't replace any of it. Any food that is highly processed is going to be chromium-poor.

Watch the sugar. If you're eating a lot of sugary foods, you need extra chromium to metabolize it, plus you're actually draining the store of chromium your body has built up. Sugary foods may cause you to lose more chromium in your urine.

Instead, opt for whole grains and cereals, beans, peas, and starchy vegetables.

Exercise in moderation. Chromium is tough for your body to absorb. Exercise helps increase absorption, but too much of a workout can be counterproductive. When you exercise strenuously, your body needs more chromium because you lose more than usual.

Go easy on over-the-counter antacids. Calcium carbonate, the active ingredient in such products as Rolaids, decreases your body's ability to absorb chromium.

DO YOU NEED SUPPLEMENTS?

Chromium supplements may only help you if your body is lacking in this mineral. Unfortunately, figuring out whether you're deficient is almost impossible. Blood tests that measure chromium levels can be wildly inaccurate. That's because (1) your body has such a low level of chromium that it's hard to measure, (2) you can have chromium pools in your body that a blood test would miss, and (3) there's so much chromium in the environment that laboratories have trouble making sure it doesn't contaminate your blood sample.

The best way to find out whether you have a chromium deficiency is to take supplements and see if they help.

But don't do this without talking to your doctor first. There are still concerns regarding long-term safety and doses that are effective yet not toxic.

A low dose of chromium in a multivitamin supplement is probably a good idea for everyone.

THE WISE CHROMIUM CONSUMER

You can find chromium supplements in just about any grocery store, drugstore, or health food store. It's included in many, but not all, multivitamins. Check the label to make sure.

The chromium should be listed as chromium picolinate or nicotinate glycinate or as GTF (Glucose Tolerance Factor) chromium, which means it's combined with glycine, glutamic

THINK YOU RE GETTING ENOUGH? MAYBE NOT

The USDA's Dr. Richard Anderson believes that nine out of 10 Americans, Canadians, and British don't get the amount of chromium they need to ward off maturity-onset diabetes, hypoglycemia, and heart disease.

A diet can seem perfectly healthy, be high in most nutrients, and be low in chromium. Take a look at this "healthy" low-chromium diet Dr. Anderson used in one of his experiments:

Breakfast

Shredded wheat, egg, white bread with butter and grape jelly, whole milk

Lunch

Tuna with mayonnaise on whole wheat bread, apple, fruit punch, whole milk

Dinner

Beef cubes, white rice, peas, orange, lettuce, tomatoes, French dressing, sugar cookies, white roll with butter, whole milk

This well-balanced diet contains less than 20 mcg of chromium, much less than Dr. Anderson recommends.

acid, cysteine, and niacin. In other forms, chromium is extremely difficult for your body to absorb, making it of little benefit.

To get the most out of your chromium supplements, store them in a cool, dry place away from direct light, and don't freeze them.

CHROMIUM CAUTIONS

If you have diabetes, you need to talk to your doctor before taking supplements. Chromium could change the amount of insulin you need. You should also check with your doctor first if you have lung, liver, or kidney disease. Women who are pregnant or nursing should not take a chromium supplement.

A study released in 1995 suggested that chromium picolinate produced chromosome damage in the ovarian cells of hamsters, but chromium expert Dr. Richard Anderson strongly rejects the results of the study. He says that the rodents received a dose several thousand times higher than the typical supplement taken by humans.

In other studies, animals given 10,000 times more than the recommended dosage haven't had any side effects. The only cases of chromium poisoning have been from industrial overexposure in such jobs as abrasives manufacturing, diesel-locomotive repairs, fur processing, and oil drilling.

Of course, large doses of any nutrient could be harmful. In a laboratory test tube, large chromium doses slowed cell growth and blocked iron uptake.

In one fascinating study on chromium and aging, 10 lucky rats were fed extra chromium picolinate their whole lives. Those 10 rats lived 25 percent longer than the other 20 rodents in the experiment.

No one could understand it. Why were residents of "civilized," industrialized countries more likely to have heart disease and colon and rectal cancer than people in less "advanced" parts of the globe? We were plagued with more gallstones, diverticulosis, hemorrhoids, appendicitis, hiatal hernias, and varicose veins, too. It wasn't until 1970 that researchers uncovered the answer to the mystery. The Western World paid attention when British doctor Denis Burkitt reported that the fiber-rich diets eaten in less-developed countries appeared to be the lifesaving difference.

FIBER

Our language today is filled with references to the centuries-old process used to grind wheat into flour. We use the phrase "A millstone around your neck" to describe a heavy burden that weighs down your mind and spirit. Years ago, millstones rubbed together to crush kernels of wheat.

The next step in the process was to sift out or blow away the chaff, the inedible outer covering of the wheat kernel. Hence the term, "separating the wheat from the chaff," for keeping that which is good and nourishing — the wheat — and discarding that which has no useful purpose — the chaff.

Somewhere along the way, though, modern man determined that the time-honored milling process was more than just inefficient. It was inferior. With the introduction of new machinery, it was possible to remove the bran and the germ of the wheat and produce a whiter, smoother flour that consumers considered to be higher quality. Capitalism being what it is, white bread was born.

From a nutritional standpoint, the milling process had been essentially reversed. The nourishing portion was now being tossed to the wind, and the useless leftovers were being baked up and served to the king.

The fad escalated, and bread — a once healthful staple — now lacked a host of vitamins, minerals, and fiber. When the problem was finally recognized, the U.S. government passed the Enrichment Act of 1942. That law required the addition of niacin, thiamin, riboflavin, and iron to all refined grain products. Fiber was not deemed a necessary additive, although it's almost completely absent in enriched white bread.

Because of our refined flour, most Americans only eat about a third of the fiber they need on a daily basis.

Today, we've learned that a slice of whole-grain bread is a fiber, mineral, and vitamin powerhouse, containing magnesium, zinc, folate, vitamin E, vitamin B6, and chromium. And it tastes pretty good, too.

8 WAYS FIBER FIGHTS AGING

Have you been told that the pain of constipation, hemorrhoids, and hiatal hernia are the natural result of getting older? These gastrointestinal ailments aren't a normal part of aging. They're the ravages of a lifetime of sandwiches on white bread and Saturday cookouts underscored by white, fluffy hamburger and hot dog buns. An ethnic diet won't help much, either. There's refined flour in pizza crust and pasta, white rice, tortilla shells, and bagels.

By eating the right amount of fiber, as part of a healthy diet, you can ward off problems that have been associated with advancing age, and feel and act years younger.

Cholesterol. If you're looking to lower your level of lipids (try saying that three times fast), the medical literature suggests that you check out soluble fiber. (See *All fibers aren't equal — get the right type for you* later in this chapter.)

A group of researchers reviewed 77 different studies that looked at the effect of soluble fiber on total cholesterol, and they found significant reductions in 88 percent of them. Nearly all the studies showed that you can see results from a high-fiber diet in a matter of a few weeks.

The source of the fiber varied in the studies — ranging from pectin (found in apples and other fruit) to psyllium (the primary ingredient in Metamucil), dried beans to raw carrots. In one study, total cholesterol levels went down 7 percent with daily psyllium supplements, even after researchers added six to eight eggs *a day* to the diets of the volunteers!

THE GRAINS OF GOOD HEALTH

Let's take a look at what fiber actually is and what it does for your digestive system.

First of all, it's nothing new. In the olden days, before fiber was popular in health food stores and newspaper food sections, your parents or grandparents may have fixed you a big salad or given you celery with peanut butter and talked about the importance of "roughage." That's fiber. It's found in all whole grains, peas, beans, fruits, and vegetables. You won't find it at all in animal products (meats, dairy products, and eggs).

Fiber is the tough part of the plant that supports the leaves, stems, and seeds. On a cellular level, most fibers are chains of sugars, just like starch is. When you eat starches, the sugar can be digested and used for energy. But with fiber, your body's digestive juices can't break down the chains that hold the sugar together.

The end result: The fibers pass through your body without providing any fuel. But the value of fiber isn't in what it puts into your body, it's in what it takes with it on its way out.

The review also suggested that age and gender may play a role in how the body uses fiber. In one study, women over the age of 50 had the biggest reduction in cholesterol. In another, elderly men and women showed a 20 percent drop in total cholesterol with psyllium supplements.

If you want to lower your cholesterol with soluble fiber, the reports suggest that you can expect results by consuming one of the following on a daily basis:

❦ 6 to 40 grams of pectin (one apple provides 1 1/2 grams)
❦ 8 to 36 grams (2 1/2 to 10 tablespoons) of gums — guar gum and others can be bought in powder form
❦ 100 to 150 grams (1/2 to 3/4 cup) of dried beans or peas
❦ 25 to 100 grams (1/3 to 1 1/4 cups) of dry oat bran
❦ 57 to 140 grams (3/4 to 1 3/4 cups) of dry oatmeal
❦ 10 to 30 grams (3 to 9 tablespoons) of psyllium — the main ingredient in most fiber supplements

Colon/rectal cancer. Medical and dietary literature overwhelmingly supports a high-fiber diet for reducing your risk of colon and rectal cancer. Fiber works mainly by helping move food through your digestive system more quickly. That reduces the amount of time cancer-causing agents remain in your colon. Fiber's bulk helps in two other ways, too. It dilutes bile acids that may promote cancer growth, and it revs up bacteria in your stomach that fight the toxins you unintentionally eat.

In a study conducted by the Arizona Cancer Center in Tucson, people who ate two-thirds of a cup of wheat fiber cereal a day for nine months had a 73 percent drop in bile acids. All 95 of the study participants were between 50 and 75 years old and had had surgery to remove precancerous polyps in their colons, making them at high risk for colon cancer.

Constipation and hemorrhoids. You're constipated if you're having fewer bowel movements than usual for you, and your stools are hard, dry, and difficult to pass. If you suffer from constipation regularly, you're going to get hemorrhoids, which are swollen veins in the rectum.

And if you're like most of the four million constipated Americans, you haven't visited your doctor about your condition. You're trying to treat yourself. That's why sales of over-the-counter laxatives rose to more than $500 million a year.

That sales figure is frightening. People who rely on laxatives can become addicted, doing their bodies great harm.

If you use laxatives too long, your bowels become dependent on them and may not function properly without them. You also become malnourished because nutrients are rushing through your intestines so quickly your body doesn't have time to absorb them.

Mineral oil, for example, can rob you of fat-soluble vitamins and minerals. Vitamin D and calcium dissolve in the oil and are excreted with the oil instead of being used by your body.

Instead of using laxatives, you need to change your diet. Not getting enough fiber in your diet is the single most common cause of constipation. Most people would have no problem with constipation if they doubled their fiber intakes.

Diabetes. Your diet, including fiber, can play a tremendous role in controlling diabetes and helping diabetics stay healthy.

Fiber actually helps control your blood sugar. How? It ties up the sugar in the food you eat, slowing down your body's absorption of sugars and starches. That helps blood sugar rise gradually over a longer period, instead of rising quickly after a meal.

Diverticulosis/diverticulitis and appendicitis. Half the people over age 60 have diverticula, which are sac-like swellings about the size of the tip of your pinkie finger. They grow on the wall of the large intestine, and they are the direct result of a diet high in fat and red meat and low in fiber.

Most people who have diverticulosis never even know it. They might have some mild cramping or tenderness that's relieved by a bowel movement or passing gas. But if the sacs become inflamed and infected, you may find yourself doubled over in pain and passing blood in your stools. When that happens, you've got diverticulitis.

Gallstones. Having stones in your gallbladder is normal. About one in five Americans over age 40 has them. The gallbladder is a sac connected to the liver that stores bile. Stones form out of cholesterol, bile pigment, or calcium. The stones aren't cancerous, and almost half the people who have them won't have any symptoms. However, when gallstones obstruct the flow of bile and cause symptoms, you can suffer with severe spasms, nausea and vomiting, bloating, jaundice, and an intolerance for fatty foods.

One of the risk factors for gallstones is a high-fat, low-fiber diet. Another is obesity. You should be able to beat gallstones with a diet high in fiber and low in fat and a sensible weight loss program. Don't try to lose weight too quickly, though. Rapid weight loss also has been linked to this disorder.

Heart disease. If you could do one easy thing to cut your risk of a fatal heart attack by more than half, would you do it? Most people would say "yes" in, well, a heartbeat.

A long-term study of more than 40,000 U.S. male health professionals tracked their eating habits over a six-year period. Researchers found that the risk of a fatal heart attack was 55 percent lower for the men who ate the most fiber. Most all of these men started their day off with a bowl of cold breakfast cereal.

The researchers concluded that you could cut your risk of heart attack by 20 percent just by adding 10 grams of fiber a day to your diet. That's the same impact you would get by lowering your cholesterol by 10 percent.

The American Health Foundation advocates an easy-to-remember 25/25 diet — no more than 25 percent of calories from fat and at least 25 grams of fiber every day. *The Journal of the American Medical Association* recommends a lifelong high-fiber diet starting at about age 2, using the formula "age plus 5." That means by the time you're 20 years old, you should be consuming the recommended 25 grams of fiber a day.

A high-fiber diet also is part of a regimen to reduce your risk of atherosclerosis, or hardening of the arteries, a major cause of heart attacks and strokes.

Hiatal hernia. The hiatus in a hiatal hernia is the opening in your diaphragm where your esophagus passes through on its way from your throat to your stomach. When you have a hiatal hernia, that opening is weak or stretched out. Part of your stomach is able to poke up through that opening, and stomach acid tends to splash up and irritate the esophagus.

Most common for people over 50, a hiatal hernia can cause heartburn, belching, and difficulty swallowing. Your risk for a hiatal hernia increases if you have chronic constipation and strain during bowel movements. Since a high-fiber diet is considered the most effective remedy for constipation, it stands to reason that it reduces your risk of hiatal hernia as well.

ALL FIBERS AREN'T EQUAL
GET THE RIGHT TYPE FOR YOU

Plants are made of two kinds of fiber — soluble and insoluble. Some plants just have one type; some have both.

Insoluble fiber is what most people think of as fiber. It's in whole grains, wheat bran, vegetables, seeds, peas, beans, and brown rice. It doesn't dissolve in water.

By adding bulk, insoluble fiber speeds up your food's trip through your digestive system. That reduces your risk of colon cancer, diverticulosis, and appendicitis. It also keeps your stools soft and your bowels moving regularly. That helps prevent constipation, hemorrhoids, hiatal hernia, and irritable bowel syndrome. Since the fiber absorbs water and swells, you feel full long after you eat it. That helps you lose weight.

Soluble fiber dissolves easily in water. It can make food gummy or gel-like. It's found in fruits, vegetables, seeds, rye, oats, barley, rice bran, peas, and beans. Pectin, taken from apples and other fruits, can be used to thicken jelly or hold salad dressing together.

Soluble fiber can help lower cholesterol and keep blood sugar levels on an even keel, even for people with diabetes.

YOUR ACTION PLAN

You've heard all the benefits of a high-fiber diet, so now it's time to swing into action. Here are some common questions, good guidelines, and words of caution.

HOW MUCH IS ENOUGH?

The Food and Drug Administration and the National Cancer Institute recommend between 20 and 35 grams of fiber a day. Most Americans get about 11 grams a day.

HOW TO GET MORE FIBER NATURALLY

The easiest way to add fiber to your diet is to eat a fiber-rich cereal for breakfast. It's a great way to start the day, and a large bowl helps compensate for a lack of fiber in your other meals.

You also can add fiber by eating an extra serving of fruits and vegetables a day, switching to whole-grain breads and brown rice from white, adding cooked beans to your diet every week, or adding 1/4 cup or more of miller's bran to some foods, such as cooked cereal or applesauce.

When you add fiber to your diet, you also need to make sure you are getting enough fluids. A healthy level of fluid intake is six to eight eight-ounce glasses of water a day.

Easy substitutes

Refined food item	Fiber-full option
White bread	Whole wheat bread or rolls*
White rice	Brown rice
Mashed potatoes	Baked potato in the skin
Applesauce	Unpeeled apple, or applesauce made with unpeeled apples
Orange juice	Orange
Refined cereals	Whole grain cereals (check label for fiber content)
Potato chips	Popcorn (lightly seasoned, if at all)

(continued)

Refined food item	Fiber-full option
Bread crumbs	Wheat or oat bran bread crumbs

* Make sure whole-wheat flour, not just wheat flour, is the first ingredient.

High-fiber foods

Here is a helpful chart of good sources of fiber, courtesy of the American Institute for Cancer Research.

Food	Serving size	Grams of fiber
Cereals		
All Bran or		
100% Bran	1/3 cup (1 oz)	9 - 10
Bran Chex	2/3 cup (1 oz)	5
Bran Flakes	2/3 cup (1 oz)	5
Extra Fiber		
Bran Cereal	1/2 cup (1 oz)	14
Nutri-Grain		
Wheat Flakes	2/3 cup (1 oz)	3
Fruit and Fiber	1/2 cup (1 oz)	4
Raisin Bran	1/2 cup (1 oz)	4 - 5
Shredded Wheat	2/3 cup (1 oz)	3
Wheat Chex	2/3 cup (1 oz)	3
Wheat Germ	1/4 cup (1 oz)	3
Oatmeal,		
quick or regular	2/3 cup (1 oz)	3
Bread, pasta, grains		
Bran muffins	1 regular muffin	2.5
Cracked wheat bread	1 slice	1.1
Pumpernickel bread	1 slice	1.0
Whole wheat bread	1 slice	1.6
Ry Krisp	6 crackers (1/2 oz)	3.5
Crispbread	1 - 3 crackers (1/2 oz)	2.5
Rice, brown	1/2 cup cooked	1.0
Spaghetti, whole wheat	1 cup cooked	3.9
Popcorn	1 cup	2.5
Tortilla, corn	1 tortilla	1.3

(continued)

Food	Serving size	Grams of fiber
Fruits		
Apple, with skin	1 medium	3.5
Apple, without skin	1 medium	2.7
Banana	1 medium	1.9
Blackberries	1 cup	6.6
Blueberries	1 cup	4.4
Dates	10	4.2
Orange	1	2.4
Pear, canned	2 halves	2.2
Pear, with skin	1 medium	4.6
Prunes	3	3.0
Raisins	1/4 cup	1.6
Raspberries	1 cup	5.8
Strawberries	1 cup	2.7
Vegetables, cooked		
Broccoli	1/2 cup	2.7
Brussels sprouts	1/2 cup	3.2
Carrots	1/2 cup	2.0
Corn, canned	1/2 cup	1.6
Parsnips	1/2 cup	2.7
Peas	1/2 cup	2.8
Potato with skin	1 medium	5.0
Spinach	1/2 cup	2.1
Sweet potato	1/2 medium	1.7
Zucchini	1/2 cup	1.8
Beans, peas		
Baked beans in tomato sauce	1/2 cup	8.8
Cooked kidney beans	1/2 cup	7.3
Lima beans, cooked, canned	1/2 cup	4.5
Navy beans, cooked	1/2 cup	6.1
Lentils	1/2 cup	3.7

Extra ways to add extra whole grains

Here are some simple, good tasting ideas for adding fiber grams to your daily diet:

❦ Place thin slices of whole grain bread under the broiler. Turn once they are well-browned. When slices have cooled, crumble into tiny pieces for use as bread crumbs in recipes. For herbed stuffing, sprinkle spices on the bread before toasting. Crumbs can be stored for weeks in an air-tight bag.

❦ Use rolled oats or oat bran in meatloaf, meatballs, or other dishes that require bread crumbs.

❦ Try using rolled oats, oat bran, or wheat bran and a small amount of Parmesan cheese as a topping for casseroles in place of bread crumbs and cheddar cheese.

❦ Keep oat bran muffins in your freezer for a quick breakfast. They can be thawed quickly in your microwave, and they are good to take along while traveling or for a snack at work.

❦ A handful of low-fat granola in the morning is a good, whole-grain addition to your breakfast.

❦ For dessert or snack, use oatmeal cookies or brownies made with added oat bran.

❦ You can substitute oat groats, wheat berries, or barley for rice in most recipes.

❦ Stir whole grains into soups — let the soup cook for at least 45 minutes after adding grains.

❦ Use oat or wheat bran as the "breading" on broiled or pan-broiled meats and vegetables.

❦ Serve only whole-grain breads and rolls.

❦ When eating out, try ethnic restaurants that offer more bean and meatless entrees. Good choices include Middle Eastern or Mediterranean cuisines. Chinese and Japanese dishes are often prepared with many fresh vegetables.

❦ At restaurant salad bars, fill up on high-fiber greens like broccoli and spinach.

DO YOU NEED SUPPLEMENTS?

You should be able to get all the fiber you need from natural food sources. And, a plus — many high-fiber foods, like fruits and vegetables, also are high in alkaline, a natural laxative.

Taking fiber supplements can help you, but don't take too much. And, make sure you also eat plenty of healthy foods. Pure fiber, like oat bran, wheat bran, or a psyllium supplement, doesn't contain any nutrients.

FIBER CAUTIONS

The ancient Greek dictum of everything in moderation certainly applies to fiber. We've already discussed the problems associated with too little, but there are significant reasons not to overdo.

Many people have been "turned off" to fiber because they added too much too quickly, and they suffered such unpleasant side effects as bloating, cramps, loose stools, and flatulence. All this can be minimized by gradually adding fiber from a wide variety of food sources, drinking plenty of water, and eating well-balanced meals slowly and chewing thoroughly. Within a few weeks, your intestinal system will adjust.

A special word of caution about going overboard on purified bran products, like wheat bran or oat bran: One man required emergency surgery on his intestines to remove a blockage created by eating too many oat bran muffins.

There also are special cautions for elderly people. Remember that fiber makes you feel fuller, so you eat less. That can cause deficiencies of other nutrients, as well as reduce the amount of energy your body is getting.

Do you love seafood? Your heart does. Eating just one three-ounce serving of fatty fish a week could slash your risk of heart attack in half.

FISH OIL

Remember how your mother always said eating fish would make you smart? Fish has long been considered "brain food," and studies show that old wives' tale may be true.

Fish is rich in omega-3 fatty acids. These fatty acids are necessary to keep your brain in tiptop shape. Research has shown that two omega-3 fats, eicosapentaenoic acid (EPA) and docosahexaenoic acid (DHA), are important for brain development. They also may protect your brain from damage or heal it after damage occurs.

EPA and DHA are also critical for keeping your eyes sharp. Some researchers think your eyes deteriorate as you age because you don't maintain enough omega-3 fatty acids in your retinas.

EPA and DHA are found in seafood, especially cold-water fish. Another omega-3 fatty acid is alpha linolenic acid (LNA) which is found in tofu, soybean and canola oils, and nuts.

Omega-3 fatty acids affect your body differently from another type of fatty acid — omega-6, which plays a critical role in your cell membranes. Omega-6 fats are found in vegetable oils, seeds, nuts, and whole-grain products. Both of these fatty acids are considered essential nutrients because your body can't make them — they must come from the food you eat.

While most people get plenty of omega-6 fats, they sometimes have problems getting enough omega-3. That's because these fatty acids are mainly found in fish oil, and most people just don't eat enough fish.

Looking for a quick, easy way to add fish oil to your diet? Try the two recipes found in this chapter and discover how tasty fish can be.

BROILED SESAME FISH

For a quick, low-fat main dish, try this fish recipe. It takes about 15 minutes to prepare and contains very little fat. Makes four servings.

Cod fillets, fresh or frozen	1 pound
Margarine, melted	1 teaspoon
Lemon juice	1 tablespoon
Dried tarragon leaves	1 teaspoon
Salt	1/8 teaspoon
Pepper	Dash
Sesame seed	1 tablespoon
Parsley, chopped	1 tablespoon

Thaw frozen fish in refrigerator overnight or defrost briefly in a microwave oven. Cut fish into four portions. Place fish on a broiler pan lined with aluminum foil. Brush margarine over fish. Mix lemon juice, tarragon leaves, salt, and pepper. Pour over fish. Sprinkle sesame seeds evenly over fish. Broil until fish flakes easily when tested with a fork — about 12 minutes. Garnish each serving with parsley.

6 WAYS FISH OIL FIGHTS AGING

Heart disease healer. Would you believe eating fat can make you thin? Well, a part of you anyway. Omega-3 fatty acids help thin your blood, and this may protect your heart. Like aspirin, omega-3 helps keep your blood from becoming too sticky and forming clots, which can cause heart attack and stroke. Studies show that eating one 3-ounce serving of fatty fish per week can cut your risk of heart attack in half. If you never eat seafood, but start including even a moderate amount in your diet, you can lower your risk of heart disease by 50 to 70 percent.

Fish oil also lowers your bad cholesterol and triglyceride levels, and it helps protect against irregular heartbeats. If your high blood pressure is caused by hardening of the arteries, heart disease, or high cholesterol, fish oil may be just what the doctor ordered. The higher your cholesterol levels and the worse your heart disease, the better fish oil works to lower your blood pressure.

If you're free and clear of heart disease, fish oil may or may not help your blood pressure. Studies show you have to take a lot to get any effect at all.

If you really want to live right, consider moving to Greenland. The Eskimos there are well-known for their low death rates from heart attack. Studies have shown their diet of seal, walrus, and mackerel puts them in fish oil heaven.

Takes a stab at strokes. Eating fish may be smart stroke protection for women.

A four-year study showed that white women who ate fish more than once a week suffered strokes about half as much as those who never ate fish. White men didn't show the same effect, but black women and men did.

Since stroke is the third leading cause of death in women, you may want to put fish at the top of your next grocery list.

The news isn't all bad for men, either. A 25-year study found that men who did not have strokes during that time ate almost 50 percent more fish than the men who did have strokes. The risk was lower for the men who consistently ate fish than for those who changed their eating patterns later to include fish.

Animal studies show that fish oil helps stop blood clots from forming in your blood vessels. Since blood clots can cause strokes, it makes sense that this would help prevent them.

There is a drawback, however. Fish oil's blood-thinning effect may increase your risk of stroke caused by bleeding in the brain. This only seems to occur when people eat huge amounts of fish. If you eat a sensible amount, two to three portions a week, you'll reap the benefits and not have to worry about the dangers.

Pain-free periods. Nausea, bloating, headaches, cramps. Does this sound like your monthly horror show? Omega-6 fatty acids may be partly responsible for your uncomfortable menstrual symptoms. They help produce certain substances, called prostaglandins and leukotrienes, which cause those unwelcome and painful conditions.

But omega-3 fats come to the rescue, so to speak. They compete to make the same substances, and this interaction helps reduce the inflammatory effect omega-6 has on your body.

A study with adolescents found that omega-3 supplements did just that, resulting in less-painful periods.

Attacks arthritis. Arthritis acting up? Dig in to a seafood dinner several times a week and keep those joints moving.

In a recent study, people with rheumatoid arthritis who took 3 to 6 grams of an omega-3 supplement reported a fewer number of tender joints and a shorter period of morning stiffness. They were able to stop their anti-inflammatory medications, and the relief lasted up to eight weeks after stopping the supplements.

Eating fish, especially the dark, oily kind like salmon, sardines, anchovies, tuna, mackerel, and bluefish, is the best way to get your fish oil. But although it may help soothe your pain, you shouldn't depend on diet alone to control your arthritis. You'd need to eat a salmon or mackerel every day to get 3 grams of omega-3 fatty acids. The recommended two or three servings of fish a week wouldn't do it.

Good for diabetics. Eskimos who eat a lot of fish don't seem to get diabetes as often as most people. With diabetes, your body is "glucose intolerant," meaning it has a hard time regulating your sugar levels. Fish oil has been shown to reduce this glucose intolerance, but it has to be eaten every day. If you have mild diabetes, you may benefit from fish oil, but if you have a severe form of diabetes, it probably won't help.

Prevents relapse in Crohn's disease. Crohn's disease is a painful condition that can affect any part of your gastrointestinal tract from your mouth to your bottom. The most common place for problems is at the end of your small intestine where it joins the large intestine. Fish oil may prevent a relapse of this disease because it keeps the inflammation from flaring up.

YOUR ACTION PLAN

HOW MUCH IS ENOUGH?

Neither omega-6 nor omega-3 fatty acids have a Recommended Dietary Allowance (RDA), but scientists may agree to include them in the future. Meanwhile, experts say you should eat fish two or three times a week, as well as small amounts of vegetable oils, to get the right balance between those two essential nutrients. You should try to eat one omega-3 food for every four omega-6 foods. Scientists say this ratio may be critical to maintaining the proper balance for your health.

HOW TO GET MORE FISH OIL NATURALLY

Simple — eat fish, especially fatty, cold-water fish. Some of the more common varieties include anchovies, bluefish, herring, mackerel, mullet, salmon, sardines, sturgeon, trout, tuna, and whitefish.

Cod is a cold-water fish, but it stores omega-3 in its liver rather than its flesh. Many doctors advise against a regular supplement of cod liver oil, since too much can cause overdoses of vitamins A, D, and E.

Shellfish like lobster, crab, and shrimp have smaller amounts of omega-3, as do mollusks like scallops and clams.

Can you get this important nutrient from plants? Sure, but plant sources are generally lower in omega-3 than the same amount of fish. Oat germ is an exception — it's better than all but 15 kinds of oil-rich fish. Other plant sources include flaxseed, dry beans, tofu, soybean products, walnuts, wheat germ oil, and purslane, a type of lettuce used in soups and salads in Mediterranean countries.

Margarine is also a rich source of omega-3, mainly because it's made from soybeans. Unfortunately, it also has more saturated fat than fish or other plant sources.

So go ahead and enjoy some anchovies on your pizza, whip up a tuna casserole, or treat yourself to a thick salmon steak. You'll give yourself a hearty dose of fish oil in the best way possible — naturally.

DO YOU NEED SUPPLEMENTS?

Let's face it, some people just can't stand fish. If you're one of those who would rather swim with the fish than eat them, you can turn to fish oil capsules to get the fatty acids you need. Just make sure you don't overdo it. The effective dose is between 3 and 5 grams daily.

FISH OIL CAUTIONS

It's easy to overdose on fish oil supplements because the oil in a pill is more concentrated than in the fish itself. And if you take too much, you can change your blood fat levels and worsen type 2 diabetes. It can also harm your immune system, which makes it easier for you to develop infections or even cancer.

Fish oil supplements are made from fish skins and livers, which may contain toxic pesticides and other contaminants. Fish oil contains high levels of vitamins A and D, which can also be toxic if you take too much.

You're also risking free radical damage. Since omega-3 fatty acids are unsaturated, they're open to attacks by free-radical oxygen. This starts a chain reaction that can easily damage your cell membranes and may lead to cancer and heart disease. If you get too much omega-3 fat, you could be letting yourself in for more than you bargained.

Any benefits you'd get from fish oil supplements are probably outweighed by the dangers. Your best bet is to go straight to the source — eat fish.

CITRUS FISH FILLETS

Add a citrus tang to this fish recipe with orange and lemon juice. Makes four servings.

Cod fillets, fresh or frozen	1 pound
Orange juice	2 tablespoons
Lemon juice	1 tablespoon
Orange rind, grated	1 teaspoon
Rosemary, crumbled	1/2 teaspoon
Ground ginger	1/4 teaspoon
Salt	1/8 teaspoon
Pepper	1/8 teaspoon
Garlic, minced	1 clove
Margarine, melted	1 tablespoon
Orange	2 slices
Parsley, chopped	1 tablespoon

2 to 24 hours ahead:

Thaw frozen fish in refrigerator overnight or in microwave oven. Separate fish into four fillets or pieces. Place fish in glass or stainless steel dish. Mix juices, orange rind, rosemary, ginger, salt, pepper, and garlic. Pour over fish; cover and refrigerate for 2 to 24 hours. Turn over once or twice.

To prepare:

Drain fish; discard marinade. Place fish in baking pan; brush with margarine. Broil 4 inches from heat 8 to 10 minutes or until fish flakes easily with a fork. Garnish with halved orange slices and parsley.

The same plant that may have provided material for your table-cloth or blazer could also help you live longer. The seed of the flax plant, which is the source of linen cloth, has been found to reduce cholesterol and protect against hormone-dependent cancers like breast cancer and prostate cancer.

FLAXSEED

Cotton may be king, but the humble flax plant has helped keep people fed, clothed, and healthy for centuries. In fact, flax was probably one of the first crops cultivated by man, perhaps as long ago as 8000 B.C. Even the Bible makes note of the many uses of this versatile plant. The flax plant was used for the thatching of roofs, and fibers from the stem of the plant provided flax for weaving cloth, either fine linen for clothing or coarse cloth for tents. The seeds of the plant were eaten or pressed to make linseed oil for cooking.

According to other historical records, linseed oil has been used internally, as a laxative, and externally, to soften and soothe skin. Linseed oil is found today as an ingredient in paints, varnishes, and printer's ink.

The medicinal qualities of flax throughout the years have ranged from treating colds to helping remove foreign objects from the eye.

Modern medical research has confirmed some of the traditional benefits of flax and has found many others. For example:

❦ Lowers cholesterol
❦ Provides heart-healthy omega-3 fatty acids
❦ Protects against certain cancers
❦ Increases the amount of fiber in your diet
❦ Stimulates your immune system

4 WAYS FLAXSEED FIGHTS AGING

Heads off heart disease. Are you careful to keep the oil changed in your car because you know that smoothly flowing oil will make your car last much longer? You should try to keep your blood flowing smoothly, too, so your body can function like a well-oiled machine. The smoother and easier your blood flows, the less work your heart has to do. Your blood tends to get thicker and stickier with age, just like the oil in your car. While you can't run to the nearest quick-change shop and get a fresh supply of blood, adding a little flaxseed to your diet may be the next best thing.

Flaxseed or linseed is the best vegetable source of omega-3 fatty acids. Omega-3s help keep your blood from becoming sticky, lowering your risk of heart attack and stroke.

Controls cholesterol. Your daily bread can help keep damaging cholesterol under control. One study found that when people with high cholesterol ate six slices of flaxseed bread a day, their cholesterol levels dropped significantly, compared with those who ate six slices of wheat bread. Whenever you break bread, maybe you should make sure it has some cholesterol-clobbering, heart-protecting flaxseed inside.

Puts cancer to rest. Can a simple plant fight the most deadly of diseases — cancer? Studies show that flax is one plant that may help put the squeeze on this killer disease. Lignans, a type of phytochemical or natural disease fighter that comes from plants, have been shown to prevent or slow the growth of several types of cancer. When researchers studied foods in an attempt to identify those that contained substances that make up lignan, they found that flaxseed contained 75 to 800 times more of those substances than other foods.

One study found that rats fed flaxseed and then exposed to cancer-causing substances cut their risks of developing colon cancer by more than half. Flaxseed may be especially effective at guarding against hormone-related cancers like breast cancer and prostate cancer.

Gives kidneys a kick. Flaxseed may give failing kidneys a boost. Researchers conducted a study to see if people with systemic lupus erythematosus, a disease of the immune system, might be able to benefit from adding flaxseed to their diet. Lupus causes connective tissue to become inflamed, eventually causing damage to internal organs, particularly the kidneys. Sometimes the kidneys begin to fail, resulting in the need for dialysis or a kidney transplant. The study participants

---

FLAXSEED PANCAKES OR WAFFLES

1-1/2 cups whole wheat flour
1/2 cup flaxseed flour (contains 35 percent oil; add 1 or 2 tablespoons of vegetable oil, if desired)
1-1/2 cups pancake mix or all-purpose flour
1/4 teaspoon baking powder (double if you use flour rather than pancake mix)
1/4 teaspoon baking soda (double if you use flour)
3 tablespoons sugar (if desired)
1/4 teaspoon salt
1 teaspoon cinnamon
1 egg (or 2 egg whites)
3 cups buttermilk

Combine dry ingredients in a large bowl; add eggs and buttermilk. Bake on griddle or electric skillet at 375 to 400 degrees, or cook waffles on waffle iron. Makes about 2-1/2 dozen 4-inch pancakes or about 8 waffles.

---

stirred between 15 and 45 grams of flaxseed into their breakfast cereals, orange juice, and other beverages. Researchers found that the flaxseed improved kidney function and reduced the scarring of the kidney tissue that accompanies the disease.

YOUR ACTION PLAN

HOW MUCH IS ENOUGH?

The average adult only needs about three teaspoons of flaxseed a day.

FLAXSEED MUFFINS OR

QUICK BREAD

3 cups all-purpose flour
1 cup flaxseed flour
1 teaspoon salt
1 teaspoon baking powder
1 teaspoon baking soda
1 teaspoon cinnamon
2 cups milk
4 egg whites or 2 eggs
1/2 teaspoon vanilla extract
1/2 cup honey or sugar
Grated peel from 2 lemons or oranges
2 cups dried fruit*

Combine dry ingredients in a large bowl. Add fruit to dry mixture. Mix together milk, eggs, sugar, vanilla, and grated lemon peel and add to dry mixture.

Bake in loaf pans, about 3 by 7 inches, or muffin tins at 350 degrees for 40 minutes. Makes 2 loaves or about 2 dozen muffins.

How to get more flaxseed naturally

Flaxseed is easy to add to your diet. You can sprinkle a couple of spoonfuls of these nutty-tasting seeds on your cereal in the morning, or you can bake it into breads and muffins.

Do you need flaxseed?

Almost everyone needs to eat more food high in fiber, and flaxseed is an excellent source of fiber.

The wise flaxseed consumer

Health food stores carry several different flaxseed products — flaxseed flour, meal, oil, and ground flaxseed. Flaxseed oil becomes rancid quickly, so it's probably a good idea to buy small amounts at a time and make sure you store it properly. Many flaxseed products should be refrigerated, or at least stored in a cool, dry place.

Flaxseed cautions

Because flaxseed is high in fiber, it may cause gas until your body gets used to it, so start with small amounts. People with diabetes or hemophilia, a blood clotting disorder, should consult their doctors before adding flaxseed to their diet. Flaxseed may cause changes in your blood, which could affect the treatment of these diseases.

Garlic is the most widely used herb in the world and for good reason. No other herb has served mankind as food and medicine for so long and in so many ways. Modern research now bolsters ancient claims of garlic's powers to treat every ailment from the common cold to heart disease, cancer, and infections — America's top three killers.

GARLIC

"Eat leeks in March and wild garlic in May,
And all the year after physicians may play."
Old Welsh rhyme

Garlic's mellow taste and aroma spice up gourmet dishes and peasant casseroles the world over. Popular with health-conscious cooks because it adds flavor without fat, some folks still object to the herb's strong odor. But garlic's health and anti-aging benefits are nothing to sniff at. Modern science has come a long way toward proving the herb's ability to rev up the immune system, battle some kinds of cancer, and control infection and heart disease. Truly, garlic is nature's herbal wonder drug, a potent weapon against premature aging.

Cultivated since Neolithic times, garlic is one of the world's oldest crops. According to legend, garlic was said to strengthen the heart; protect against the plague; cure colds, athlete's foot, toothache, and snakebite; repel vampires and demons; grow hair; stimulate sexual performance; and rid the dog of fleas. Always a popular remedy for colds, sore throats, and coughs, your grandmother may have prescribed it eaten raw or boiled into a syrup. There are plenty of reasons to celebrate this easy-to-find, inexpensive "white pearl."

In ancient Egypt, garlic was worshiped as both food and medicine. Cloves of garlic were unearthed in King Tut's (the Pharaoh Tutankhamen's) tomb. Slaves building the pyramids refused to work because their daily meals did not include sufficient garlic and onions to boost their physical performance, according to an Egyptian papyrus dated 1600 B.C.

Scientists all over the world are examining folklore's claims of garlic's benefits, especially its ability to strengthen the immune system and fight damage from free radicals, the potentially harmful atoms that cause aging and cancer.

"Because garlic has the power to save from death,

Endure it, though it leaves behind bad breath."

— Duke Robert I of Normandy

8 WAYS GARLIC FIGHTS AGING

Garlic's complex chemistry has long been the subject of scientific study. In the last 50 years, researchers have published more than 2,000 scientific papers documenting the herb's potency against bacteria, cancer, hardening of the arteries, and other threats to the heart.

Of garlic's more than 100 chemical parts, one of the strongest is allicin, an amino acid that's released when a clove is crushed. It is a powerful antibacterial and antiviral agent. Allicin is what gives off that pungent aroma particular to garlic and its cousins in the allium family (leeks, chives, shallots — all relatives of the elegant lily.) Garlic is also rich with the vitamins A, B, and C; the minerals calcium, potassium, and iron; and the antioxidants germanium and selenium.

Lengthens cell life. In a recent Danish study, researchers added garlic extract to laboratory dishes of human skin cells. The cells reproduced while scientists checked their health and life spans. The cells exposed to garlic were healthier and lived much longer than the cells deprived of garlic.

In a Japanese study, researchers found that mice fed garlic lived significantly longer than the control mice, plus their learning ability and memory were much improved. Dr. T. Moriguchi at the University of Tokyo, Japan, who conducted the study, wrote that garlic "might be useful for treating physiological aging and age-related memory deficits in humans."

"Russian penicillin." During World War II, the Soviet Army used so much garlic as a remedy that the herb earned the nickname "Russian penicillin" for its ability to help the body fight off infections, particularly respiratory and digestive infections. The great French research biologist Louis Pasteur studied garlic's antibiotic power in 1858. In a more recent study, Boston University medical school researchers claimed that garlic works like an antibiotic against strep, staph, and fungus and yeast infections, as well as numerous strains of the flu.

In the Orient, garlic has been in use since the 6th century, and it's still extremely popular for dysentery, parasites, and other stomach infections. Traditionally, the Chinese have considered garlic a tonic for older people to improve digestion and circulation.

Allicin is the remarkable agent that fights bacteria. It seems to even fight some infections that are normally resistant to antibiotics. Such power may account for garlic's legendary reputation in folk remedies.

In Germany, where garlic has government approval for its heart-healthy benefits, garlic supplements are the top-selling over-the-counter medicine in drugstores. An estimated 12 percent of the population over age 14 takes garlic preparations.

Battles cancer. Scientists have long known that people who traditionally eat a lot of garlic, like the Chinese and Italians, have lower rates of stomach cancer. In 1988, The National Cancer Institute reported on a study of 1,695 Chinese. Of the 564 participants with stomach cancer, most ate little or no garlic. A 1991 study concluded that two of garlic's sulfur compounds (ajoene and diallyl sulfide) appear to fight cancer.

Garlic may battle breast cancer, too. Pennsylvania State researcher Dr. John A. Milner exposed rats to huge amounts of chemicals that cause cancer. Then he gave some of the rats chow full of garlic. The rats who ate garlicky chow had 50 percent fewer precancerous changes in their breasts.

Stay heart-healthy with garlic. If you live in the United States, your chances of having dangerously high cholesterol levels and hard, stiff arteries are greater than 50 percent.

Excess cholesterol in your body builds up on blood vessel walls, reducing the amount of oxygen and nutrients that get to your brain and putting a strain on your heart. Blood clots can form around these fatty deposits. In an artery supplying the heart, such clots can lead to chest pain and heart attack. If a blood vessel nourishing the brain becomes clogged, the result could be a stroke.

Taking small amounts of garlic daily can lower the "bad" LDL (low-density lipoprotein) cholesterol while raising the "good" HDL (high-density lipoprotein) cholesterol. HDL cholesterol prevents the build up of fatty deposits in your arteries.

One-half to one clove of garlic a day (or the equivalent in garlic supplements) may be all that's needed to decrease total cholesterol levels from 9 to 17 percent. Look for results after a month.

Garlic may even protect you after you've suffered a heart attack. In a three-year study in India, 432 heart attack survivors who drank the juice of six to 10 garlic cloves a day had almost half as many deaths as the group who drank fake garlic juice.

Protects against blood clots. One of garlic's 33 sulfur-rich compounds, known as ajoene, helps prevent blood clots. As you age, your blood can become "sticky" as blood platelets clump together and attach to artery walls, eventually forming dangerous clots. Some scientists believe that ajoene is as strong as aspirin in thinning the blood.

Lowers high blood pressure. There's even some evidence that garlic may also lower high blood pressure.

Eases painful leg cramps. Because garlic stimulates the circulatory system, researchers believe the herb may help treat the painful condition known as "intermittent claudication." That's the leg cramps and aches you get when you don't have enough blood flowing to your legs. Doctors often advise a walking program to help ease the pain of claudication, but walking more than short distances hurts! People participating in a recent study in Germany took 800 milligrams of garlic powder for 12 weeks and were able to walk farther without the cramping pain.

Richest in antioxidants. Garlic is extremely rich in antioxidants, which block free radicals — the potentially harmful elements that circulate in the body and may lead to cancer and heart disease. The U.S. Department of Agriculture recently analyzed the antioxidant content of several nutritious vegetables. Garlic topped the list, by far, outranking even spinach, sweet potatoes, and broccoli.

YOUR ACTION PLAN

HOW MUCH IS ENOUGH?

So just how much garlic do you need to eat, and what's the best way to take it? The boom in garlic research during the past 20 years has produced conflicting recommendations, but many experts agree you'll get the most benefits from garlic if you eat it fresh, from one-half to three cloves a day.

HOW TO GET MORE GARLIC NATURALLY

Look for fresh garlic at your supermarket or farmer's market. Try to buy heads with big, plump, firm cloves, and avoid those in the little plastic-wrapped packages. Garlic keeps well for a month in an airy place out of the sun. Keep it away from the stove and sink. Don't store it in the refrigerator and never freeze — it turns mushy.

You might want to take your garlic with a little milk or slice it up on a hunk of dark bread. Take it just before a meal to lessen any stomach distress. Or cut up a clove into chunks, swallowing them like pills. Try to keep your tongue out of the way. A cup of peppermint tea or a sprig of parsley may freshen your mouth after your garlic treatment.

Drying and cooking destroys some of garlic's beneficial compounds. Allicin is unstable and sensitive to heat. Cook the garlic lightly, if at all, and always mince it to release the most allicin.

GARLIC-LOVER RECIPES

It's easy to increase the amount of garlic you use in your kitchen. Just add a few more cloves to soups, casseroles, stir-fries, sauces, and pasta dishes. Refer to the quick recipes in this chapter to get you started.

PESTO

In summer, when fresh basil is plentiful, try this sauce which is rich in uncooked garlic. It is very easy to prepare in a blender or food processor.

In a food processor with a metal blade, process 2 1/2 cups fresh basil leaves (or 2 1/2 cups fresh spinach and 3 tablespoons dry basil). Add 1 cup grated Parmesan or Romano cheese, 3 to 6 cloves of fresh garlic, peeled, and 1/4 cup walnuts or pine nuts. With the motor running, slowly add 1/3 cup olive oil and process until well-mixed.

Pesto will keep in the refrigerator up to a week if well-covered. Or you can freeze it in small portions. Toss pesto with freshly cooked and drained spaghetti, spread it on toasted French bread, use as a topping for baked mushrooms or tomatoes, or add a tablespoon or two to sautéed vegetables.

GARLIC VINAIGRETTE

An easy way to get your daily dose of garlic — just add it to a homemade salad dressing.

In a small bowl, mix 2 tablespoons vinegar or lemon juice with 1/2 teaspoon to 1 teaspoon (or more) minced garlic. Add salt and freshly ground pepper to taste. Slowly whisk in 1/2 cup olive or salad oil. Toss with salad greens and fresh vegetables for a tasty salad.

OIL AND GARLIC SPAGHETTI

In Italy, this simple sauce is a favorite late-night snack or side dish to a family meal. Try to time it so the sauce is finished when the pasta is just cooked and drained. Start peeling the garlic while the pasta water is heating.

Heat a large quantity of water for the pasta. Add pasta when water comes to the boil. Meanwhile, peel and finely slice 4 to 5 cloves of garlic. In a tall, narrow saucepan over medium heat, warm 1/4 cup olive oil. Add garlic and reduce heat to very low. Cook garlic very slowly, (about five minutes), stirring until it is golden but not burnt. Drain the pasta and transfer to a warm serving dish. Immediately pour garlic sauce over it. Season to taste with salt and pepper. Toss with grated Parmesan or Romano cheese if desired

CUBAN GARLIC SOUP

Once you've come to love garlic, try this robust soup.

16 cloves garlic
8 slices bread, cubed, crust removed
1/2 cup extra virgin olive oil
2 quarts chicken stock
3 eggs
2 large white onions, coarsely chopped

Heat oil in a large, deep skillet. Coarsely chop garlic and lightly fry in oil until garlic is crisp, but not burnt. Remove garlic with slotted spoon or pour through strainer and reserve. Return oil to skillet, reheat, and add bread cubes, stirring and frying until crisp. Remove bread cubes and reserve. Return oil to heat, adding more if needed to sauté onions until translucent. Add chicken stock. Finely chop crisp garlic and add to stock. Bring almost to a boil. While stock is heating, beat eggs into a small bowl. Pour 1/2 cup of hot stock slowly into eggs, continuing to whisk. Remove boiling stock from heat and add egg mixture, whisking briskly so that eggs cook and thicken. Add salt and pepper to taste.

Ladle soup into large serving bowls, add reserved croutons, and enjoy. Serves six.

Do you need supplements?

Garlic is one of the best-selling herbal dietary supplement products in the United States. And there's good reason — garlic supplements have some advantages over the fresh herb. First, there's no garlic breath, and second, many capsules are "enteric coated" to keep allicin from being released before it reaches your small intestine. Some researchers think this may lessen intestinal trouble. Garlic is available in capsules at health food stores and some pharmacies.

The wise garlic consumer

Only a few of the 70 or so garlic products on sale produce the amount of allicin available in 4 grams of fresh garlic, the recommended daily dose. Most preparations are so lacking in active ingredients that they have no health benefits.

The labels on garlic products can be confusing. Some products do not list amounts for allicin, garlic's key antibiotic agent. Instead, they list quantities of "high potency garlic" or "raw garlic concentrate" or "whole garlic clove."

The best-selling supplement, Kyolic, made of aged garlic extract contains no allicin, but offers standardized levels of another compound, SAC, which the company says is just as beneficial.

Here's a look at some of the brands available in health food stores:

Brand	Quantity	Allicin(mcg)
Garlinase 4000	1 tablet	5,000
Nutrilite Garlic Heart Care Formula	2 tablets	6,000
Puritan's Pride	1 tablet	6,500
Spring Valley	2-3 tablets	3,600
Vitamin World	1 tablet	6,500

GARLIC CAUTIONS

Although garlic is considered a safe herb with no side effects, some people are allergic, and large quantities can cause heartburn and gas, or even bleeding in your stomach. If you're taking any anticoagulant medication, be sure to ask your doctor about eating garlic because it does have a blood-thinning action.

GARLIC'S ILLUSTRIOUS HISTORY

Current research verifies garlic's amazing infection-fighting abilities, but as long ago as the 7th century, the prophet Mohammed used garlic to treat scorpion stings. Albert Schweitzer, in his African mission hospital work, treated amoebic dysentery, cholera, and typhus with garlic, and British soldiers in World Wars I and II were fed garlic to guard against infection and gangrene.

Garlic may have originated on the high plains of Central Asia and spread east and west with nomadic tribes. It was cultivated in the Middle East for more than 5,000 years. Then the Turks brought garlic to northern Europe in the siege of Vienna in 1683. When the Turkish army fled the city after a long siege, they left behind huge stocks of garlic, thus introducing garlic to the West. American Indians were familiar with a native species of garlic that they used for medical problems ranging from snakebite to intestinal worms. New England settlers strapped garlic cloves to the feet of smallpox victims, a treatment they may have brought with them from the Old World.

Like most anti-aging nutrients, ginger is a powerful antioxidant. In fact, one study suggests that ginger is one of nature's most potent antioxidants. Ginger contains 12 elements that are each more powerful than vitamin E. One of ginger's major elements actually beat vitamin E's antioxidant potential 40 times over. That's pretty impressive considering vitamin E has been praised as the body's most powerful defender against the ravages of time.

GINGER

Everything good is found in ginger.
Ancient Indian proverb

Chinese sailors may have been the first to discover ginger as a good remedy for seasickness. Early Arab traders may have taken advantage of the Chinese sailors' solution for motion sickness as they transported their ginger supplies along closely guarded trade routes to the Greeks and Romans.

The ancient Greeks welcomed the arrival of ginger and quickly put it to good use as a digestive aid. To lighten the load a big meal placed on the digestive system, the Greeks would end an evening of fabulous feasting by eating some ginger wrapped in bread. Eventually, this practice evolved into the world's first cookie — gingerbread.

Still, it was many years before common folks could feast on gingerbread or any other form of ginger. Generally, ginger only graced the dinner tables of wealthy or royal people. In the Middle Ages in England, one pound of ginger sold for about the same price as a sheep.

But by the time of the United States' Revolutionary War days, ginger was a regular part of every soldier's rations. New Englanders regularly made and ate ginger jam to prevent belching and gas.

Although ginger is used today primarily as a culinary spice, this popular plant (almost 100,000 tons of ginger are produced around the world each year) does have potent healing powers.

Although ginger is a powerful antioxidant, that's not what gives ginger its super herb status. Instead, researchers believe it's something called eicosanoids. Your body gets eicosanoids from the fat you eat. It then breaks them down into various elements, including several different types of prostaglandins.

These prostaglandins affect how sticky your blood platelets are. Your prostaglandins must be balanced for you to have healthy circulation and to avoid migraine headaches and disorders like rheumatoid arthritis. Several studies show that ginger contains the elements that can keep eicosanoids working for your body instead of against it.

7 WAYS GINGER FIGHTS AGING

Takes ache out of arthritis. Recent research suggests that ginger may work as a natural anti-inflammatory, reducing the redness, pain, and swelling that often accompanies arthritis. A 2 1/2 year study conducted in Denmark of 56 people who suffered with arthritis or muscle pain found ginger relieved muscle discomfort, pain, and swelling in three-quarters of the study participants.

The people who experienced relief with ginger took an average of 5 grams of fresh ginger or 1 gram of powdered ginger daily. Some people in the study decided to take extra ginger and took up to 4 grams of powdered ginger a day. The lead researcher, Krishna Srivastava, Ph.D., noted that the more ginger people took, the greater their relief.

Another study of seven people with rheumatoid arthritis found that ginger provided substantial pain relief while the conventional drugs they were taking only provided partial or temporary relief. Six of the participants in this study took 5 grams of fresh ginger or 0.1 to 1 gram of powdered ginger daily. One participant consumed 50 grams of lightly cooked ginger each

SPICE UP BATH TIME WITH GINGER

According to Asian accounts, ginger is a good bath buddy. It helps to relieve tension as well as minor aches and pains. Some say a ginger bath will even remove unwanted toxins from your body. If you're suffering with a stuffy nose caused by allergies, sinus problems, or a cold, a ginger bath will clear out clogged nasal passages.

If a ginger bath sounds like just what you need, first grate 5 ounces of fresh ginger. Next, fill your bathtub with water as hot as you can stand it. Now, take your gratings and squeeze the juice from them into the bath water. To make squeezing ginger simple, wrap gratings in a double thickness of cheesecloth, then squeeze the juice out. Throw gratings away, and hop in the tub.

Soak for 15 minutes, then get out and wrap yourself in something warm and comfy. It's especially important to put something on your feet to keep them warm. Now, snuggle into bed and enjoy the gentle healing effects of your ginger bath.

If getting in the bathtub is something that generally gives you more pain than pleasure, then try a ginger footbath. Grate enough ginger to make 1/2 of a cup. Squeeze grated ginger into a pan full of hot water. Soak your feet for 15 minutes. You may want to place a large towel over the pan to keep the water warm while your feet are soaking. When your foot soak is finished, wrap your feet warmly.

day. All of the people in this study reported better joint movement and less pain, stiffness, and swelling.

None of the people in the study reported any serious side
effects from taking ginger.

A natural remedy for arthritis is welcome news to people
who regularly relieve their pain with nonsteroidal anti-inflammatory drugs (NSAIDs). NSAIDs, such as aspirin and ibuprofen, are notorious for causing ulcers, which lead to thousands of
deaths each year. All of the 200 drugs currently used to relieve
arthritis pain have side effects.

Blood clot buster. A 1980
study reported in *The New
England Journal of Medicine*
was the first to note ginger's
remarkable ability to inhibit the
formation of blood clots by
interfering with platelets' ability

to clump. Since then, at least 20 studies have confirmed ginger's
good effect on the circulatory system.

A 1994 study conducted in India revealed that 5 grams of
ginger a day significantly inhibits platelets' ability to clump,
which in turn reduces the risk of clogged arteries in people
with heart disease. Less blood clotting means less risk of a
heart attack.

In response to these studies, an outpatient cardiology clinic
in Israel now routinely recommends 1/2 teaspoon of ginger
daily for its patients.

Clobbers cholesterol. Ginger helps lower the amount of cholesterol in your bloodstream by improving the digestion of fats.
Ginger does this by aiding the liver and gallbladder in their production and transportation of bile to the intestines where it
helps your body digest fat.

Eases common cold and flu symptoms. For centuries, natural
healers have used ginger to fight off flu and colds. Traditional
folk wisdom maintains that ginger can prevent colds, as well as
cut a cold's time short.

Scientific research has documented ginger's ability to boost
the immune system, fight inflammation, reduce fevers, and

suppress coughs. To win a war against the flu or a cold, take 1/2 to 1 gram of powdered ginger every hour for two to three days.

If you feel like a bout of the stomach flu is settling in, take four to six ginger capsules at the first sign of nausea. This can help you avoid some of the unpleasant symptoms of stomach flu.

Stomach soother. Ginger relieves the uncomfortable feeling caused by overeating by increasing the speed that the stomach empties. To relieve indigestion or calm a troubled tummy, pour 1 cup of boiling water over 2 teaspoons of powdered ginger or grated ginger root. Cover the tea and steep for 10 minutes. Strain, then sip slowly.

However, Dr. Daniel B. Mowrey, author of *Herbal Tonic Therapies* and director of the American Phytotherapy Research Laboratory in Salt Lake City, maintains that although ginger teas and other ginger drinks are pleasing to the palate, it is difficult to drink enough of them to experience any benefit. He suggests powdered ginger capsules instead. The capsules will enable you to get the amount of ginger you need without suffering the burning sensation that swallowing plain powdered ginger can cause.

His rule of thumb for taking ginger is to take it 'til you taste it. According to him, you've taken enough when you develop a ginger taste in your mouth or feel a very slight burning in your esophagus (the tube that runs from the back of your throat to your stomach).

In contrast to Dr. Mowrey's method for deciding a ginger dosage, the German Commission E (an organization similar to the United States Food and Drug Administration) suggests a very specific amount of ginger to aid digestion and ease nausea. They recommend 2 to 4 grams (1/2 to 1 teaspoon) a day.

According to a 1987 study conducted at the University of Alabama, ginger is even helpful in relieving nausea caused by chemotherapy. People in the study reported that their nausea was less severe and didn't last as long after taking ginger.

Many people find themselves feeling nauseated after surgery, especially if they've been under anesthesia. Several studies report that ginger may be an even better solution to this problem than the anti-nausea drugs that are available.

A 1990 study of 60 women who underwent gynecological surgery revealed that women who took 1 gram of powdered

A SWEET SOLUTION FOR MOTION SICKNESS

Motion sickness can make even the most enthusiastic traveler miserable.

If motion makes you queasy, no doubt you've tried Dramamine and other over-the-counter remedies. Sure, you don't get sick, but it's hard to remember any of the sights when you were sleeping the whole trip. Guess what? Ginger is not only good for slowing down the aging process, it's the best known natural remedy for motion sickness. It also won't cause the drowsiness or dry mouth over-the-counter drugs can. A 1982 study revealed that people prone to motion sickness who took ginger lasted 57 percent longer in a computerized rocking chair than people who took Dramamine. Ginger can also be helpful in treating nausea caused by dizziness.

Another study showed that taking two to four capsules of dried ginger before traveling in a car, boat, plane, or train prevented motion sickness in 90 percent of the people who participated in the study. The German Commission E, which has approved ginger as being an effective treatment for motion sickness, suggests 2 to 4 grams of ginger a day to prevent motion sickness.

Herbal expert Dr. Varro E. Tyler recommended taking the 2 to 4 grams on the following schedule. Take two 500 mg capsules of ginger 30 minutes before your trip. Take one to two more about every four hours or as symptoms of motion sickness begin to occur.

If you prefer not to take ginger capsules, consider candied ginger. You can find it in Oriental food markets or, if you prefer, you can make your own (see recipe on page 108). A piece 1 inch square and one-quarter inch thick is about equal to one 500 mg ginger capsule.

ginger had fewer bouts of nausea after surgery than women who didn't take ginger. An additional benefit of the ginger is that it did not cause side effects common to many anti-nausea prescription drugs, such as itching, unusual movements, or vision problems.

To prevent nausea after surgery, take 1 gram of ginger a day. Be sure you talk to your doctor before taking ginger. Although none of the studies on ginger for post-surgery nausea reported any side effects, there has been some concern that ginger could cause excessive bleeding.

Ginger also helps your body produce good bacteria. In addition to being a good source of vitamin K and several B vitamins, these bacteria help protect your intestines against potentially bad bacteria, such as *E. coli* and salmonella. This means that ginger may be able to protect you from food poisoning.

Makes mincemeat of migraine headaches. At least one report suggests that ginger may be helpful for migraine headaches. A woman who had suffered with migraines for 16 years finally experienced relief when researchers from Denmark's Odense University gave her 500 to 600 milligrams (mg) of powdered ginger whenever she felt a headache coming on. Within 30 minutes, her migraine would be gone.

ROOT OR RHIZOME?

Despite ginger's popularity through the centuries, there is still a little confusion about its status as a root. Herbal experts insist that ginger is a rhizome and not a root. Yet grocery store after grocery store insist on labeling its fresh ginger as ginger roots, not ginger rhizomes.

While both grow underground, rhizomes have leaves roots don't. Still, try telling that to your local grocer and convincing him to change the way he labels ginger. Chances are, fresh ginger in your grocery store will remain labeled as ginger root.

After this, the woman began taking 1.5 to 2 grams of powdered ginger every four hours. Eventually, she switched to eating fresh ginger every day. She reported having both fewer and less intense migraines. Although more research remains to be done to confirm ginger's good effect on migraines, this report may finally help researchers solve the mystery of migraines.

Ousts ulcers. Several animal studies lead researchers to believe that ginger may be an effective treatment for ulcers. Ginger appears to protect against ulcers caused by alcohol, stress, or drugs like aspirin. This is encouraging news for ulcer sufferers who spend millions of dollars each year on traditional treatment and medicine.

YOUR ACTION PLAN

Ginger is not only good for what ails you, it's also a good source of several vitamins and minerals. About 26 teaspoons, or 100 grams, of fresh ginger contains 6 mg of vitamin C, 60 mg of phosphorus, and 20 mg of calcium. Ginger is also a good source of the mineral manganese.

HOW MUCH IS ENOUGH?

Although there is no Recommended Dietary Allowance (RDA) for ginger, most herbalists base their ginger recommendations on the 2 to 4 daily grams of ginger established by the German Commission E to aid digestion and ease nausea. Most herbalists suggest dividing your ginger into two or three doses throughout the day.

When eating fresh ginger, start out with small amounts and gradually work your way up to larger amounts of ginger. This will help prevent a burning sensation in your mouth or stomach.

For certain conditions, such as arthritis or migraines, you may need more than 2 to 4 grams a day. Experiment to see what works best for you.

How to get more ginger naturally

Just adding a little ginger to your favorite recipes here and there probably won't give you the health benefits you're hoping for. The best way to get more ginger naturally is to eat 2 to 4 grams of a combination of fresh ginger and dried ginger every day. If ginger's burn bothers you, buy ginger in gelatin capsules.

Do you need supplements?

If you don't plan to use fresh ginger to get in your 2 to 4 grams of ginger each day, then you'll probably want to consider supplements. Of course, you can take the regular dried ginger you probably have sitting in your spice rack, but swallowing plain, dried ginger can cause an unpleasant burning sensation in your esophagus and stomach. To prevent this problem, you can buy powdered ginger in gelatin capsules. Normally, you get 500 mg of powdered ginger per capsule. In order to get 2 to 4 grams of ginger, you'll need to take four to eight capsules.

The wise ginger consumer

Among the more than 400 elements that make up ginger, gingerol and shogaol are two of several that possess healing powers. Gingerol gives ginger its distinctive bite. Gingerols that are heated or dehydrated convert into shogaols. To take advantage of all ginger's health benefits, most herbalists recommend eating both fresh and dried ginger. Supposedly, powdered ginger is a more potent anti-inflammatory, while fresh offers the best protection against liver damage and parasites.

Ginger comes in a wide range of flavors, from modestly mild to sizzlingly spicy. Herbal experts generally agree that the milder forms of ginger, found in China, are better for cooking, while their spicier sister varieties, said to come from Africa, have more healing power.

If you want fresh ginger, you can find it in the produce section of your grocery store. Look for a plump, hard chunk of ginger. Stay away from ginger that looks moldy, shriveled, or shrunken. Wrap fresh, whole ginger in a paper towel, place in a plastic bag, and store in the refrigerator. It will keep for three weeks.

You can also store fresh, whole ginger in a plastic bag in the freezer if you're planning on grating or juicing it. For other preparation methods, frozen ginger will be too soggy when thawed. If you prefer to cut your ginger into slices, place them in a glass jar, cover with sherry or vodka, put on the lid, and store in the refrigerator. Sliced ginger stored in sherry or vodka will keep for three to six months.

GINGER CAUTIONS

Ginger is classified by the Food and Drug Administration as GRAS (generally recognized as safe). Although side effects are rare, they can occur. Some people who are sensitive to its taste report heartburn. However, there are a few people who should take extra precautions when using ginger. Talk to your doctor before using it if you ...

❦ have gallstones.
❦ are pregnant.
❦ take heart medicine. Ginger may intensify the effects of heart drugs, which can be dangerous.
❦ are scheduled for surgery. Ginger may interfere with your blood's ability to clot.

Some studies have suggested that very large doses may slow down the central nervous system and lead to irregular heartbeats. Ginger may also worsen problems in women who have high estrogen levels.

NATURAL GINGER ALE

1 teaspoon finely ground fresh ginger root
1/4 cup sugar
3 cups plain water
1/4 teaspoon lemon juice
1 cup carbonated water (optional)

Bring grated ginger and plain water to a boil. Turn heat to low and simmer for 20 minutes. Remove from heat. Strain ginger water through a sieve into a bowl. Stir in sugar and lemon juice. If desired, add carbonated water. (If excess gas is causing part of your stomach discomfort, you may want to leave out the carbonated water as it can add to your discomfort by creating more intestinal gas.)

Makes four servings if you add carbonated water or three servings without. Serve hot or cold as desired.

GINGER ALE: A GOOD SOURCE OF GINGER?

Once ginger made its way to the West Indies, the Jamaicans lost no time in concocting a drink to aid digestion — ginger ale. Meanwhile, folks in 17th century England and the American colonies soothed their upset stomachs with a similar drink they called ginger beer.

These days, ginger ale is still recommended to calm a troubled tummy. However, if you commonly turn to grocery-store ginger ale for your tummy troubles, you may not find much relief. That's because it usually doesn't contain enough ginger to be helpful, according to herbal expert Dr. Varro E. Tyler. In fact, Canada Dry ginger ale contains no fresh ginger at all, only ginger flavoring.

If you hope to experience the stomach-soothing effects of ginger ale, you'll either need to buy natural ginger ale brands from a health food store or make your own. The next time tummy troubles strike your home front, try the recipe for natural ginger ale on page 106. It will ease stomach aches that grocery-store ginger ale can't.

CANDIED GINGER

2 cups fresh, sliced ginger
1/2 cup orange juice
1 cup sugar
2 tablespoons corn syrup

Slice ginger into 1/4-inch pieces. In a saucepan, cover ginger with water. Bring to a boil. Let boil five minutes. Drain ginger. Cover with water, boil, and drain again. Cover with water and bring to a boil once more, put on the saucepan lid, then reduce heat and simmer until tender, about one hour. Drain ginger, remove from saucepan and set aside.

Using the same pot, bring sugar, corn syrup, and orange juice to a boil. Add ginger slices and return to boil. Reduce heat and simmer ginger for one hour or until it is translucent. Stir occasionally.

Use a slotted spoon to transfer ginger to a wire rack to cool. Place tray underneath to catch extra ginger juice. Once ginger is dry to the touch, roll lightly in sugar. Store in a glass jar.

Although the amount of magnesium in the body of the average person is small (about 1 3/4 ounces), adequate magnesium is vital for over 300 life-sustaining processes in the body. In fact, to develop properly and function perfectly, your body must have adequate magnesium from the moment you are conceived until the day you die. The scary part is that despite the incredibly important role magnesium plays in the body, as much as three-quarters of the U.S. population may have a dietary magnesium deficiency.

MAGNESIUM

Magnesium is an important mineral for preserving your body's youthfulness. A lack of magnesium in the body makes cells more vulnerable to damage by free radicals, which speeds up the aging process. Ongoing magnesium deficiency also saps stores of vitamin E, making you age even faster.

The irony is that as you grow older, several factors dramatically increase the likelihood that you will be magnesium deficient. This means you won't benefit from the age-slowing effects of magnesium unless you make a dedicated effort to maintain adequate amounts of magnesium in your body.

With age, most people tend to get fewer calories from a smaller variety of foods, which increases the risk of not getting enough magnesium in the diet. And older people may not absorb magnesium well and excrete more of it as waste.

Among healthy older folks, magnesium absorption at age 70 is only about 65 percent of what it was at age 30. In addition, hormone changes and certain medicines can contribute to magnesium loss.

8 WAYS MAGNESIUM FIGHTS AGING

Magnesium's major role is to keep nerves and muscles functioning properly. It is also essential for helping your body make protein and release energy. In addition, it helps protect your teeth from decay. Even a slight deficiency of magnesium can cause nausea, muscle weakness, irritability, and mental difficulties.

Defeats diabetes. Researchers have known for a number of years that diabetes is linked to a deficiency of magnesium in several ways. First, people with low levels of magnesium are more likely to develop diabetes. Second, diabetics who take insulin often develop a magnesium deficiency, which further increases their risks of complications.

Evidence suggests that normal amounts of magnesium can help prevent common diabetic complications such as heart disease, eye disease, kidney disease, and high blood pressure. In fact, diabetics who are given extra magnesium often have better blood sugar control and require less insulin.

Even if you're not diabetic, low levels of magnesium can increase your risk of becoming insulin resistant, which can raise your risk of heart disease, cancer, and diabetes.

Boosts heart health. Magnesium is a critically important mineral for your heart. Low levels of magnesium can cause a number of problems, including skewing normal sodium and potassium levels, which help maintain the proper electrical function of your heart.

In addition, a 10-year ongoing study of 2,182 men ages 45 to 59 suggests that dietary magnesium may provide long-term heart protection, according to Dr. Peter Elwood of the Medical Research Council Epidemiology Unit in South Wales. A good supply of magnesium can also protect your heart from the ravages of high cholesterol, which increases your risk of heart disease.

❦ **Halts heart artery spasms.** Plenty of magnesium boosts your heart health in many ways, but it seems particularly effective at protecting your heart from artery spasms. The lower your body is in magnesium, the less able your heart is to stop the spasms, which can lead to death. Magnesium can be especially helpful for heart rhythm irregularities that occur after a heart attack has damaged the heart muscle.

❦ **Heads off high blood pressure.** Some studies show that magnesium lowers blood pressure. Researchers suspect magnesium does this by relaxing blood vessels, which allows them to open more widely. Wider blood vessels give blood more room to flow and reduce blood pressure.

❦ **Backs off blood clots.** A study led by Dr. Jerry L. Nadler at the City of Hope Medical Center in Duarte, Calif., suggests that magnesium can help prevent blood clots, which can block arteries and lead to heart attacks. Magnesium does this by slowing the release of thromboxane, a substance that makes blood platelets more sticky and more likely to clot.

❦ **Help for a heart attack?** Several small studies have suggested that magnesium given during the acute phase of a heart attack can reduce the risk of complications and death. However, injections of magnesium following a heart attack remain controversial. A recent study of 58,050 heart attack victims revealed that magnesium injections may have no effect. Critics of the study contend that magnesium had no effect because it wasn't administered at the proper time. More studies need to be done to determine magnesium's true effect on heart attack victims.

KO's kidney stones. In people prone to develop kidney stones, extra magnesium appears to reduce the number of new stones formed. Researchers speculate that people who have problems with kidney stones are probably magnesium deficient. In other words, the lack of magnesium lead to the stones.

Takes the misery out of migraines. Several studies have shown that migraine sufferers often have low levels of magnesium. Magnesium is sometimes called nature's calcium channel blocker, a drug that is used to prevent migraines. Researchers theorized that since magnesium acts like a calcium channel blocker, it would likely affect migraines the same way.

Several studies support this theory including a study of 3,000 women who were given 200 milligrams (mg) of magnesium a day. About 80 percent, or 2,400, of those women experienced relief from their migraines.

Outwits osteoporosis. Low intakes of magnesium have been linked to bone loss. Although calcium and estrogen are commonly recommended to combat osteoporosis, magnesium is just as important.

That's because calcium has to work with magnesium in order to activate the chemical reactions that form new bone. A deficiency of magnesium slows bone formation.

Could put a stop to PMS. A few studies have suggested that low levels of magnesium contribute to premenstrual stress. Supplements of magnesium appear to reduce the severity of PMS. Researchers speculate that a lack of magnesium can cause certain brain chemicals to fall too low, contributing to the emotional swings common to premenstrual syndrome.

May slash risk of stroke. Some research suggests that maintaining normal magnesium levels may help prevent the intense blood vessel spasms in the brain that can lead to stroke.

Aces asthma? Some preliminary research has also indicated that magnesium may also be helpful in the treatment of asthma.

YOUR ACTION PLAN

HOW MUCH IS ENOUGH?

The Recommended Dietary Allowance (RDA) for healthy adults is 320 mg for women and 420 mg for men.

If you have diabetes; heart disease; or take digitalis, diuretics, or have recently taken antibiotics, it is important to have your magnesium level tested. Several studies have shown that people taking the heart drug digitalis are likely to be deficient in magnesium.

HOW TO GET MORE MAGNESIUM NATURALLY

Generally, your best sources of magnesium are unprocessed foods. If you get enough magnesium on a regular basis, you shouldn't have any problem with a deficiency unless you have trouble absorbing the mineral. People who might have trouble absorbing magnesium include those with irritable bowel syndrome, Crohn's disease, ulcerative colitis, or any other disorder that interferes with intestinal absorption.

Good natural sources of magnesium include beans, brown rice, grains, popcorn, nuts, spinach, soybeans, broccoli, green peas, corn, acorn squash, potatoes, sweet potatoes, molasses, oatmeal, cornmeal, shrimp, clams, oysters, crab, and skim milk.

Since magnesium is easily washed or peeled away from foods, it's best to eat magnesium-rich foods that have been processed as little as possible. Also, limit fat in your diet, since a high-fat diet can interfere with magnesium absorption.

Eating lots of sugar will cause you to lose more magnesium in your urine, increasing your magnesium needs. A high protein diet will also increase your magnesium needs.

DO YOU NEED SUPPLEMENTS?

You only need a supplement if you can't get enough magnesium through your diet. A normal multivitamin-mineral supplement usually provides 100 mg.

THE WISE MAGNESIUM CONSUMER

Magnesium supplements are available in a variety of forms. Magnesium oxide is high in pure magnesium but is often not well-tolerated. Generally, the easiest absorbed types of magnesium are magnesium chloride, magnesium lactate, magnesium aspartate, and magnesium gluconate. However, these forms do contain a little less pure magnesium.

Dr. Lorraine Tosiello of Overlook Hospital in Summit, N.J., suggests magnesium chloride as the preparation of choice. She also notes that magnesium-containing antacids are a convenient source of magnesium, offering 400 mg per dose. If you choose antacids, just be sure not to overdo it.

Generally, 350 mg of pure magnesium or less is considered safe unless you have kidney or heart disease or have had a heart attack. If any one of those conditions applies to you, you must get your doctor's approval before you even consider taking magnesium supplements.

If you take magnesium supplements, you will need to monitor your calcium intake. That's because calcium and magnesium are absorbed the same way. Therefore, how much you get of one can affect how much you get of the other. Experts aren't definite, but they generally recommend that you get twice as much calcium as magnesium.

Getting more than twice as much calcium as magnesium may interfere with your absorption of magnesium. Too much magnesium can also interfere with your absorption of calcium. This is just one more reason to try to get the nutrients you need from food sources. Nature has already seen to the proper balance of things, and you usually don't have to worry about getting too much of one nutrient and too little of another.

MAGNESIUM CAUTIONS

Moderation is the magic word when it comes to magnesium. That's because too much can make you very sick, causing nausea, vomiting, or even paralysis and death.

If you regularly consume large amounts of over-the-counter antacids, laxatives, or pain relievers that contain magnesium, you may be poisoning yourself. One woman who had been taking two bottles of magnesium-containing antacids a day for several months learned that lesson the hard way. She ended up

MAGNESIUM'S INTERACTIONS WITH CERTAIN VITAMINS, MINERALS, AND MEDICINES

Interacts with:	Effect:
Calcium	May reduce the absorption of magnesium.
Folic acid	May increase magnesium needs.
Vitamin D	Decreases absorption of magnesium.
Vitamin E	Vitamin E deficiency can reduce tissue levels of magnesium.
Iron	May decrease absorption of magnesium.
Potassium	Increases loss of magnesium through the kidneys.
Cellulose sodium phosphate	May prevent cellulose sodium phosphate from working correctly. Take magnesium supplements one hour before or after taking cellulose sodium phosphate.
Digitalis	Magnesium deficiency can cause heart rhythm disturbances.
Sodium polystyrene sulfonate	May lessen effectiveness of magnesium supplements.
Ketoconazole	Reduces absorption of ketoconazole. Take magnesium supplements and ketoconazole two hours apart.
Mecamylamine	May slow urinary excretion of mecamylamine. Avoid combining mecamylamine and magnesium supplements.
Tetracycline, oral	May prevent tetracycline from working correctly. Take magnesium supplements one to three hours before or after taking tetracycline.

paralyzed, in a hospital on life support, before routine blood work uncovered her massive magnesium overload.

She was one of the lucky ones. According to a study from the Food and Drug Administration, 14 people have died and several others have been hospitalized or disabled from magnesium poisonings since 1968.

Older people are particularly prone to magnesium poisoning because they often have indigestion and constipation and frequently turn to over-the-counter remedies for relief. In addition, many people think if a little works well, a lot works better, so they take far more than recommended. Problems also arise because older people's kidneys don't work as well as they used to, and they don't remove excess magnesium from the body as well as they should.

If you have a stomach or intestinal disorder and take several drugs, especially narcotics or anticholinergics (drugs used to block impulses from the central nervous system, including some antidepressants, antihistamines, anti-parkinsonism drugs, and muscles relaxers), you have an especially high risk of experiencing side effects from a magnesium overdose.

Signs of a magnesium overdose include lightheadedness, low blood pressure, muscle weakness, confusion, heart rhythm abnormalities, nausea, and vomiting. If you have any of these symptoms, stop taking the magnesium supplements and see your doctor immediately.

For a more complete list of interactions, see the magnesium interaction chart on the preceding page.

Some researchers think primitive societies avoid high blood pressure, the leading cause of stroke and heart attack, not because of their low sodium intake but because of their high potassium intake.

POTASSIUM

A human body powered by electricity ... you may think that sounds like something out of a science fiction story. Well, there have been science fiction stories written about electrically powered human bodies. But, guess what? Electrically powered humans aren't so far-fetched as they might seem. If you want to see one, go look in the mirror.

Potassium and sodium chloride are the two essentials that let you literally become a walking power plant. Your body's electricity is similar to the regular electricity that illuminates light bulbs. Too little voltage (potassium) and the light (your body) won't work. Too much voltage (potassium) and you destroy the object (your body) you're trying to electrify.

The mineral potassium is an electrolyte, which means that in water the mineral completely dissolves into separate components called ions that conduct electrical charges. Potassium is a positively charged ion.

The body also contains sodium and chloride, both of which are electrolytes and conduct electrical charges, too. Sodium is also positively charged, while chloride is negatively charged.

Potassium, sodium, and chloride work together by way of their positively and negatively charged electrons to maintain fluid balance inside and outside your body's cells. This arrangement, which works like a tiny battery, creates enough electricity to let nutrients and waste products in and out of your cells. Your body's "battery" is essential for maintaining normal function of your heart, brain, muscles, and kidneys.

In addition to providing your body's battery with what it needs to function, potassium also inhibits the formation of free radicals, which further slows down the aging process.

5 WAYS POTASSIUM FIGHTS AGING

Breaks you out of the bone loss cycle. Several studies indicate that getting plenty of potassium may reduce the loss of calcium from your body. Keeping all the calcium you can in your body is essential for maintaining strong bones.

Puts the brakes on high blood pressure. Since the 1920s, various studies have observed potassium's potential for lowering blood pressure, especially in people who tend to have high blood pressure. Lower blood pressure means a lower risk of heart attack and stroke. Even in people with perfectly normal blood pressure levels, a serving or two of fresh fruits and vegetables every day can reduce the risk of stroke.

In people with high blood pressure, the power of potassium is even more amazing. Not only does a little extra potassium in the diet significantly lower the blood pressures of people taking high blood pressure medicine, it also reduces the need for blood pressure medicine at all.

African Americans respond exceptionally well to potassium's blood pressure lowering effects. This may be partially due to their tendency to eat fewer foods containing potassium than other people.

Makes sure the beat goes on. Potassium is critical for maintaining your heartbeat. Too little potassium can lead to arrhythmias, or heartbeat irregularities, which may be fatal. This is especially true for people taking digitalis. In addition, the sudden deaths attributed to fasting are thought to be caused by potassium loss.

Maximizes muscle power. Your body must have potassium for your muscles to contract. Too little potassium can cause muscle weakness, cramps, restless legs, progressive muscle loss and, eventually, even paralyze your respiratory system.

Kicks kidney stones. Low potassium leads to less acid in your urine, a condition that favors the development of kidney stones. Plenty of potassium in your diet can prevent this painful problem.

YOUR ACTION PLAN

HOW MUCH IS ENOUGH?

Are you getting enough? Probably not. According to the Intersalt study, most Americans aren't. The major reason for the deficiency is too many fast foods and too few fresh fruits and vegetables. Another common cause of low potassium is overuse of diuretics.

Most people, especially older adults and African Americans, could probably benefit from extra potassium. Although there is no Recommended Dietary Allowance (RDA) for potassium, experts estimate that healthy adults need at least 3,500 milligrams of potassium a day.

Since potassium is present in many unprocessed foods, most people can easily get all the potassium they need by eating a well-rounded diet. If you choose processed foods, be sure to check the labels because many food companies are now adding potassium to these foods.

HOW TO GET MORE POTASSIUM NATURALLY

The best way to pump up your potassium is to eat plenty of unprocessed foods, especially vegetables, beans, peas, and fruits, many of which are naturally good sources of this essential mineral. If lower blood pressure is your main goal, you should also reduce the amount of salt, saturated fat, and alcohol in your diet.

Listed below are some foods that really pack a potassium punch.

Food/Milligrams of potassium	Amount
Acorn squash, cooked/896	1 cup
Apricots, dried/482	10 halves
Banana/451	1 medium
Broccoli, frozen, cooked/332	1 cup
Cantaloupe/412	1/4
Dates, dried/541	10
Kidney beans, cooked/713	1 cup
Milk, skim/406	1 cup
Orange, raw/250	1 medium
Potato with skin, baked/844	1 large
Raisins/553	1/2 cup
Spinach, cooked/838	1 cup
Sunflower seeds, dry roasted/241	1 ounce
Tomato, raw/254	1 medium
Watermelon/186	1 cup
Wheat germ, toasted/268	1/4 cup
Zucchini, cooked, sliced/456	1 cup

DO YOU NEED SUPPLEMENTS?

Because of the dangers of overdose, don't take a potassium supplement unless your doctor recommends it.

If your doctor does recommend or prescribe a supplement, be sure you follow the instructions on the supplement bottle carefully. This will reduce your risk of side effects and make sure you get the most benefits.

Generally, when taking potassium supplements, you should not use salt substitutes, drink low-sodium milk, or eat low-sodium foods, especially canned foods and certain breads, because these products are likely to contain potassium. Also, check with your doctor before beginning an exercise program, especially if you are out of shape. Exercise can increase the amount of potassium in your blood.

Contact your doctor at once if you pass black stools. This may indicate intestinal bleeding. You should also see your doctor if you feel confused; develop a slow or irregular heartbeat; have difficulty breathing; or feel unusually tired, weak, or anxious.

THE WISE POTASSIUM CONSUMER

To get more potassium from your diet, avoid processed foods as much as possible. Processing foods strips them of their natural potassium and adds extra sodium, a very unhealthy combination, especially for your heart.

Try to get most of your potassium from unprocessed fruits and vegetables. Since potassium dissolves in water, you'll get the most potassium possible from fruits and veggies if you eat them raw instead of cooked. Certain vegetables, like potatoes, that are commonly cooked in their skins, retain their potassium even after being cooked. Instant mashed potatoes have about the same amount of potassium as fresh potatoes.

POTASSIUM CAUTIONS

Don't take a potassium supplement without talking to your doctor. If your doctor decides you need supplements, he should monitor you carefully as potassium supplements can interact with a number of drugs and foods — and even exercise. To prevent potentially harmful reactions, make sure your doctor is aware of all vitamins, minerals, and medicines you are taking.

Also, never stop taking any high blood pressure medicine your doctor may have prescribed even if you are eating a diet that gives you plenty of potassium. If your goal is to get off your blood pressure medicine by eating foods full of potassium, you must work closely with your doctor.

Certain conditions can also make you more susceptible to the adverse effects of potassium supplements. Be sure to let your doctor know if you have Addison's disease, diabetes, kidney disease, heart disease, or a stomach ulcer or intestinal blockage. If he suggests potassium supplements, also let him know if you've recently had diarrhea or been dehydrated.

Taking too much potassium can be toxic, and your body will try to get rid of the excess by vomiting. Too much potassium can be fatal to babies and people with weak hearts who aren't able to withstand the trauma of an overdose.

POTASSIUM DEFICIENCY — ARE YOU AT RISK?

Take this easy quiz and find out.

❦ Are you over age 55?

❦ Do you drink more than three cups of coffee a day?

❦ Do you regularly engage in vigorous activities that require a lot of endurance?

❦ Do you take laxatives once a week or more?

❦ Do you smoke?

❦ Have you recently had surgery or been through a very stressful experience?

❦ Have you recently been severely injured or burned?

❦ Do you take water pills (diuretics), digitalis, or cortisone drugs?

❦ Have you had part of your gastrointestinal tract removed?

If you answered yes to more than one question, you may have a potassium deficiency. Ask your doctor if you need potassium supplements. Remember ... don't take potassium supplements without your doctor's approval. Overdosing on potassium can be deadly.

The death rate from cancer is 25 percent lower in Cheyenne, Wyo. than in Muncie, Ind. What's the difference? Cheyenne has one of the highest levels of selenium in the country, and Muncie, one of the lowest. Research shows that states rich in selenium suffer fewer deaths from this devastating disease.

Selenium may not only slash your cancer risk, it can benefit almost every part of your body. Studies suggest this superstar mineral can halt heart disease, improve your energy level, relieve arthritis, prevent cataracts, and much more.

SELENIUM

Selenium remained one of nature's well-kept secrets until the 1930s. Ironically, it first made nutrition news for poisoning cows. Cows eating grass grown in high selenium soil developed problems ranging from liver cirrhosis and hoof malformations to muscle and hair loss.

It was more than 20 years before nutritionists realized selenium was an essential nutrient in humans. And it wasn't until 1979 that Chinese scientists discovered selenium supplements could prevent a serious condition called cardiomyopathy, a potentially fatal weakening of the heart.

Although labeled as a micromineral, meaning your body only requires minute amounts, selenium is one of the strongest mineral antioxidants. It is absolutely vital for good health, as various soil studies around the world have shown.

In fact, parts of the Carolinas and Georgia that are extremely low in selenium are sometimes referred to as the "stroke belt" because strokes and heart attacks are so common. Researchers suspect a link between the low selenium levels and the large number of those serious illnesses.

China, Finland, and New Zealand are among the countries low in selenium. The Ministry of Agriculture and Forestry in Finland recently started supplementing fertilizer with selenium to correct the deficiency. In the U.S., you can check with your local agricultural agent to find out the selenium content of soil in your area.

8 WAYS SELENIUM FIGHTS AGING

Besides being an antioxidant itself, selenium increases the antioxidant effects of vitamin E and vitamin C. It also joins forces with vitamin E to create the powerful antioxidant glutathione peroxidase. Adding vitamin C to that combination can raise your glutathione levels fivefold. Glutathione is an important amino acid that neutralizes free radicals, particularly those that attack fat molecules and turn them rancid. It is also vital for promoting a healthy immune system.

If you're trying to keep your aging body firm and flexible, selenium will move you closer to your goal. This mineral helps keep body tissues elastic, which slows the aging process even more.

Takes agony out of arthritis. Glutathione helps soothe your joints by reducing the production of the prostaglandins and leukotrienes that make them ache. If you take selenium with vitamin E, you can reduce your pain and stiffness even more. For relief, experts recommend taking 100 to 200 micrograms (mcg) of selenium per day along with 100 to 200 milligrams (mg) of vitamin E.

Aces asthma. If your diet is low in selenium, you may increase your risk of developing asthma. A New Zealand study by the Wellington School of Medicine and the University of Otago showed that study participants with the lowest blood levels of selenium had nearly twice the risk of asthma. Several other studies have reported similar findings.

Cuts cancer risk. When scientists studied the selenium levels in more than 20 countries and compared them to cancer rates, guess what they found? The lower the selenium, the higher the risk of cancers of the bladder, breast, colon, lungs, ovary, pancreas, rectum, and skin. Leukemia rates also rose.

The latest studies on selenium and cancer continue to suggest a strong link between low selenium levels and a high cancer risk. The most recent study found that taking 200 mcg of selenium a day may slash your risk of prostate, colon, and lung cancer in half.

Researchers suspect selenium fights cancer by boosting immune function, preventing cancerous mutations, and repairing damaged cells.

Minds your mental health. Finnish researchers studying a small group of senior citizens found that vitamin E and selenium supplements improved the seniors' ability to care for themselves. They also felt more alert, and less anxious and hostile.

Another selenium study at University College in Swansea, Wales produced similar results. Every day for five weeks, each member of the study group took either 100 mcg of selenium or a placebo (a fake pill). The participants taking the selenium supplement improved in mood and anxiety level. Those taking the placebo reported no improvement.

Interestingly, the changes appeared to be linked to how low a person's selenium level was before the study. The more deficient he was, the more likely he was to report feeling tired, depressed, or anxious, and the more he was helped by even a moderate amount of selenium.

Eases eyesight problems. Selenium also may prevent one of the most common eye complications of aging — cataracts. Glutathione helps protect the lens of your eye from damaging free radicals that can lead to cataracts. Since you can't make glutathione without selenium, you may get cataracts more easily if you lack this important mineral. Studies do show that a lens obscured by a cataract only contains 15 percent of a normal lens' level of selenium.

In a similar way, selenium and vitamin E also may help protect your retina from macular degeneration, a common disorder in older people that causes gradual vision loss.

Keeps heart healthy. Selenium improves the supply of oxygen to the heart. It also helps form prostaglandins, hormone-like fatty acids that can help lower blood pressure and prevent blood clots.

A selenium deficiency can lead to free radical damage that may cause the LDL "bad" cholesterol to clog up your arteries more easily, increasing your risk of heart disease.

A study in Denmark found that men with the lowest blood levels of selenium were 1.7 times more likely to suffer from cardiovascular complications. And in nearby Finland, a country plagued by heart disease, researchers found that people who had high blood selenium levels were 60 percent less likely to develop heart problems than those with low levels.

Invigorates your immune system. As you age and your body begins to break down, you become more susceptible to different diseases. It doesn't help that your normally vigilant immune system begins to slack off on its duties, too. However, here's where selenium can help you beat Mother Nature at her own sly game.

A supplement of selenium and beta carotene significantly improved immune functions in a group of older folks, according to a recent study at the University of Arizona. And pairing selenium with vitamin E helps your body produce glutathione, which boosts the efficiency of your immune system and reduces your risk of infection and cancer.

Studies with rats suggest selenium may prevent normally harmless viruses from turning vicious or actually undergoing genetic changes that make you sick. If researchers find they can apply these results to other viruses, such as hepatitis, influenza, or the AIDS virus, they may hold one of the critical keys to controlling such devastating diseases.

Supports your sex life. If you're a man, almost half your body's supply of selenium is located in your testicles and in the semen ducts next to your prostate. Sperm cells also contain a good supply of selenium. Every time you ejaculate, you lose some selenium. To keep sexual satisfaction at its highest, it's important to get enough selenium in your diet to replace those lost stores.

YOUR ACTION PLAN

HOW MUCH IS ENOUGH?

The Recommended Dietary Allowance (RDA) for selenium is 55 mcg a day for adult men and women. Although most experts think up to 400 mcg of selenium is probably safe, they

Low

Adequate

This map shows areas of the United States and Canada where soil levels of selenium are adequate or low. Areas that aren't marked vary widely in their selenium concentrations.

Used with permission from SELENIUM IN NUTRITION: REVISED EDITION, copyright 1983 by the National Academy of Sciences. Courtesy of the National Academy Press, Washington, D.C.

strongly caution against going above that amount. Side effects from too much selenium are unpleasant and can be deadly.

How to get more selenium naturally

Good natural sources of selenium include bran, Brazil nuts, brewer's yeast, broccoli, cabbage, celery, chicken, cucumbers, eggs, garlic, kidney, liver, milk, mushrooms, radishes, and seafood. Most meat will have adequate levels since the Department of Agriculture allows animal feed to be fortified with small amounts of selenium.

However, you should keep in mind that the selenium levels of vegetables, grains, and nuts can vary according to where they were grown. Generally, the Southeast and Northeast have the lowest levels of selenium. The Southwest has average selenium levels, and the Northwest, except for certain areas of the Pacific coast, the highest levels.

An easy way to boost selenium is to choose whole grains over refined foods whenever possible. Also, limit vegetable cooking time. Boiling veggies reduces their selenium content by almost half. A high-sugar diet also contributes to selenium deficiency.

Do you need supplements?

Strangely enough, if you work in a job where you're around a copy machine all day, you may not. That's because copy machines use selenium plates that emit a form of selenium into the air. You also should not take supplements if you work at an industrial site that manufactures glass, pesticides, rubber, semi-conductors, copper, or film. In fact, you should probably monitor yourself to make sure you show no signs of overdose.

The wise selenium consumer

If you decide to take supplements, choose an amino acid chelate (also called organic selenium), such as L-selenomethionine. Your body can absorb chelated selenium more quickly and completely than other types of supplements. It also has fewer side effects.

Be sure you take any supplement with a full glass of water or other beverage. Don't chew or crush it. Take the supplement with meals, or one to 1-1/2 hours after meals.

SELENIUM CAUTIONS

Taking more than 400 mcg of selenium a day can be toxic. Also, too much selenium may actually impair your immune system. One early sign of overdose is a metallic taste in the mouth. Other indicators include dizziness; diarrhea; nausea; persistent garlic breath; and loss of hair, nails, or teeth.

Trade your Big Mac for a soy burger, and you could beat cancer and other age-related diseases. Soybeans are a staple of Asian cooking and may be the reason the Japanese have very low death rates from breast and prostate cancers. Researchers find that Japanese who move to the West, and replace their typical diet of soy foods with American steaks, burgers, and fries, have cancer rates just as high as Westerners.

SOY

Creamy tofu, soy milk and flour, tempeh and miso — their names may be unfamiliar to you, but these soy products are treasure troves of protein, fiber, and valuable life-extending minerals.

Soybeans contain more protein than any other legume, and they are the only vegetable food whose protein is complete. That means there's no need to pair them with rice or pasta to get nutritional benefits.

Like other fruits and vegetables, soybeans have no cholesterol to clog your arteries. Plus, they are rich in fiber — the "roughage" or "bulk" that protects your digestive system. Soy has both kinds of fiber: water-soluble fiber that helps lower cholesterol and control blood sugar and insoluble fiber that produces larger stools and helps fight stomach and colon cancers. Insoluble fiber also helps prevent gallstones and relieve constipation.

Soybeans may be high in protein and fiber, but they do contain polyunsaturated fat. That's not as harmful as the saturated fat in meat and dairy products, but you should take it into consideration if you're trying to eat less fat. Luckily, there are plenty of low-fat forms of soy products to choose.

The humble soybean is also the vegetable world's richest source of lecithin, a compound that plays many roles in fighting off disease and aging. Lecithin lowers cholesterol, helps the body digest fats, and prevents the buildup of fat in the arteries.

Soy products have other powerful weapons in the arsenal against aging: They are packed with calcium to help prevent bone density loss in women after menopause. And soy is rich in linolenic acid, one of the omega-3 oils that helps reduce the risk of heart disease and stroke.

Nutritionists claim soy protein is the best vegetable food for maintaining normal blood sugar levels, an important factor for people with diabetes or for those who get dizzy between meals.

6 WAYS SOY FIGHTS AGING

Soybeans, known as the "greater bean" in the Chinese language, have reigned supreme as a food and traditional medicine in Asian culture for 1,000 years. Current scientific research reveals that this ancient plant has earned its anti-aging reputation.

A recent Chinese study revealed that soy actually slowed the aging of red blood cell membranes and heart muscle membranes. Researchers fed small amounts of special soybean paste to humans and guinea pigs for two months. They found that blood fat levels were reduced, and cells aged more slowly.

Asians eat 20 to 50 times more soy per person than Americans. Nutritionists urge all of us to eat more fruits, vegetables, legumes, and grains in place of meat, poultry, dairy products, and eggs. If you substituted vegetable protein for the animal protein in your meals, you would automatically eat less fat and more fiber and help ward off the menaces of old age — cancer, heart disease, and stroke.

Medicine-free menopause. Oddly enough, not all women in all parts of the world have similar symptoms during menopause. About 75 percent of European women have hot flashes compared with only 18 percent of Chinese women. In Japan, the symptoms are so rare there's not even a word in the Japanese language for "hot flash." Scientists suspect that the natural plant estrogens in soybeans are the secret to an easy passage through menopause.

Doctors often prescribe Hormone Replacement Therapy (HRT) or powerful drugs to relieve the hot flashes, night sweats, insomnia, and mood swings associated with menopause. But some studies show HRT may increase the risk of breast cancer. One researcher thinks soybeans promise a bright, drug-free future for women facing menopause. Mark Messina, Ph.D., coauthor of *The Simple Soybean and Your Health,* says that one day a soybean-based diet may be prescribed in place of HRT.

Soy's healing power may come from phytoestrogens, a group of natural plant estrogens that act like very weak forms of the human hormone estrogen. Several dozen other plants like rye, wheat, apples, and carrots also contain phytoestrogens, but soybeans have a special kind called isoflavones.

Isoflavones' estrogen-like effects may also block the buildup of fatty deposits or plaque in the arteries and prevent the bone density loss that occurs in older women. Soy's natural plant estrogens don't seem to have the harmful, cancer-causing effects on breast and uterine tissues that human estrogen can have.

Goes to bat against cancer. One of soy's natural estrogens — genistein — may be the key to preventing breast and prostate cancers.

Dr. Stephen Barnes is studying genistein at the University of Alabama at Birmingham. He says this very weak plant estrogen mimics the action of human estrogen — just like a Little League baseball player imitates the pros. Both human and plant estrogens go to bat against menopause symptoms, osteoporosis, and heart disease.

But sometimes, genistein interferes with human estrogen — like a Little League player let loose in the World Series. That's a good thing, too, because human estrogen contributes to breast cancer.

Investigators at the University of Alabama recently exposed rats to powerful carcinogens and then fed them soy protein. The rats developed half as many tumors as rats who ate milk protein. When the rats' food was washed with alcohol to get rid of the genistein, the cancer-fighting properties disappeared.

Researchers are intrigued with the possibility that soy foods can lower the risk of prostate cancer. In Japan, the risk of prostate cancer is low in men, and breast cancer is rare in women. Many Japanese families start the day with a bowl of miso soup, a broth made of fermented soybeans, so rich in antioxidants that miso may cut the risk of stomach cancer by one-third.

Soybeans also contain a protease inhibitor, which keeps cells from multiplying. Dr. Ann R. Kennedy of the University of Pennsylvania thinks the protease inhibitor is a more likely candidate than genistein to win soybean's cancer-fighting honors.

Soybeans keep arteries clean. No question about it. Soybeans lower cholesterol levels and help keep arteries young and clear. In a major review of 38 clinical trials involving 730 volunteers, University of Kentucky researchers found that soybean eaters reduced their total cholesterol levels about 9 percent on average.

The study participants ate an average of 47 grams of soy protein per day — some ate more, some less — but all of them lowered their cholesterol levels. Volunteers with the highest cholesterol levels had the most dramatic results. On average, they reduced their total cholesterol levels by nearly 20 percent.

Even better, the soy protein reduced only low-density lipoprotein cholesterol (LDL), the so-called "bad" cholesterol. Levels of high-density lipoprotein cholesterol (HDL), the "good" cholesterol, remained the same and sometimes increased.

Two strikes against stroke. As you know, the fatty deposits that build up on your artery walls over the years can lead to a stroke. Soybeans have plenty of power to combat this buildup.

In animal studies, soy's wonder chemical genistein helped keep fatty deposits from building back up on arteries that were surgically widened.

Soybean oil is also a rich source of alpha-linolenic acid, a chemical that researchers believe can lower your risk of stroke.

Protects liver, and that's no monkey business. Ever seen a drunk baboon? Researchers in New York City had a theory that the lecithin found in soybeans would protect the liver and maybe even prevent cirrhosis, the liver disease associated with alcoholism.

So they took 30 baboons and gave 15 of them a diet like a chronic alcoholic's — half of a day's calories for an alcoholic come from alcohol. Some of the baboons also got three table-spoons of soy lecithin in their food every day.

Every "alcoholic" baboon who didn't get lecithin developed severe scars on his liver, and two of the animals had full-blown cirrhosis. But the animals that got the lecithin were almost completely protected against the alcohol. Their livers showed very little scarring.

Beans build up your bones. Dowager's humps, broken hips, and fractured wrists don't have to be your fate as you age. The Osteoporosis Foundation recommends tofu, or soybean curd, as a rich source of calcium to help fight the loss of bone mass. One 4-ounce serving of tofu provides twice the calcium of one cup of plain yogurt. In addition to calcium, researchers think the estrogen-like effects of genistein also prevent loss of bone.

UNDERSTAND THE DANGERS OF SOY

A few years ago, Dr. Lon White and his fellow researchers at the Pacific Health Research Institute in Hawaii examined the eating patterns of more than 8,000 Japanese-American men over a period of 30 years.

They found that those who ate two or more servings of tofu a week were far more likely to have memory problems as they got older than those who ate little or no tofu. And the more tofu they ate, the greater their memory and learning difficulties.

White suggests you eat soy only in moderate amounts.

YOUR ACTION PLAN

HOW MUCH IS ENOUGH?

You might not want to start the day the Japanese way — with a bowl of miso soup for breakfast — but substituting lots of soybean products for meat, cheese, and vegetables in your diet is a good idea. Scientists disagree on the exact amount of soybeans you need for heart and cancer protection, but huge amounts aren't necessary. One serving a day should give you some protection against cancer, heart disease, or uncomfortable menopause symptoms.

Here are some typical servings along with the average amount of isoflavones, the estrogen-like, cancer-fighting plant substances unique to soybeans, they provide:

1/2 cup of soy flour = 50 milligrams (mg) isoflavones

1 cup of soy milk, 1 ounce of soy nuts, or 1/2 cup of tofu or tempeh = 40 mg isoflavones

1/2 cup cooked soybeans or textured vegetable protein = 35 mg isoflavones

If you really want to lower your cholesterol, shoot for three daily servings of soy foods. You might start slowly by substituting one soy meal a week for a meal based on animal protein, but over time, try to replace 50 percent of the animal protein you now eat with vegetable protein. Look in bookstores and libraries for cookbooks specializing in vegetarian, bean, and tofu cooking.

> "Consuming Metamucil and skim milk is one way to achieve a low-fat, high-fiber diet, but it is not the same as basing one's diet on beans and grains, which also are low in fat and high in fiber."
> — Mark Messina, Ph.D., coauthor of *The Simple Soybean and Your Health*

HOW TO GET MORE SOY NATURALLY

Your goal is to replace high-fat, low-fiber meats with soy-based foods. Don't just add soy products to a typical American diet. Most Americans eat too much protein already, and if you add protein-rich soybeans to a meat-heavy diet, you're likely to have kidney trouble. Your kidneys will have to work overtime to excrete all the waste that is produced when your body metabolizes proteins.

Although lower in fat, especially in saturated fat, than most animal proteins, soybeans still contain 19 percent polyunsaturated fat. One ounce of regular tofu has 41 calories and more than 2 grams of fat. To keep those fat grams under control, look for the low-fat soy products that are available, like low-fat soy milk and tofu.

Soybeans aren't a magic potion guaranteeing eternal youth, but adding them to your daily diet will help keep you feeling young and fit for years to come.

DO YOU NEED SUPPLEMENTS?

Some of soy's benefits can be found in pills and powders, but most researchers do not recommend them. Studies on soybean phytochemicals, the plant's natural disease fighters, are only a decade old, and many questions about side effects and safety still remain unanswered.

Plus, pills and powders alone don't supply all the good phytochemicals that soy foods provide.

If you eat a soy-based diet, you automatically reduce the overall fat and saturated fat content in your daily diet. You can't improve your health and fight off old age by eating a pint of ice cream and popping a soy pill. To get the maximum cholesterol-lowering, cancer-preventing benefits, you should use soy to replace the high-fat meat and dairy products you now eat.

THE WISE SOY CONSUMER

A few years ago, if you had a yen for soybean products, you could only find them in health food stores or Asian markets. Now most supermarkets stock tofu and tempeh among the fresh produce, while other soy items are found in the health food section. More than 2,000 new soy foods were introduced in the last decade, and several researchers are hoping that the latest studies will spur food companies to develop more.

The technology exists to add soy to hot dogs, brownies, blueberry muffins, and ice cream without an unpleasant "beany" taste. Soy is already used in baby formula and in some commercial baked goods, but not in high enough amounts to give you its many benefits. Researchers hope if the public demands more soy protein, food companies will provide it.

Meanwhile, look in your supermarket or health-food store for the following:

Tofu. Sold in small blocks, this creamy, high-protein soybean curd is extremely rich in calcium. (Look for "calcium sulfate" on the label for even more calcium.) It has a custard-like texture and can be used in soups, salads, stir-fries, dips, spreads, salad dressings, and even in thick milkshakes and cheesecake. Slice it, dice it, mash it, or eat it raw, steamed, broiled, grilled, or baked. Tofu has about 145 calories per 3 1/2 ounces and almost 9 grams of fat. Even though it is mostly unsaturated, use the low-fat versions.

Tofu is quite perishable. Choose fresh-looking tofu sold in dated, sealed, refrigerated packages and heat for two minutes in boiling water before using it. Avoid buying tofu from markets where it is left in unrefrigerated trays of water. That's an open invitation to high levels of bacteria.

Tempeh. A useful meat substitute, tempeh is made from cooked, fermented soybeans and contains even more protein than tofu, but it has a slightly stronger flavor and a firmer texture. It can be sliced; made into patties; or diced and added to chili, sloppy joes, burgers, stews, or stir-fries. It can be refrigerated for up to 10 days or frozen for as long as two months. A 3 1/2 ounce serving has about 200 calories; 8 grams of fat; and is rich in calcium, iron, and vitamin B12.

Soy milk. Made from cooked, ground soybeans, soy milk is available in low-fat versions and in powdered and flavored forms. Substitute it for dairy milk in cooking and baking, or pour it on cereal or into a tall glass and enjoy. Try mixing it 50-50 with regular milk at first. Soy milk could be your easiest way to enjoy soy's benefits.

Miso. A salty seasoning paste rich in B-complex vitamins and iron, miso is made from fermented soybeans and grains, such as rice or barley. It has a distinct flavor that makes a tasty soup base or seasoning, but its sodium content is very high, so use it in moderation. It's an ingredient in some instant soups and ramen noodle products. Look for it in health food stores. Refrigerated, it keeps indefinitely.

Soy cheese. Similar to tofu, but it has a firmer texture. Soy cheese comes in flavors like cheddar, mozzarella, and spiced jack. Keep it refrigerated.

Soy flour. Made from finely ground roasted soybeans. Adds a nutty flavor to baked goods, breads, and cakes. Substitute soy flour for up to one-quarter of the flour called for in recipes for baked-goods, but don't use it in recipes calling for yeast. Soy interferes with the rising process.

Texturized vegetable protein (TVP). Made from compressed soy flour, it has a texture similar to ground beef and can be substituted for all or a portion of ground beef in your regular recipes.

Meatless meat. New soy products include mock bacon, sausage, hot dogs, turkey, chicken, and beef. Some products even have a smoked taste. Watch out for high levels of sodium and fat. Read those labels.

According to legend, this delightfully healthy brew was first discovered by the Chinese emperor Shen Nong, often called "The Divine Healer," when tea leaves accidentally fell into some water being boiled for him. Inquisitive by nature, he decided to try the new concoction and found it invigorating. Today, more tea is consumed around the world than any other beverage except water.

TEA

For over 4,000 years, healers worldwide have used tea to soothe digestive distress, relieve headaches, fight infections, control coughing, boost energy levels, and soothe sunburn, just to name a few of tea's traditional uses.

Just what is it that makes tea so good for you anyway?

It's probably the plant tea comes from that deserves all the praise, the *Camellia sinensis*. This plant, which may either be a shrub or a tree depending on the variety, is the source of all teas — green, black, and oolong. The only difference between them is how they are processed. The processing difference means green tea ends up with more polyphenols than black tea.

And it's those polyphenols that researchers think give green tea, and possibly to a lesser extent black tea, its healing properties. Active antioxidants, polyphenols provide protection against free radical damage that may lead to cancer and heart disease.

The polyphenols in green tea are called catechins. Catechins are the most important components of green tea because of their ability to scavenge free radicals. Catechins are also present in black tea, although to a lesser extent than in green tea.

"One sip of this will bathe the drooping spirits in delight,
beyond the bliss of dreams."

John Milton, author of Paradise Lost, on tea.

6 WAYS TEA FIGHTS AGING

Combats cancer. Animal studies provide convincing evidence that green tea can inhibit a variety of cancers, including stomach, esophageal, gastrointestinal, liver, lung, and pancreatic. Several other studies have found that black tea also reduces the risk of certain cancers. Although the results from human studies have been less clear due to the number of variables associated with tea drinking (such as how hot it's taken or whether milk, sugar, or lemon is added), the most recent studies provide strong support for the theory that tea can prevent cancer in humans.

Several studies have found that drinking as little as one cup of green tea a week can slash your risk of developing cancer of the esophagus (the tube that carries food from your throat to your stomach) by as much as 50 percent.

A 27-month investigation of tea drinkers in Shanghai showed that people who drank at least one cup of freshly brewed green tea a week for six months or more had a 30 percent lower risk of stomach cancer than people who didn't drink tea.

Some research even suggests that drinking green tea may block some of the damage caused by smoking cigarettes. Although Japanese men smoke more cigarettes than American men, studies show a lower rate of lung cancer death for the Japanese men. One possible explanation may be the Japanese custom of drinking green tea.

Additional studies have found that green tea reduces the risk of the following cancers: gastric cancer among Swedish teens, cancer of the mouth among northern Italians, pancreatic cancer among older people in Poland and in the United States, and colon cancer among Japanese men.

A natural heart healer? Animal studies have found that hamsters given green and black teas have lower cholesterol levels. In rats, tea has anti-clotting effects. For humans, these studies could mean fewer or less severe heart attacks, or it could mean that humans just have to drink a heck of a lot of tea to experience any benefits at all. The hamsters studied were drinking quantities of tea that would be about equal to two quarts of tea a day for humans.

That may, in fact, be the case. A recent study of 1,371 Japanese men found that drinking more than 10 cups (8 cups equals 2 quarts) of green tea a day reduced total cholesterol levels and increased the "good" HDL cholesterol, both benefits when it comes to preventing heart disease. Consuming green tea also reduced the risk of clogged arteries. Another study of elderly Dutch men provides additional support for tea's good effect on the heart. That study found regularly consuming tea reduced the risk of coronary heart disease.

Staves off strokes. Tea may also protect against strokes. A study of 552 men ages 50 to 69 revealed that those who drank more than 4.7 cups of black tea a day had a 69 percent reduced risk of stroke compared with the men who drank less than 2.6 cups of tea a day. Researchers suspect tea protects against stroke by preventing blood clots and by hindering LDL "bad" cholesterol from clogging arteries.

Inhibits infections. Several studies have found green tea to be useful in preventing infections, especially diseases that cause diarrhea like cholera and typhus. Other studies have indicated that green tea may be useful in preventing the flu and may even protect against the AIDS virus. One animal study has also found that green tea appears to boost the immune system, which would further boost your body's ability to fight infections.

Crushes cavities. Green tea also appears to offer powerful protection against cavities by killing the bacteria that commonly lead to tooth decay. It may also increase the resistance of your tooth enamel to decay.

Loves your liver. The Japanese study that revealed 10 or more cups of green tea a day offered heart protection also revealed that green tea protected against liver cell damage.

> "If you are cold, tea will warm you;
>
> If you are too heated, it will cool you;
>
> If you are depressed, it will cheer you;
>
> If you are excited, it will calm you."
>
> *William Gladstone, former British Prime Minister*

YOUR ACTION PLAN

HOW MUCH IS ENOUGH?

No one really knows for certain, according to Joe Vinson, Ph.D., professor of chemistry at the University of Scranton in Scranton, Pa. Studies surveying populations that drink green tea have found four cups to be better than two. Those studies also show that spreading your tea drinking throughout the day is better than drinking it all at once.

The only specifics researchers have to rely on for making tea drinking recommendations come from the studies themselves. For example, a recent Japanese study found that 10 cups or more of green tea a day lowers cholesterol. Dutch research revealed it takes a little over four and a half cups of black tea a day to reduce the risk of stroke. To protect yourself from esophageal cancer, researchers think as little as one cup of green tea a day may do the trick.

If you're primarily a black tea drinker, Dr. Vinson sees no reason for you to switch to green. According to him, black tea also contains good antioxidants, and population studies have shown a positive link between black tea and good health.

Instant tea and iced tea also contain the health-promoting antioxidants. Just don't leave iced tea uncovered or sitting out of the refrigerator too long, or its antioxidant levels will drop.

Do you need supplements?

No one really needs tea supplements of any sort since you can get all the benefits by just drinking a cup of tea.

However, if you can't stand the taste of green tea, you may find supplements a satisfactory substitute. Most health food stores carry green tea capsules containing standardized extracts of polyphenols, the antioxidants that give tea its healing powers. Polyphenol concentrations may range from 15 to 50 percent.

How to brew an excellent cup of tea

You don't have to cook up a tempest in a teapot to brew an excellent cup of tea. Follow these four golden rules and you'll always find yourself sipping an exquisite blend.

❦ Prerinse the teapot or teacup you'll be using for your tea with hot water. This will ensure that your tea stays warm while brewing.

❦ Fill your tea kettle with fresh, cold water. Reheated water gives tea a flat taste. Bring water to a rolling boil. If you're brewing green tea, remove the kettle from the heat and let it sit with the lid open for a few minutes. Green tea needs to be steeped at cooler temperatures than black or oolong teas. For black tea, use water immediately.

❦ Use one tea bag or 1 teaspoonful of tea for every cup of water. Pour water over the tea. Although with loose tea you normally start with 1 teaspoonful of tea, you may want to experiment with different amounts, more or less, to see what taste suits you best.

❦ Watch the clock. Tea should be brewed for three to five minutes. The color of tea is not a good indicator of its strength. If you find that the tea is too strong for you after it's finished brewing, add a little warm water.

THE WISE TEA CONSUMER

You can find tea in a variety of places, from specialty shops to the local supermarket. Black tea may be the easiest to locate, but you can find green tea in natural health food stores or Asian food markets. Green tea in tea bags is now widely available in grocery stores.

If you're buying your tea fresh, look for leaves that have an even color and a delicate, not strong, aroma. Since top grades of tea are handpicked, you should see fewer stems in more expensive varieties. Tea leaves of top grade teas are also more tightly rolled than lower grade teas. This gives tea a more consistent flavor. It also means that a pound of high-quality tea will look smaller than a pound of lower quality tea.

As more studies show a link between green tea and good health, the popularity of green tea grows. Due to the studies showing that green tea may protect against skin cancer, you can now purchase a variety of personal care products that contain green tea, from moisturizers and sunblocks to shampoos and deodorants.

Do you take milk with your tea? Many people do. However, if you're drinking tea for your health, adding milk may do more harm than good.

A recent Italian study showed that people who added milk to their tea in about a four to one ratio — 80 percent tea, 20 percent milk — found that milk inhibited the antioxidant potential of tea.

Researchers suggest milk proteins may attach themselves to the antioxidants in tea, making them ineffective. This means the normally protective antioxidants in tea won't be able to protect your body from the health risks free radicals can cause, such as cancer and heart disease.

Green tea is even turning up in toothpaste. Once manufacturers learned of green tea's ability to reduce plaque formation and strengthen tooth enamel, they didn't let any grass grow under their feet getting their new green tea toothpaste on store shelves.

If you're considering purchasing any of these products, just keep in mind that most studies were done using green tea, not a green tea extract.

TEA CAUTIONS

Don't take your tea too hot. Studies show that extremely hot tea can actually increase your risks of esophageal and stomach cancers.

Better to be deprived of food for three days than of tea for one.

Ancient Chinese saying

Powerful protection against heart disease, cancer, infection, and vision loss is as close as your grocery store's produce department. A generous helping of deep orange or dark green vegetables and fruit every other day provides high levels of vitamin A and beta-carotene, two important weapons in your anti-aging arsenal.

VITAMIN A

If a little vitamin A is good for you, then a lot must be better, right? Nothing could be further from the truth.

Your body must have this fat-soluble vitamin for a host of critical functions. Vitamin A plays an important role in vision, fighting infection and bacteria, maintaining your skin and body linings, bone and body growth, reproduction, and normal cell development. Several foods, such as liver, sweet potatoes, and carrots, are extraordinarily rich in vitamin A.

Its plant source, beta-carotene, is one of a group of acknowledged antioxidants that fight heart disease, cancer, memory loss, rheumatoid arthritis, respiratory distress syndrome, liver disease, age-related eye disease, Parkinson's disease, and complications of diabetes.

But studies have shown this essential vitamin can be harmful — and in rare cases, fatal — in large doses. In recent studies, megadose supplements of vitamin A did nothing to help prevent heart disease and might even have caused cancer. Large doses increased the risk of lung cancer in smokers and those exposed to asbestos, so much so that the National Cancer Institute shut down a vitamin A/beta-carotene supplementation study almost two years early because a troubling number of the participants had died.

The study's authors said they could not support taking supplemental beta-carotene or vitamin A, especially for those at high risk for lung cancer. But they did recommend eating fruits and vegetables as sources of these important nutrients.

6 WAYS VITAMIN A FIGHTS AGING

Picture, if you will, a city under siege. The bombardment is constant, and it seems that at any moment, the invaders will rush in and destroy everything the city's residents have spent a lifetime building and nurturing. The only hope is the tireless warriors protecting the city walls.

If it sounds a bit dramatic, it's actually a fairly accurate metaphor for a battle that researchers believe takes place every day in your body. Fortunately, the body has at its disposal a large, highly skilled defense force known collectively as antioxidants.

One of the battalions in the force of free radical fighters is the carotenoids, which occur naturally in such foods as broccoli, cantaloupe and spinach. Beta-carotene is among the fiercest carotenoids. Working together, beta-carotene and vitamin A boost immunity to form a protective shield against free radicals and the diseases they cause. Beta carotene is particularly good at quenching a type of free radical called singlet oxygen.

Needless to say, it's important to keep your troops reinforced. But like many people, you may not get as much as you need of either of these front-line fighters.

Keeps eyesight sharp and clear. They might not have understood the reason, but ancient Egyptians saw the results of treating vision problems with vitamin A. For night blindness and other eye disorders, Egyptian doctors prescribed eating liver or applying juice squeezed from cooked liver to the eyes.

Nowhere is the need for vitamin A more dramatically displayed than in our vision. Half a million children worldwide go blind every year because they don't get enough vitamin A. This deficiency also contributes to age-related macular degeneration and cataracts.

Want to know why your eyes can't do without vitamin A? The vitamin is actually in your light-sensitive eye pigments. When light hits your retina, it bleaches the pigment. The vitamin A breaks away from the pigment. That sends a signal to your brain's optic center, registering the sensation of sight. The vitamin then reconnects with the pigment.

This process occurs continually when your eyes are open. Naturally, a little bit of vitamin A is destroyed every time it happens, so your blood has to deliver a fresh supply.

Night blindness. Do you have trouble seeing at night? Night blindness — when a bright flash of light temporarily blinds you — is one of the first symptoms of a vitamin A deficiency. When the light bleaches your retina, there's a lag before the signal hits your brain. For several seconds, you can't see a thing.

Cloudy corneas and cataracts. Without vitamin A, a protein called keratin can build up and cloud your cornea, the clear lens that covers the retina. (Keratin is what makes your hair and fingernails tough.) This can lead to a drying of the cornea called xerosis. Then, if you continue to lack vitamin A, the protein can thicken and cause permanent blindness.

For us Westerners with healthy diets, cloudy corneas usually mean cataracts. Beta-carotene may help with those, too. Experts think free radicals damage your eyes and cause cataracts. In a 15-year study in Finland, people who took in the fewest antioxidant vitamins, including beta-carotene, were three times more likely to develop cataracts than people with vitamin-rich diets. In a U.S. study, the cataract rate was five times higher for people who didn't get enough vitamins.

Macular degeneration. An uncommon genetic eye disorder that leads to blindness, Sorsby's fundus dystrophy, can be successfully treated with high doses of vitamin A. That has some researchers suggesting that vitamin A treatment might benefit victims of macular degeneration. Macular degeneration is the leading cause of blindness for people over 50 in the Western world, and it's similar in many ways to Sorsby's disorder.

Fends off infection. The cornea isn't the only protective covering in the body that needs vitamin A to function properly. Without vitamin A, that active protein keratin can also build up on your skin and all your internal linings, drying and hardening the surfaces. They begin to crack, making them susceptible to infection.

The master gland of the immune system, the thymus, also gets a boost from vitamin A. In a trial in Indonesia, preschool children received one megadose of vitamin A two weeks before getting a tetanus vaccination. Three weeks after the shot, the children given the vitamin A supplement had a significantly higher level of protection than children taking a placebo.

Another study noted that half the children who get measles in U.S. cities have a vitamin A deficiency. The worse the deficiency, the more severe the measles. This study's researchers recommended giving vitamin A supplements to everyone hospitalized with measles.

However, too much vitamin A may be as bad as too little. In a study in northern Haiti, where vitamin A deficiency is chronic, children took megadoses every four months to see if the supplements affected diarrhea and respiratory disease. They did, but not in the way expected. Children taking the megadoses tended to get worse. The researchers concluded that you can harm your immune system response both by taking too much vitamin A and by taking too little.

Natural help for cancer. While many experts take a dim view of supplementing your diet with vitamin A and beta-carotene, it's a well-known fact that a diet high in fruits and vegetables — especially when they're eaten raw — gives you a hedge against several kinds of cancer.

In fact, we could bore you to tears by discussing the number of studies proving the cancer-fighting powers of vitamin A and beta carotene. Let's just say an incredible amount of research has shown that lacking these powerful nutrients can put you at risk for cancer of the lung, breast, uterus, prostate, stomach, mouth, esophagus, head and neck, as well as leukemia.

One study even suggested that vitamin A and beta-carotene, along with vitamins E and C, may reverse some types of cancer cells to a normal state.

Other experiments showed a reversal, too. Leukemia cells treated with retinoic acid, an active form of vitamin A, stopped dividing and developed the characteristics of mature white blood cells. Clinical studies showed that certain leukemia patients went into remission after treatment with retinoic acid. A California study of adults with chronic leukemia showed that those who took high doses of vitamin A along with their chemotherapy treatments lived longer.

Of course, no one with leukemia should go out and buy vitamin A supplements. Talk with your doctor about these studies to see if retinoic acid is an option for you.

Prevents heart disease. Eating foods rich in beta-carotene may be a powerful weapon in the fight against heart disease. That's because beta-carotene is an efficient scavenger of free radicals. Free radicals can turn LDL cholesterol molecules into fatty cells that damage and clog arteries.

In one study, a large group of male doctors with heart trouble took 50 mg of beta-carotene every other day. Compared with men who took nothing, they had almost half the number of heart attacks and strokes. It did take two years of taking supplements before they saw any positive results.

A study of nearly 1,300 elderly Massachusetts residents had similar results, as did the Nurses' Health Study, with a smaller dosage. Women who ate more than 15 to 20 mg of beta-carotene a day had a 40 percent lower risk of stroke and a 22 percent lower risk of heart attack, as compared with women who ate less than 6 mg a day.

It may be particularly important for smokers to eat a diet rich in beta-carotene. In a study of men who suffered heart attacks, smokers who had only small amounts of carotenoids in their bloodstreams were at much greater risk for heart problems than smokers with above average amounts.

Staves off memory loss. You may be more concerned about losing your memory and your mental faculties than you are about your physical health. Recent research shows that eating a diet with even a modest amount of beta-carotene may help keep your brain powered up.

In a Dutch study of more than 5,100 people ages 55 to 95, barely 1 mg a day of beta-carotene made a tremendous difference in brain power. People who took less than 0.9 mg per day were almost twice as likely to have memory loss, disorientation, and difficulty solving problems as those who ate 2.1 mg a day or more.

Boosts growth hormone levels? The effect of human growth hormone on aging is big news in certain circles, so you may be interested in this study. Researchers in France looked at slowly growing children with delayed bone age.

These children secreted low levels of growth hormone (which you only produce during deep sleep), and their diets were significantly low in vitamin A and beta-carotene. The children took vitamin A supplements for three months, and for nine out of the 12 children, their growth hormone levels increased between 28 percent and 219 percent.

YOUR ACTION PLAN

In fruits and vegetables, vitamin A exists in a form called a precursor or a provitamin. These provitamins for vitamin A are called carotenoids, and there are about 600 different kinds. Only 10 or so can convert to vitamin A in the body. The best of the bunch is the antioxidant giant, beta-carotene. Your body needs both vitamin A and beta-carotene.

Your body contains three active forms of vitamin A. One is retinol. It's stored in the liver and converted into the other two forms, retinal and retinoic acid, as needed. You can get these active forms straight from animal sources — meats and dairy products.

HOW MUCH IS ENOUGH?

The amount of vitamin A you need varies, depending on your weight, age, and sex. A man over 50 needs a daily average of about 900 RAE (retinol activity equivalents). A woman over 50 needs about 700 RAE. On supplement bottles, you may see vitamin A amounts expressed in IUs (international units). The

Recommended Dietary Allowance (RDA) for a man is approximately 3,000 IU and, for a woman, approximately 2,300 IU.

Since vitamin A is stored in the body, though, this RDA is truly an average. You don't have to get the vitamin on a daily basis.

For math lovers only

For those of you who like to be truly correct, don't use international units when you're talking about the RDA for vitamin A. Retinol activity equivalents are more correct. A retinol activity equivalent is the amount of retinol your body will get from any kind of food, whether it contains beta-carotene or vitamin A itself.

The only reason we are even mentioning IUs is that vitamin supplement labels still tend to use those units. Here's how to properly convert IUs to retinol activity equivalents:

Vitamin A from animal sources
(preformed vitamin A): 1 RAE = 3.33 IU
Vitamin A from vegetables and fruits
(beta-carotene): 1 RAE = 20 IU

How to get more vitamin A naturally

It's virtually impossible to get too much vitamin A from your diet unless you're a liver fanatic. Animals store much of their vitamin A in that vital organ so you have to be careful not to eat too much of it. In fact, arctic explorers exclude polar bear livers from their diets because the bears eat whole fish whose livers also contain large amounts of vitamin A. So if a sizzling plateful of liver and onions is your idea of heaven, try to limit yourself to a weekly treat.

If you eat too much beta-carotene, your skin color will turn a rather unsettling bright yellow. That's because beta-carotene is an orange pigment in plants. It won't harm you, but it is a signal to cut back on your carrots and cantaloupes.

Although vitamin A has an RDA, beta-carotene does not. The average daily National Cancer Institute and USDA menu for healthy eating contains 5.2 to 6 mg of beta-carotene. Most Americans eat about 1.5 mg a day. That means you need to pile more fruits and vegetables in your shopping cart.

A good guideline is to choose deep orange or dark green fruits and vegetables, like winter squash, cantaloupe, spinach, broccoli, sweet potatoes, carrots, pumpkin, and apricots. Try to eat them at least every other day to get a healthy level of beta-carotene and vitamin A. Liver, cheese, butter, cream, eggs, and fortified milk also are good sources.

Do you need supplements?

With the serious risks associated with vitamin A overdose (vomiting, headaches, itching, joint pain, severe liver damage, among others) the medical community almost unanimously recommends against vitamin A supplements, and certainly not any in excess of the RDA.

In one case, a woman taking 25,000 IU of vitamin A per day (more than 10 times the RDA) experienced hair loss, dry mucous membranes at the lips, and symptoms of depression. Two months after stopping the supplements, her symptoms improved.

Another documented case was of a woman who took 5,000 IU a day of vitamin A — the amount typically found in a multivitamin — for 10 years. She was diagnosed with liver disease. When she stopped taking the supplement, her condition cleared up.

Vitamin A cautions

If you do use multivitamins or other supplements, read the labels carefully to determine how much vitamin A is present. Experts caution against taking supplements that provide more than the RDA of vitamin A.

A 1989 study suggested those over age 60 who take vitamin A supplements may be at an increased risk for vitamin A overload. These researchers recommended lowering the vitamin A RDA for the elderly.

Because of the danger of spontaneous abortion and birth defects, pregnant and nursing women should not take vitamin A supplements.

FOODS HIGH IN VITAMIN A

Food	Serving size	Amount of vitamin A in IUs
Cooked carrots	1 cup	38,304
Baked sweet potato	1 potato	31,860
Raw carrots	1 cup	30,942
Cooked spinach	1 cup	14,742
Pumpkin pie	1 piece	12,431
Sweet red pepper	1 cup	8,493
Mango	1 mango	8,061
Cooked butternut squash	1 cup	8,014
Cantaloupe	1 cup	5,158
Canned apricots	1 cup	4,126
Raw spinach	1 cup	2,015
Romaine lettuce	1 cup	1,456
Raw broccoli	1 cup	1,357
Paprika	1 teaspoon	1,273
Grapefruit juice	1 cup	1,087

Vitamin C may be the single most influential vitamin you consume. Your body needs it to produce collagen, the protein building block of bones, teeth, blood vessels, and scar tissue. It's also a vital antioxidant and works hard to protect your body from the common cold and other infections.

VITAMIN C

Collagen is one of today's buzzwords. Everywhere you turn, you hear of women getting collagen injections to plump up their skin and smooth out their wrinkles. Just what is this secret beauty ingredient anyway?

Collagen is the main protein that helps hold together all the cells and tissues of your body, including ligaments, tendons, and scar tissue. It also supports your bones and teeth. What's the vitamin C connection? Vitamin C helps your body produce and maintain this wonder protein. If you don't get enough vitamin C, you may suffer from such things as gum disease and arthritis, or have problems recovering from burns.

An 18th-century British doctor first discovered the role collagen plays in the body while searching for a cure for scurvy. In this condition, your body makes very little collagen, which weakens your blood vessels until they break apart. Picture an old, brittle, leaky garden hose. That's what your blood vessels would look like without collagen to reinforce them.

British sailors often came down with scurvy on long voyages, because they couldn't get enough fresh fruits and vegetables to eat. Dr. James Lind discovered that feeding the sailors lemons, limes, or oranges helped them recover from this horrible disease. What was the secret ingredient? Vitamin C, of course.

Eventually, the British government ordered sailors to drink lime juice every day to protect them from scurvy, earning them the nickname "limeys." It also led to vitamin C being named "ascorbic acid," or "no-scurvy" acid.

You'd think a disease with such a simple cure would no longer be a problem. But scurvy is still a risk for elderly people, alcoholics, and babies who drink cow's milk instead of mother's milk or formula.

12 WAYS VITAMIN C FIGHTS AGING

Boosts your brain power. When you think of "C," think of clear thoughts. According to Michael Lesser, author of *Nutrition and Vitamin Therapy,* large doses of a certain form of vitamin C (potassium ascorbate) make your brain more active. Higher blood levels of vitamin C are related to higher IQ scores.

If you're low on vitamin C, you may have problems with reasoning and other thinking skills, particularly if you're older. Studies show that low vitamin C is associated with poor cognitive performance, which includes perception, memory, and judgment, in the elderly.

First line of defense against free radicals. Sound the alarm! Call out the troops! When bacteria, viruses, cancer cells, or any foreign objects invade your body, this is how you respond. Your immune cells rush to attack and drive out the invaders, helped along by their protector, vitamin C.

Your defense cells win their battles by creating free radicals and dumping them on the hostile invaders to kill them. Vitamin C jumps in first to protect the immune cells from attack by rampaging free radicals. Your defenders can then store and carry their own free radical toxins without risk to themselves.

If your immune cells are attacked by free radicals, they can no longer defend your body. Think of the devastating effects of AIDS and cancer, and you'll get a picture of what happens when your immune system is destroyed by free radicals.

When you're low on vitamin C, your defense system may take longer to respond to your body's SOS signals. You may not make as many antibodies to fight infection, and the ones you do make may not have the killer instinct they need to do the job.

Studies have shown that elderly people who are sick tend to die more often no matter how serious their illnesses if they are low on vitamin C.

Relieves colds and other respiratory infections. Do you suffer through the cold and flu season? If you followed Dr. Linus Pauling's advice, you'd take large amounts of vitamin C to help you through your misery. Dr. Pauling believes colds can be prevented by taking megadoses of vitamin C. Other research says vitamin C doesn't prevent colds, but it may relieve your symptoms and make you feel better faster.

What about the misery of allergies? If you sneeze and sniffle your way through the spring or fall, you may want to try some extra vitamin C. A host of research says vitamin C helps seasonal allergy symptoms, probably by reducing the release of histamines.

Vitamin C supplements also have helped elderly people with severe respiratory infections such as bronchitis or pneumonia. Researchers think it's because vitamin C boosts your immune system response and helps prevent damage caused by inflamed bronchial tubes.

If you have asthma, you need all the relief you can get. Studies have shown that a diet low in vitamin C is a risk factor for asthma. Vitamin C supplements may help decrease your symptoms.

Cancer connection. Vitamin C, along with other vitamins found in fruits and vegetables, seems to protect against cancers of the mouth, larynx, esophagus, stomach, colon, and breast. Some doctors are testing the use of megadoses of vitamin C to treat cancer.

Love to sprinkle salt on your foods? Why not try a shaker of vitamin C instead? Lots of processed meats and other foods contain nitrates and nitrites as preservatives. Vitamin C helps keep them from turning into cancer-causing nitrosamines. Sprinkle a few on your ham casserole or hot dogs and beans to give yourself added protection.

Focuses your eyes. Did you know you have a projection screen in your eyes? The back of your eyeball is lined with special cells, called the retina, which act like a projection screen. When light strikes these cells, they go through a complex process to make your brain see an image.

The most sharply seeing part of your retina is the macula. As you age, the macula starts wearing out, a condition called macular degeneration. If this happens, you won't be able to read, drive a car, or even recognize familiar faces. It's said to be the most common form of untreatable blindness in the elderly.

Vitamin C, along with other antioxidants and carotenoids, may help prevent this disease. Sending in the vitamin C troops boosts your other antioxidant nutrients, which help protect your retinas from being damaged.

Do you see spots before your eyes? If you have cataracts, you won't actually see spots, but your lenses will have spots, sort of like flaws in a diamond. These flaws will make things look foggy to you. Medical research shows that if your diet is low in vitamin C, you'll have a greater chance of developing cataracts.

If your vision is starting to fog, you can turn to vitamin C for help in slowing or stalling the change in your eyesight. A combination of vitamin C and vitamin A is even better — it seems to stop cataracts in their tracks and helps keep you away from the surgeon's table.

Keeps your heart and circulation healthy. Want another way to protect yourself from the ravages of heart disease? Studies show vitamin C lowers your cholesterol and blood pressure and strengthens your capillaries. It also lowers your risk of angina. In one study, researchers showed that taking an extra 60 milligrams (mg) of vitamin C a day — about one orange — helped lower heart disease.

If you don't have enough vitamin C, your body makes more fat to patch the damaged walls of your arteries. These patches are the beginnings of cholesterol plaques, which plug up and harden your arteries.

If you already have coronary artery disease, your blood vessels will sing the praises of vitamin C. It helps open those clogged vessels when your heart needs more blood during work or exercise. Team it with vitamin E for an extra-effective boost.

Combats blood sugar assaults. If you have diabetes, vitamin C plays a critical role in maintaining your health. It strengthens your blood vessels, which improves circulation. As an antioxidant, it fights the constant assault on your tissues from high blood sugar.

It also helps you tolerate carbohydrates, break down fats and sugars better, and lower your "bad" cholesterol, as well as other fats in your blood.

Stroke protector. Vitamin C may protect against declining mental ability and stroke. In studies with elderly people, researchers found that low vitamin C levels contributed to slower reasoning skills, which was a strong factor in their dying from stroke.

Prevents sore joints and muscles. Have a tough workout this morning? Or perhaps you're still smarting from that pulled muscle you got the other day. If you increase your vitamin C intake, it may help prevent these aches and pains.

Your body needs more vitamin C when it's injured or infected, especially when an area becomes inflamed. Remember, vitamin C is a potent antioxidant. When enemy cells attack an area of your body, your immune cells dump toxins on the invaders to get rid of them. These toxins generate free radicals, and vitamin C helps lessen the damage they cause.

You may be used to taking aspirin or phenylbutazone (a prescription anti-inflammatory drug) to relieve inflamed joints and muscles. Studies with animals have shown vitamin C to be more potent than either of these.

You may want to take an extra 500 mg of vitamin C, above what you normally take, four times a day when you have any type of inflammation. If you take it before you work out, you may keep your muscles from getting sore at all.

Vitamin C can also help if you suffer from arthritis, because it builds and repairs the cartilage, ligaments, and tendons around your bones. As an antioxidant, it keeps your tissues from aging as quickly, which slows down the development of osteoarthritis.

Detoxifies your system. Alcoholism is a serious illness. If you have a drinking problem, vitamin C may help by improving your body's ability to detoxify and clear the alcohol from your system. It also prevents some of the liver damage alcohol causes.

Vitamin C also helps your body get rid of poisons you pick up from your environment, such as cigarette smoke and other pollution.

Enhances iron absorption. Love spinach salad? Make sure your recipe includes some orange slices. Not only will you get some vitamin C, but you'll get more iron from the spinach. Vitamin C improves your ability to absorb iron from your intestines, so combining vitamin C with iron-rich foods does your body a double favor.

If you tend to be anemic, vitamin C will give you new ammunition to fight your iron deficiency. Also, if you suffer from a heavy menstrual flow, vitamin C plus bioflavonoids, which are available in a combined tablet form, may help reduce it.

Contributes to emotional well-being. Are you feeling tired, listless, or generally depressed? Could be your vitamin C levels are

---

SIGNS OF VITAMIN C DEFICIENCY

- ❦ Shortness of breath
- ❦ Digestive difficulties
- ❦ Easy bruising
- ❦ Swollen or painful joints
- ❦ Nosebleeds
- ❦ Anemia: weakness, tiredness, paleness
- ❦ Frequent infections
- ❦ Slow healing of wounds
- ❦ Scurvy: muscle weakness, swollen gums, loss of teeth, tiredness, depression, bleeding, under skin, bleeding gums

---

low. Vitamin C makes your brain produce serotonin, a chemical that helps you sleep and makes you feel good.

It teams up with vitamin B6 to change a certain amino acid into "norepinephrine," a mood-boosting chemical. This chemical regulates your "fight or flight" response when danger threatens.

Vitamin C also helps you make other hormones, such as thyroxin, which regulates your metabolism and body temperature. And it raises your level of red blood cell glutathione, which gives you more antioxidant protection during normal everyday activities.

Depression is one of the earliest symptoms of a lack of vitamin C. Even a mild deficiency can make you lose your sense of well-being. If you find yourself feeling low, make sure you eat lots of fruits and vegetables. While you're at it, relax with a cup of green tea. It helps your body retain vitamin C.

YOUR ACTION PLAN

HOW MUCH IS ENOUGH?

That's a good question. The Recommended Dietary Allowance (RDA) for vitamin C is 90 mg for men over 50 and 75 mg for women over 50. However, since Dr. Pauling's research on the positive effects of vitamin C, many people have been taking 1,000 mg or more each day.

Recent studies show that 200 mg is the point where vitamin C saturates your cells and blood. That means your body can't absorb any more and will simply excrete it. So taking large doses may not do you any good, and it may even be harmful if it builds up in your bloodstream. Some experts believe it contributes to kidney stones, but others think 1 to 5 grams per day may actually keep stones from forming.

HOW TO GET MORE VITAMIN C NATURALLY

"Breakfast without orange juice is like a day without sunshine."

Anita Bryant

If you're trying to get more vitamin C in your diet, you're lucky — you have plenty of natural sources to choose from.

Take Anita Bryant's advice and start your day with a glass of "liquid sunshine." You'll meet your RDA for vitamin C before you even finish your breakfast. Just eat four more servings of fruits and vegetables high in vitamin C throughout the day, and you'll get more than enough vitamin C for your daily needs.

Among the fruits and vegetables high in vitamin C are lemons, oranges, grapefruit, strawberries, tangerines, black currants, broccoli, brussels sprouts, cabbage, collards, peppers, kale, potatoes, spinach, tomatoes, and watercress.

How about trying something exotic? Kiwis, guava, mangos, papayas, and rose hips may be just what you need to spice up your life — and your health.

HOW TO GET YOUR DAILY DOSE
OF VITAMIN C

Orange juice, fresh	1 cup	124 mg
Broccoli, cooked	1 cup	116 mg
Cantaloupe	1/2	113 mg
Sweet red pepper, fresh	1/2 cup	95 mg
Brussels sprouts, cooked	1 cup	96 mg
Green pepper	1 whole	66 mg

DO YOU NEED SUPPLEMENTS?

You probably don't need a supplement if you're eating the recommended five servings of fruits and vegetables each day. Chances are you're already getting close to 200 mg a day, which is more than double the current RDA. But if you're fighting specific health problems, you may want to increase your daily dosage. Some recommendations go as high as 4,000 mg per day, but it's best to check with your doctor before taking so much.

Additional vitamin C may help if you are:

- ❦ undernourished or not getting enough calories.
- ❦ over 55 years old.
- ❦ pregnant or breast feeding.
- ❦ an alcohol or drug abuser.
- ❦ a smoker.
- ❦ fighting an infection.
- ❦ suffering from a chronic wasting illness, acute illness with fever, hyperthyroidism, tuberculosis, or cold exposure.
- ❦ stressed out for long periods or have recently undergone surgery.
- ❦ involved in athletics or vigorous physical activities.
- ❦ recovering from severe burns or injuries.
- ❦ receiving kidney dialysis.
- ❦ someone who has had part of his gastrointestinal tract removed.

THE WISE VITAMIN C CONSUMER

Experts say it's better to get your vitamin C and other antioxidants from food rather than supplements. It's more satisfying too! Wouldn't you rather bite into a big, juicy orange or a tangy tangerine than pop a vitamin pill? You have so many wonderful fruits and vegetables to choose from, it's a shame not to take advantage of them.

Your best bet is to eat your food raw or minimally cooked. You can shorten cooking time by putting vegetables in small amounts of water. Avoid soaking your vegetables, leaving food at room temperature for long periods, or overexposing them to air and light. These tips will help you get the most vitamin C out of your foods.

If you want to take a large amount of vitamin C, you have a number of options. Vitamin C comes in different types of tablets that you can either swallow, chew, or dissolve in liquid. Powdered vitamin C can be diluted in water or sprinkled directly on food. You can even be injected with vitamin C, but you must see a doctor or nurse if you choose this option.

VITAMIN C CAUTIONS

Even though vitamin C is considered one of the safest vitamins, it does cause problems in some people.

You may be one of those who can't break down vitamin C normally, which makes you more likely to develop kidney stones. If you have this problem, you should drink lots of fluids and avoid taking large doses of vitamin C.

Don't take extra vitamin C if you have sickle cell disease, because it may make your condition worse. Also, don't take it if you're on any medication that contains aluminum. Vitamin C makes your intestines absorb aluminum better, and too much aluminum can be toxic.

Other medicines also interact with vitamin C. For example, aspirin, mineral oil, sulfa drugs, tetracyclines, and salicylates all lower the effect of vitamin C. If you take barbiturates, you'll not only decrease the amount of vitamin C in your body, you'll increase the effect of the drug, which could be dangerous.

If you're convinced vitamin C is the best thing since white bread, just be smart about it. Treat it like a drug, avoid doses larger than 2,000 mg, and keep close tabs on your blood iron concentrations. High doses put some people at risk for iron overload.

Finally, if you don't want to spend extra time in the bathroom, be sure to take your supplements after meals so your body can absorb them better. Large amounts of vitamin C can cause diarrhea, as well as abdominal cramps and nausea.

Vitamin D — the "sunshine" vitamin. Without the light of the sun, your body can't produce this essential nutrient. And, in fact, it's the only vitamin your body can manufacture by itself. Vitamin D helps regulate the calcium and phosphorus in your body so you can grow and maintain healthy bones, teeth, and muscles.

VITAMIN D

Vitamin D is a "quiet" vitamin. If you hadn't seen "fortified with vitamins A and D" on the side of a milk container, you might not even know it exists. But without vitamin D, calcium — the body's most common nutrient — couldn't be used. And without calcium, your body simply couldn't function.

The scientific community first recognized vitamin D in the 17th century. At this time, nutrition was a budding science, and vitamin D was almost classified as a hormone because it acts like one. Even today, some experts consider it more of a hormone than a vitamin.

This vitamin attracted a lot of attention after the industrial revolution hit England in the 18th century. Children were suffering from a bone disease called rickets in epidemic proportions. It was caused by a lack of vitamin D, although no one realized it at the time. These children worked in England's factories and mines from dawn until night and ate very little meat or milk. It's no wonder they were victims of vitamin D deficiency.

Did your mother ever make you take cod-liver oil to keep you healthy? If so, she was relying on a treatment that developed during this period. Doctors found that cod-liver oil could cure rickets, because vitamin D occurred naturally in cod and other fish. Researchers finally realized that sunlight was the best cure for this bone-deforming disease. But people decided cod-liver oil was good for any ailment, so the practice of dosing the family with cod-liver oil became a popular remedy.

9 WAYS VITAMIN D FIGHTS AGING

Protects your bones from osteoporosis. You know how critical calcium is to your bones. Vitamin D works hand-in-glove with calcium to give your body the building blocks it needs to produce and maintain strong bones and teeth. Vitamin D helps your body absorb the calcium it takes in. No matter how much calcium you have, your body can't use it without vitamin D.

This tightknit relationship often puts elderly people at high risk for osteoporosis. If you stay indoors, you're not exposing yourself to those wonderful healthy sunbeams that stimulate your skin to make vitamin D. If you don't drink enough fortified milk, you also increase your risk for a vitamin D deficiency. The result can be a loss of calcium that can lead to osteoporosis.

Do you live in the north and suffer through lots of cold, bleak winter days? If so, it can be even harder for your bones to get enough sunshine-loving vitamin D. Studies have shown that hip fractures are more common at this time of year. Snowy, icy sidewalks are one reason, but if you're low on vitamin D, your bones may become weak and break more easily. In one study, women who took a vitamin D supplement every day for two years made their hip bones stronger even without extra calcium.

Ask your doctor about vitamin D supplements, and take advantage of sunny winter days to boost your vitamin D level naturally. But don't think you can just sit by the window to reap the sun's benefits. That warm ray of sunlight won't do you any good unless you're outside. Studies have shown that glass and most plastics absorb the UV waves your skin needs to make vitamin D.

Keeps arthritis in check. Are your knees so stiff that it's excruciating to walk even a few short steps? According to an eight-year study, osteoarthritis of the knee may be controlled by taking higher levels of vitamin D than normally recommended. Check with your doctor to see if extra vitamin D might relieve your arthritis.

May reduce your risk of cancer. When it comes to colon cancer, sunshine may be just what the doctor ordered.

Although it's not quite that simple, studies have shown that calcium and vitamin D may reduce your risk of colon cancer. Apparently, vitamin D helps stop the cancerous cells from spreading, either by something it does directly or by increasing the amount of calcium your body absorbs.

Vitamin D also may be a factor in surviving breast cancer. It seems to keep the cancer cells from growing and spreading.

Keeps your blood pressure low. Calcium helps flush out excess salt from your body, which lowers your blood pressure. Since vitamin D helps your body absorb calcium, it's an important link in preventing high blood pressure.

Gives your heart rhythm. Your heart is a natural pacemaker, and you need calcium to help fire it up. Remember — your body can't use calcium unless it has vitamin D to help it along. If you have a heart rhythm problem, it may be harder to treat if you're short on vitamin D.

Strengthens your jaw and gums. If you suffer from gum disease, you may benefit from supplements of vitamin D, calcium, and magnesium. Research shows these vitamins may help prevent bone loss in your jaws, which can cause gum infections.

Tunes up your ears. Not hearing so well these days? You may need to spend more time outdoors. A vitamin D deficiency may contribute to hearing loss and inner ear problems. Get enough vitamin D, and you'll be able to enjoy those beautiful songbirds in your garden.

Relieves migraine headaches and PMS. If you suffer from premenstrual syndrome or menstrually related migraines, studies show that extra doses of vitamin D and calcium may relieve your symptoms.

Gives your bowels a boost. Having a little problem with your back end? Then you'd better make an extra effort to soak up the sunshine. Vitamin D deficiency often occurs in people who have bowel conditions and diseases, such as Crohn's disease and irritable bowel syndrome. This is probably because an inflamed bowel can't absorb the vitamin from fortified foods.

Try to spend 30 minutes every day sitting, walking, or exercising in the sun to make sure you get enough vitamin D.

YOUR ACTION PLAN

HOW MUCH IS ENOUGH?

Your body needs only a small amount of vitamin D. The RDA for healthy adults, age 50 to 70, is 10 micrograms (mcg) a day. If you're outdoors a lot, you probably get about 75 percent of the vitamin D you need from the sun.

But modern living sometimes makes that difficult. We live in cities full of pollution and skyscrapers that block the sun. We spend most of our lives indoors, and when we do go out, we cover ourselves with heavy clothing or sunscreen. Our skin doesn't get much of a chance to feel the warmth of the sun. If that's your situation, you need to make an extra effort to get your vitamin D from the foods you eat.

Some people may need even more vitamin D than the recommended amounts. If you're over 55 years old, you will probably benefit from more vitamin D, especially if you're a postmenopausal woman. As you get older, your body can only change about half as much of the sun's rays into vitamin D as it did when you were younger.

If you have a chronic illness, undergo long periods of stress, or have recently had surgery, you also need more vitamin D. Alcohol or other drug abuse and a poor diet are also good reasons for taking more vitamin D.

HOW TO GET MORE VITAMIN D NATURALLY

Let the sun shine in! The best way to boost your vitamin D level is to enjoy at least 30 minutes of outdoor sunlight each day. Take a walk, tend your garden, or read your favorite book out on the porch. While you relax and absorb the sun's warm rays, your body will be busy making one of your most essential nutrients.

Fortified milk is your richest food source of vitamin D. You can also find it in other fortified dairy products and cereals, egg yolks, liver, and fatty fish such as salmon, tuna, and sardines.

DO YOU NEED SUPPLEMENTS?

The change of seasons, time of day, where you live, aging, sunscreen use, and the pigment of your skin can all affect how much vitamin D your body makes. If you don't get enough sunshine, you may want to take supplements.

Homebound elderly people are at particular risk for vitamin D deficiency. They not only lack sunlight but tend to have a poor diet as well.

Are you a strict vegetarian who does not eat animal products? You also may lack this important vitamin, since animals are the only natural food source for vitamin D. Unless you're a construction worker or lifeguard, you'd better add a supplement to your diet.

One reminder — if you do take extra vitamin D, make sure you get enough magnesium as well. Studies have shown that vitamin D needs magnesium to work effectively with calcium.

VITAMIN D CAUTIONS

Be careful when taking vitamin D supplements. This vitamin is fat-soluble, which means it's stored in your body instead of excreted. Too much vitamin D — only five times the RDA — can cause high blood pressure, irregular heartbeat, seizures, liver and kidney damage, and heart disease.

If you're over 55, you're more likely to experience bad reactions and side effects from vitamin D supplements. Watch for symptoms such as irritability, weakness, abnormal thirst, increased urination, nausea, vomiting, headache, and depression.

Certain drugs and conditions may cause vitamin D deficiencies. Check with your doctor about taking supplements if you have epilepsy, chronic diarrhea, intestinal problems, sarcoidosis or any disease of the heart, kidney, liver, or pancreas.

Vitamin E could be your body's most powerful defender against the ravages of time. Vitamin E sacrifices itself in order to protect more important substances in your body from being damaged.

VITAMIN E

Vitamin E, or tocopherol, is like the Arnold Schwarzeneggar of the antioxidant world. It uses its antioxidant muscle to protect your cells by breaking up free radical reactions. Vitamin E is the most effective "chain-breaking" antioxidant. Some antioxidants prevent oxidation, but chain-breakers like vitamin E can repair oxidation after it has occurred.

As you know, free radicals are unstable molecules that have become oxidized. This means they lack an electron and try to steal one from the cells in your body. When vitamin E encounters these free radicals, it gives them an electron, making them stable once again, but the vitamin E becomes oxidized in the process. Fortunately, the oxidized form of vitamin E is relatively harmless and can be repaired to function as an antioxidant once again.

The repair process for vitamin E requires a little help, mostly from vitamin C and the amino acid glutathione. Although vitamin E is a fat-soluble vitamin and vitamin C is a water-soluble vitamin, they cooperate to form a tag team to fight free radicals. While vitamin E and vitamin C are both antioxidants in their own right, when vitamin E sacrifices itself to break up a free radical, vitamin C steps in. It helps recycle vitamin E so it can return to its job as a free radical buster.

Because vitamin E is a fat-soluble vitamin, it is stored in fat cells in your body. This is important because fat is particularly susceptible to free radical damage. Vitamin E helps protect these fats, especially polyunsaturated fats, from becoming oxidized.

Vitamin E doesn't just sit in one place, waiting for free radicals to show up so it can do its job. Vitamin E is much busier than that. It travels all over your body to seek out and destroy free radicals and prevent damage to important cells. This is how vitamin E protects every part of your body from free radical damage — from your heart to your skin.

8 WAYS VITAMIN E FIGHTS AGING

It's tough to get scientists to agree on anything, but most researchers think there is strong evidence that antioxidants help your body fight disease. Of all the known antioxidants, vitamin E probably has the most convincing evidence of its disease-fighting capabilities.

Fires up your immune system. Have you noticed that it takes you just a little bit longer to walk to the mailbox than when you were younger? Most people begin to move a little more slowly as they get older. Your immune system begins to move more slowly, too. As you age, it takes longer for your body to fight off bacteria and infection. This gives disease more time to become firmly established in your body's cells. Vitamin E stimulates your immune system, making it work more quickly and efficiently. Studies show that when elderly people are given vitamin E supplements, their immune response times improve.

This helps increase resistance to the damaging effects of viruses, strokes, infections, and even smog.

Heads off heart disease? Once the hero of heart health, vitamin E's reputation has diminished lately. Several new studies have found no conclusive evidence that vitamin E provides any benefits to your heart. But don't dismiss this nutrient just yet. There is research supporting the heart-protecting effects of vitamin E.

For example, one study found that women who ate foods high in vitamin E were 62 percent less likely to die from a heart attack as women with low vitamin E intakes.

Another study found that people who already had symptoms of heart disease could benefit from vitamin E supplements. People with heart disease symptoms who took supplements of 400 to 800 International Units (IU) of vitamin E daily were about three times less likely to suffer a heart attack as those who didn't take supplements.

How does vitamin E work its heart-guarding magic? Most researchers think vitamin E stops oxidation of LDL, the "bad" cholesterol. As LDL cholesterol travels through your bloodstream, it often likes to cling to the walls of your blood vessels. This eventually causes clumps that make your arteries much narrower, causing your hard-working heart to work even harder to pump blood through these tiny passageways.

Oxidation of LDL cholesterol by free radicals makes it more likely to stick to your artery walls. Vitamin E stops free radical damage and keeps LDL cholesterol where it belongs — on the move.

Stops strokes. Vitamin E's ability to stop LDL cholesterol from clinging to your blood vessel walls may also help prevent another potential killer — stroke. The clots that form on artery walls sometimes break loose and travel to your brain where they can cause a stroke.

Vitamin E also fights stroke by making your blood more slippery and less likely to form clots. A study on the effects of another well-known anticoagulant, aspirin, found that people given 400 IU of vitamin E and 325 mg of aspirin to prevent blood clots were about half as likely to form clots as people taking aspirin alone.

Prevents cancer? Could vitamin E hold the key to safer cancer treatment and prevention? Although it is doubtful that one substance will ever be able to fend off all cancers, vitamin E may at least help. Researchers say vitamin E may help defend DNA against damage that can set off the growth of cancer.

❦ Low levels of vitamin E are associated with an increased risk of breast cancer. A high fat intake is also associated with an increased risk of breast cancer. Researchers think vitamin E may protect against breast cancer by preventing the development of cancer-causing substances that are created when fat is metabolized.

❦ A recent study found that people who took a vitamin E supplement regularly for at least six months were half as likely to develop oral cancers as other people.

❦ A study on esophageal and stomach cancers in Japan found that people who took a supplement of vitamin E, beta carotene, and selenium lowered their risks of dying from cancer by 13 percent.

❦ Vitamin E supplements have been shown to slow the rates of tumor growth in people who have leukemia or lymphoma. This is probably due to vitamin E's effect in enhancing immune system response.

❦ Men who were given 50 IU of vitamin E daily for five to eight years were less likely to develop prostate cancer than those who did not take vitamin E.

Enhances exercise. Since free radicals are produced from oxygen, and your oxygen intake increases during exercise, wouldn't your level of free radicals also increase? Yes, it does. Does that mean you should stop exercising and become a couch potato? Hardly. The benefits of exercise far outweigh the damage a few extra free radicals can do. But if you truly want to make the most of your exercise, you can counteract the effects of increased free radicals by getting plenty of vitamin E. Studies show that vitamin E can reduce the muscle damage caused by free radicals during exercise, particularly in older people.

Aids against asthma. As an antioxidant powerhouse, vitamin E may cut your risk of asthma. A study in Saudi Arabia found that children who had the least vitamin E in their diets were three times more likely to get asthma. Research also shows that vitamin E helps protect you from developing this condition as an adult.

Counteracts excessive iron. Your body needs iron for healthy blood, but too much iron can lead to liver damage or cirrhosis, a chronic disease of the liver. Since your liver performs many important functions in your body, including cleansing your blood of toxic substances, liver damage can be deadly. Vitamin E may protect your liver from excess iron, which will help keep this vital organ functioning properly.

Shields skin and eyes from light damage. Do you love the beach? Do you spend a lot of time in your garden? Does your job keep you outdoors a lot? Being outdoors in the bright sunshine can be invigorating, but too much exposure to sunlight can damage your skin and eyes. If you love to have fun in the sun, make sure you get plenty of vitamin E. It may help protect your skin and eyes from damage caused by excessive light exposure.

YOUR ACTION PLAN

HOW MUCH IS ENOUGH?

The Recommended Dietary Allowance (RDA) for vitamin E is 15 mg (22 IU) for people over 50. International units or IU is a term you will see on supplement labels, even though nutrition experts no longer use it. The term they use for measuring vitamin E is tocopherol equivalents, which is expressed in milligrams. The experts believe it better reflects the vitamin's various forms and the different ways vitamin E is absorbed and used by the body.

To help you calculate, remember that 1 IU of vitamin E equals 0.67 milligrams. For example, 15 mg divided by 0.67 equals 22.39 or 22 IU. To change IU to milligrams, multiply the IU amount by 0.67.

How to get more vitamin E naturally

Vitamin E is widely available in plant foods. Vegetable oils and related products like margarine, salad dressing, and shortening contain vitamin E, but much of it is lost if the oil has been heated to frying temperatures. Other sources include green leafy vegetables, wheat germ, whole-grain cereals, peanut butter, nuts, and eggs.

Do you need supplements?

The average daily intake of vitamin E from food sources is between 7 and 10 mg. However, in order to get the amount most experts recommend for heart and immune system protection, around 100 to 400 IU daily, you would have to take a supplement.

Certain conditions, such as smoking, increase your need for vitamin E. And although fish oil provides anti-aging benefits of its own, you should be aware that an increased intake of fish oil may increase your need for vitamin E.

Also keep in mind that most fat-soluble vitamins can cause serious side effects if taken in large quantities be-cause they are stored in the body. Although vitamin E seems to be relatively safe, even in large doses, make sure you check with your doctor before taking more than the RDA.

The wise vitamin E consumer

Natural vitamin E usually comes from soybeans or wheat, while synthetic vitamin E is created in a laboratory. Many experts think natural vitamin E is more potent than synthetics. The systems of measurement, International Units or tocopherol equivalents, supposedly correct for that, making them equal, but new studies show that your body may retain natural vitamin E better than the synthetic kind.

Vitamin E cautions

Ask your doctor's advice before taking vitamin E supplements if you have any health problem or if you are taking blood thinning medication, like Coumadin.

Although vitamin E is relatively safe when compared with other fat-soluble vitamins, large doses — over 400 IU — taken over a prolonged period of time may cause blurred vision, diarrhea, dizziness, headaches, nausea, or unusual fatigue.

VITAMIN E CONTENT OF VARIOUS FOODS

Food	Amount	Vitamin E (IU
Wheat germ oil	1 tablespoon	25
Sunflower seeds	1 ounce	21
Almonds, dried	1 ounce	11
Safflower oil	1 tablespoon	8
Avocado, California	1 medium	3
Brown rice	1 cup	3
Mango	1 medium	3
Margarine	1 tablespoon	3
Mayonnaise	1 tablespoon	3
Peanuts, dry roasted	1 ounce	3
Asparagus	4 spears	2
Soybean oil	1 tablespoon	2
Spinach, raw	1 cup	1

Picture yourself on a desert isle with nothing to eat or drink. How long do you think you would survive ... 10 days? ... 20? ... a month? Actually, you'd probably last about 45 days without food. But without water, you'd be lucky if you lasted 10. Of all the vital nutrients you need to survive, water is the one you simply can't do without.

WATER

Have you ever stopped in the middle of a busy day and realized it's been hours since you've had a drink? Suddenly, you feel like you're dying of thirst.

Actually, you are. By the time your brain's thirst center wakes up, you've already lost 2 percent of the water in your body. And if you don't replace it, your body will begin to shut down.

After all, water makes up more than 60 percent of your body weight, and if you don't get enough, any other nutrients you take in will be left high and dry. A lack of water affects everything from your digestive tract to your immune system. It also helps regulate your body temperature.

Your body is so busy that it loses 10 to 12 cups of water per day just from all the normal things you do. When you sweat, urinate, excrete waste, or even just breathe, you're getting rid of some of that moisture.

So how does your body know when it needs more, and how does it get that message to you?

Think about the last time you had "cotton" mouth. That's one way your body gets you to drink. When your blood needs water, it sometimes borrows it from your salivary glands. Your mouth feels dry, and you reach for a drink to "wet your whistle."

The hypothalamus, the part of your brain that regulates many basic body functions, also kicks in when your body is low on water. It watches for changes in your blood, then signals you it's time to drink. Unfortunately, this switch is not always on the ball and sometimes forgets to tell you you're thirsty until way past the time you need water. That's why experts tell you to drink throughout the day even if you don't feel thirsty.

In times of real trouble, the hypothalamus calls out the antidiuretic hormone (ADH). This hormone tells your kidneys to send some of the water they are holding for excretion back into the bloodstream. If your body has too much water, ADH will tell your kidneys to release it. But it always makes sure you only get rid of water you don't need.

9 WAYS WATER FIGHTS AGING

Feeds and cleans your cells. Water constantly moves in and out of your cells — dissolving nutrients, delivering them where they need to go, and carrying waste out of your body. Water plays a big part in feeding your cells so you get all the energy you need. Think of it as your own personal transportation system.

Improves your digestion. Like oil in a machine, water helps your digestive system run the way it's supposed to. Without it, your "machine" will get sluggish.

Suffer from constipation? Water helps soften your stools so you can pass them more easily.

Ever get that painful, burning sensation in your chest? Heartburn is an uncomfortable fact of life for many people. You get it when acid in your stomach backs up into your esophagus and irritates it.

Water helps wash the acid out and gives your stomach a fighting chance to do its job properly. Try drinking water about an hour before or after meals to keep your stomach from bloating. A bloated stomach is more likely to overflow, which is exactly what you don't want.

Water also helps antacids and other medicines do their jobs faster and more efficiently.

Keeps your body temperature even. When exercise or fever makes you sweat, the water evaporating off your skin actually helps cool you down — call it natural air conditioning.

Your body has a hard time handling extreme heat or cold, so during a summer heat wave or winter freeze, you need to drink even more water. If you don't, your body may shut down altogether, leading to serious problems such as heatstroke or frostbite.

Heatstroke often affects older people because they sweat less and don't feel as thirsty as they used to. If you have diabetes or heart disease, you're even more at risk. Drinking lots of water will keep you from getting dehydrated and help prevent heatstroke.

In cold weather, hypothermia, or loss of body heat, is as serious as heatstroke. And dehydration is the number one cause of frostbite, say nurses in an Alaskan hospital's thermal unit. It's easy to forget to drink in chilly weather, but your body still sweats and needs fluids. Make drinking water a year-round habit.

Helps your body heal itself. If you're sick or having surgery, drinking water is an easy way to put yourself back on the road to recovery. After surgery, your body retains water to help it heal, so adding to your supply gives your body an extra boost when it needs it most.

Water is also one of your best bets to prevent bladder or urinary infections. It helps flush the infection from your system before it gets a good grip.

Six to eight glasses of water a day will also help you beat a cold or the flu.

Lubricates and cushions your joints. Water molecules are like people — they don't like to be crowded together. This aversion actually helps protect your joints. By spreading out, water forms a cushion that helps lubricate your joints, which makes them easier to bend and move around.

When arthritis makes you stiff and achy, your first thought should be, "I need some water." This simple solution may help you feel better and even reduce your painful swelling.

If you're bothered by gout, you especially need to drink a lot of water. It dilutes and carries away the uric acid that causes your discomfort.

Along with cushioning your joints, water acts like a shock absorber inside your eyes and spinal cord.

Moisturizes your skin and lips. Water is absolutely critical to healthy skin. Both water in the air and water you drink gives shape and nourishment to your cells. It makes your skin elastic and supple instead of dried up and shriveled like a prune.

But sometimes you can get too much of a good thing. If you love long, hot showers or baths, you may be doing your skin more harm than good. Lingering in a hot tub can strip your skin of natural oils, which help keep moisture in. Make your water temperature warm instead of hot. And if you like bath oil, add a little to your bath water after you've soaked for about 10 minutes to help seal moisture into your skin.

Try spritzing your face with cool water for a quick pick-me-up. Use a humidifier in your home for a taste of the tropics, and take a refreshing walk in the rain. Moist air means moist skin, and that means healthy skin.

And don't forget what it does for your lips. Water keeps them moist, supple, and kissably soft.

Stops stones before they start. A wrenching pain stabs you in your lower back. You groan as you realize it's another kidney stone attack.

If you'd been drinking plenty of water, this probably wouldn't have happened. Water helps flush out the building blocks that form kidney stones before they can join forces to make you suffer.

You are more likely to get a kidney stone during the summer, probably because you tend to sweat more and may not drink enough water to make up for it. Some urologists say you should increase your water intake to at least 12 to 16 cups a day to combat summer's heat and humidity.

In a recent study, coffee, tea, beer, and wine lowered the risk of kidney stones, while apple juice and grapefruit juice increased the risk. Additional studies are needed to confirm these results.

If your problem is gallstones, make water your lifelong friend. Bile, a fluid secreted by the liver and stored in the gall-bladder, helps in digestion, especially of fats. When your bile has enough water, it can easily dissolve the cholesterol that forms gallstones. This keeps your gallbladder fit and happy.

Watches your weight. Guess what's at the center of any successful weight-loss program? That's right, good old H_2O. Remember, your body needs this nutrient more than any other, and it happens to be calorie free.

Drink a glass before eating. Water fills you up, making it easier to resist that mound of food on your plate. It helps you eat more slowly. When you take your time, you end up eating less.

Drink more whenever you're active. It helps you exercise longer and harder. Walk one more mile. Swim an extra lap. Pound out one more set of tennis. Your body will love you for it.

Rinses away germs. Water can do you just as much good from the outside as the inside. Remember how your mother always nagged you to wash your hands before eating ... or after blowing your nose ... or coughing ... or petting the dog? She knew a good washing gave the old "heave-ho" to germs and other nasty things living on your skin.

Soap and water is the number one way to stop germs from spreading. Fewer germs mean fewer illnesses. And that means a healthier, happier you.

YOUR ACTION PLAN

HOW MUCH IS ENOUGH?

Most people tend to drink water only when they are thirsty. Big mistake! The switch that runs the thirst center in your brain doesn't even wake up until you've already lost too much of your body fluids.

As you get older, your thirst switch becomes even more forgetful. Since you don't feel thirsty, you don't drink as much as you should, and you become dehydrated.

Heavy sweating, vomiting, or diarrhea can lead to dehydration if you don't replace the fluids you lose. These conditions are especially dangerous because they flush away your body's much-needed supply of salt. About half the elderly who suffer from this serious problem will die without treatment.

Dehydration can lead to serious problems like heatstroke (overheating) or hypothermia (loss of body heat).

Symptoms of dehydration include:

- ❦ severe thirst
- ❦ dry lips and tongue
- ❦ rapid heart rate and breathing
- ❦ dizziness
- ❦ confusion
- ❦ dry, taut skin
- ❦ dark-colored urine

Tiredness, headaches, cramps, and pale skin can mean you're critically low on salt.

If you notice any of these symptoms, see your doctor immediately. Fluids and salt must be replaced quickly, and you may require hospital care.

The easiest way to prevent dehydration is to give your body lots of water every day. Just by eating, you get some water into your system, but food provides only two to four cups of water each day. Some experts say you should drink another six to eight glasses (about two quarts) to make up for what you lose. Others recommend as much as 12 to 16 cups every day. If your urine is clear or pale yellow, you know you're getting enough.

Want an easy way to keep track of how much you drink? Try keeping six inexpensive 8-ounce cups in your cupboard. Throughout the day, use each one only once, then put it in your sink or dishwasher. By the end of the day, you'll know how much you've had to drink, and you can finish any that are left.

Of course, the amount your body needs won't always stay the same. It depends on what kind of foods you eat, how hot or cold the temperature is, or whether you're out playing a hearty game of tennis or just relaxing in front of your television.

Your body definitely needs more fluids when you exercise or have a busy day, even if you're not thirsty. Water is best because it gets to your tissues more quickly than other beverages that must be digested.

Exercise actually blunts your thirst mechanism, so by the time you feel like you need a drink, you're already in trouble. Keep a water bottle handy and keep sipping whether you feel like it or not. Water also cools your body down from the inside out.

THE WISE WATER CONSUMER

A 115-year-old man living on an island off Japan was asked how a person his age could be so healthy.

"Simple," the old man replied. "I've drunk water all my life – gallons and gallons of it."

He ended up living to the ripe old age of 120 years, 237 days.

For Shigechiyo Izumi and others on his island, water was the secret to long life. But it was a special kind of water filtered through ancient coral reefs. It gave him extra minerals and other elements that helped keep the spring in his step and a youthful song in his heart.

Today, many people hope to find that same fountain of youth in bottled water. We see exotic labels like "Artesian" or "natural spring water" and think it must be better than plain old tap water. In fact, we drink twice as much bottled water as we did five years ago.

But is it really better?

Judge for yourself. At any given moment, more than 70,000 contaminants are swirling their way through your water supply. Many can make you sick.

Lead is a particularly dangerous problem. As water travels through old pipes in your home, it can pick up lead. If you're older, you need to worry about aluminum in your drinking water. It may increase your risk of Alzheimer's disease.

One sure way you can avoid these bad guys is to use a water-treatment system in your home. There are hundreds to choose from, and they all claim to remove bacteria, chemicals, minerals, and unpleasant odors and tastes. You may already have one of the simpler models. A pour-through pitcher with a carbon filter is a cheap and easy way to take care of minor water problems.

How do you know if you need a bigger and better filtering system? First, you should find out exactly what's in your water. Remember the saying: "If it ain't broke, don't fix it." You don't need a water-treatment system unless you have a problem, so have your water tested before you rush out and plunk down your hard-earned money.

The Environmental Protection Agency's Safe Drinking Water Hotline (800-426-4791) is a good place to start. The EPA can supply you with the name of a lab in your area that will test your water for lead and other contaminants. If you decide you need a filtering system, the lab can help you determine what type you need.

Your friendly neighborhood plumber also can give you some good advice. He can even help install your water-treatment system. Just be sure that any equipment you buy has a seal from NSF International or the Water Quality Association "Gold Seal." That means the equipment has been tested and meets industry standards.

WATER CAUTIONS

Many of you swear by it. No expensive contraptions. Door-to-door delivery. Goes wherever you do. In fact, one out of every 15 families drinks bottled water because they like the taste and believe it's safer than their local water supply.

Unfortunately, some bottled water may not be any purer than your own tap water.

Remember the Perrier scare several years ago? This popular brand was recalled because it contained too much benzene, a chemical used in making many dyes and drugs. Other brands have been recalled because they smelled bad or contained unhealthy levels of organic compounds.

Let's face it, all water comes from the same place — above or below ground — so it all will be contaminated in some way. How it's filtered and purified is what makes the difference. You may be surprised to learn that a quarter of the bottled water sold is actually tap water that's been re-filtered to make it taste better.

One reason bottled water tastes better is that most bottling companies disinfect their water with ozone, which leaves no aftertaste or smell. Many local water systems use chlorine to help purify the water.

BOTTLED WATER DEFINED

Confused about the labels on bottled water? You're not alone. The Food and Drug Administration provides the following definitions to help you figure out what you're buying:

❦ **bulk drinking water** — tap or spring water that's filtered and purified with ozone. Minerals are removed and may or may not be re-added. The label must state if the bottle contains municipal tap water.

❦ **mineral water** — water obtained from protected underground sources. It's usually "sparkling," meaning it contains natural carbon dioxide that makes it bubble. The bottle must list a "high" or "low" mineral content. You'll also see a nutrition label if it's high in calcium, iron, or sodium.

❦ **spring water** — underground water that flows naturally to the earth's surface or is pumped from the source. "Natural spring water" means it has not been processed in any way.

❦ **artesian water** — well water that comes from an underground rock formation. It surfaces naturally through a man-made hole.

❦ **distilled water** — produced by vaporizing water, then condensing it in a way that takes out all dissolved minerals.

❦ **purified water** — treated by certain chemical or physical processes to remove dissolved solids, including minerals. It must meet U.S. Pharmacopeia standards because it's often used in laboratories and for medical purposes.

❦ **seltzer, soda, or tonic water** — filtered and artificially carbonated tap water that usually has added sodium or sweeteners. These are considered soft drinks and are not regulated.

The U.S. Environmental Protection Agency keeps a close watch over your tap water to make sure it doesn't contain too much of anything that can harm your health.

Since 1975, the Food and Drug Administration (FDA) has been responsible for making sure bottled water is just as safe as tap water. In 2003, the FDA set new limits for as many as 50 chemicals and other contaminants in bottled water.

The FDA also defined each type of bottled water so labels would be consistent from one state to another. Now when you see "spring water" on two different labels, you can be sure they mean the same thing.

TIPS FOR WATER SAFETY

If you drink bottled water, follow these steps to make sure it's as pure and safe as possible:

❦ Choose products from companies that belong to the International Bottled Water Association (IBWA). The IBWA supports the FDA's bottled water standards.

❦ Call the bottler (most have 800 numbers) and get a list of the contaminants it tests for. Ask about chlorine and fluoride. Most companies don't use chlorine to disinfect the water because it can combine with other materials to form cancer-causing agents.

❦ Check the source. You don't want water that comes from highly industrialized areas.

❦ Buy your water in glass containers. Plastic packaging may contaminate the water — no one is sure.

❦ Disinfect your water cooler about once a month. Run a half gallon of white vinegar through it, then rinse with four or five gallons of tap water.

❦ Just for fun, join the Water of the Month Club and sample exotic waters from around the world. For example, try super-oxygenated Angel Fire Water or Fiji Natural Artesian Water. Find them on the Internet at

<http://bottledwaterstore.com>.

If you prefer using tap water:

🐞 Run the faucets for a minute or two first thing in the morning to flush out bacteria, chemicals, and other impurities.

🐞 When you're cooking, use cold water instead of hot. Hot water from the faucet may contain more lead.

🐞 Try not to boil drinking water longer than five minutes. Because some water evaporates, you end up with a higher concentration of contaminants, including lead.

In 1910, when the Pulitzer-prize-winning Russian scientist Elie Metchnikoff claimed yogurt was the elixir of long life, he started a worldwide surge for curds and whey. Metchnikoff based his claims on his studies of the lengthy life spans of Bulgarians who traditionally ate large quantities of cultured milk. As ardent believers in Metchnikoff's work, the Spanish businessman Isaac Carasso and son Daniel began manufacturing and distributing yogurt under the name Dannoh. As a testimony to yogurt's continued popularity, their company and many other yogurt producers thrive around the world today.

YOGURT

Yogurt has been prized since it was discovered more than 4,000 years ago. In ancient Persia, today known as Iran, a woman's dowry was determined by how much yogurt her prospective husband could buy. In ancient Assyria, the word for yogurt was lebeny, which also meant life.

It certainly meant life to Genghis Khan's troops as the wandering general used it to sustain them during their marches through Mongolia and Persia. And Mahatma Gandhi dedicated an entire chapter of his book *Diet Reform* to the benefits of yogurt.

Although yogurt has been around for centuries, it gained a foothold in the American diet about 25 years ago. Since then, our love for the creamy concoction has steadily increased. A survey by the U.S. Department of Agriculture found we ate an average of 4.1 pounds of yogurt per person in 1990, four times as much as in 1970. Europeans eat even more yogurt, as much as 17 pounds per person each year, according to the National Yogurt Association. Today, people from all over the world enjoy yogurt's light, creamy taste. It is truly one product that causes no culture clash.

Yogurt's health claims are based mainly on the bacteria added during production. These bacteria, *Lactobacillus bulgaricus* and *Streptococcus thermophilus,* change ordinary milk into a creamy gel which contains solids, called curds, and liquid, or whey. They're responsible for yogurt's reputation as a cure for everything from yeast infections to cancer.

Researchers agree yogurt is a good source of calcium, protein, riboflavin, vitamin A, thiamin, niacin, vitamin C, folic acid, and even a trace of iron. But beyond providing a wide range of nutrients in a fairly low-fat, low-calorie package, yogurt's health claims have not been proven. In fact, later studies even disproved Metchnikoff's research about yogurt's ability to prolong your life.

Still, yogurt studies continue, mainly because it seems to have the potential to treat several common health conditions. One study even suggests that Metchnikoff's theory may not have been so off base after all. It speculates that scientists may one day be able to prove his claim that yogurt helps you live a longer life.

Although only a few of yogurt's health benefits are set in stone, here's what researchers have uncovered so far.

8 WAYS YOGURT FIGHTS AGING

Gives you plenty of calcium without cramps, bloating, or diarrhea. To date, this is yogurt's most credible claim to fame. Although most people know that calcium is crucial for maintaining strong bones and healthy teeth, many people still avoid milk, one of the best sources of calcium, because it gives them tummy troubles. Unfortunately, in most cases, cutting out milk means slashing your stores of calcium, one of your body's most basic needs. In fact, an ample supply of calcium is essential for living a long life.

Getting plenty of calcium can help you avoid common problems of old age, such as high blood pressure, breast cancer, colon cancer, and senility. If milk makes you miserable with cramps, bloating, or diarrhea, yogurt may come in handy. It's a real stomach-saving alternative for the 40 million Americans and others around the world who are lactose intolerant.

An eight-ounce serving of yogurt contains as much calcium as a cup of milk. Plus, your body uses the nutrients from yogurt faster since yogurt is basically predigested milk. In fact, you can digest more than 90 percent of the yogurt you eat within an hour, compared to only 30 percent of milk.

The two bacteria that turn milk into yogurt are the same bacteria that help your body break down lactose into glucose and galactose. If you're sensitive to milk, lactose is the sugar you have trouble handling. Almost everyone can digest glucose and galactose without a problem. To people with lactose intolerance, yogurt can be a real blessing.

Packs a powerful protein punch. Protein is essential for keeping your immune system in tip-top shape. It's also vital for maintaining and repairing body tissues. Although milk and yogurt are equally good sources of protein, and both provide the same amount per cup, yogurt's protein is just a tiny bit better because your body digests it more efficiently. In addition, manufacturers sometimes fortify their yogurts with non-fat dry milk solids, which raise yogurt's protein count and make it an even better source of calcium and other vitamins and minerals.

Could crush cancer. Several European studies claim that people who eat large amounts of yogurt or other fermented milk products have a lower risk of developing breast cancer. Researchers theorize that *Lactobacillus acidophilus* in the intestine prevents certain bacteria from turning food, or the bile which helps you digest fat, into cancer-causing substances.

In addition, a few studies conducted on rats in the early 1980s found that yogurt decreased colon cancer tumors in these animals.

Recently, a study conducted at Tufts University in Boston led researchers to suggest that yogurt may protect against colon cancer in people, too. The investigators studied a group of men and women over age 60 who had a stomach acid deficiency called atrophic gastritis. This condition occurs in one out of every two people over age 50.

Your body needs stomach acid because it destroys enzymes in the stomach and intestines that help colon cancer develop. In this study, the participants who ate yogurt had much less enzyme activity, which the researchers speculate could mean a lower risk of colon cancer.

Cholesterol-soaking sponge. Linking yogurt and cholesterol causes more controversy than consensus, but early research shows some strains of the *Lactobacillus* bacteria may indeed lower cholesterol. Researchers at Oklahoma State University have found that certain strains work like sponges and actually soak up cholesterol in the intestines before it can be absorbed by the body. Since this research in still in the early stages, however, you won't find any of these cholesterol clobbering yogurts at your local grocery.

Other scientists have explored whether yogurt can reduce blood cholesterol levels. Studies of Masai warriors in East Africa found that when the Africans ate large quantities of yogurt, they lowered their cholesterol levels even though they gained weight. The American Heart Association doesn't agree with these results, however. It says the key to lowering your cholesterol levels is to reduce the amount of saturated fat in your diet.

Boosts immune system. Studies at the University of California suggest that eating yogurt with live active cultures can give your immune system a boost. People in the study who ate two cups of yogurt containing live active cultures every day for several months produced more gamma interferon than people who ate yogurt without live bacteria. Researchers suspect that yogurt revs up your immune system by increasing your body's production of gamma interferon, a protein that helps your body's white blood cells fight disease.

Won't yield to yeast infections. After menopause, the lining of your vagina becomes dry and thin, increasing your risk of yeast infections. Yogurt may be the key to helping your body stop these annoying infections.

A small study of 13 women conducted at the Long Island Jewish Medical Center supported this theory. Every day for six months, the women ate a cup of yogurt containing a bacteria called *Lactobacillus acidophilus*. For the next six months, they ate no yogurt at all. Researchers found the women suffered only a third as many yeast infections during the time they ate yogurt as when they didn't.

A more recent study conducted at Central Emek Hospital in Israel found that eating just a little more than half a cup of yogurt cultured with *Lactobacillus acidophilus* significantly lowered the number of vaginal infections caused by various bacteria.

Interestingly, this study also found that both pasteurized and nonpasteurized yogurts containing the *Lactobacillus acidophilus* bacteria worked almost equally well at treating yeast infections. This may mean that something besides the bacteria in yogurt fights off yeast infections. Whatever conclusion researchers come to, it's still good news for women plagued by this uncomfortable condition.

Yogurt may help in other ways as well. Some researchers have focused on using yogurt in the vagina to treat bacterial infections. A study conducted in Japan on 11 women, ages 20 to 60, found that an intravaginal application of commercial yogurt containing the *Lactobacillus* bacteria totally relieved the infection in six of the women and partially relieved the infection in three others.

Immobilizes other infections, too. Yogurt works like a natural antibiotic against some bacteria, such as *salmonella typhimurium*. Researchers in the Netherlands found that rats who were given yogurt resisted salmonella infections better than rats fed plain milk or acidified milk. Laboratory tests also show that yogurt can kill 11 strains of *Campylobacter jejuni,* a bacteria that causes intestinal problems, in 25 minutes or less.

Defeats diarrhea. Certain antibiotics cause diarrhea because they kill off your intestines' good bacteria along with the bad. Some researchers say yogurt can help stop the diarrhea caused by taking antibiotics.

Mona Sutnick, a registered dietitian and spokeswomen for the American Dietetic Association, says she thinks the jury is still out on this question. However, she's seen enough research to suggest it may be possible. She suggests trying yogurt if you're suffering from antibiotic-induced diarrhea because it may help, and it certainly won't hurt.

If you're traveling and worried about getting diarrhea from some unfamiliar bacteria, you can safely savor at least one food. That's right — yogurt. According to nutrition scientist Dennis Savaiano, yogurt is unlikely to contain disease-causing bacteria even if it's been left out in the open air. Savaiano and his colleagues at the University of Minnesota came to this conclusion after they added strains of *E. coli,* the most common cause of traveler's diarrhea, to unpasteurized yogurt. Within nine hours, the yogurt had killed all the *E. coli.*

YOUR ACTION PLAN

HOW MUCH IS ENOUGH?

Yogurt has no recommended dietary allowance, so it all depends on the health benefits you're looking for. If you just want to prevent yeast infections or protect your intestines from antibiotic-induced diarrhea, one cup a day is plenty. To boost your immune system, you probably need two cups a day. Researchers found that amount helps rev up your body's defenses. But if yogurt is your main source of calcium, try and enjoy two to three cups a day. That way, you'll get all the health benefits your body needs.

DO YOU NEED SUPPLEMENTS?

If you simply can't stand yogurt, but would like to take advantage of its benefits, you can always turn to supplements. To get the most from yogurt supplements, take them near the end of the meal when your stomach is less acidic. If you can tolerate milk, drink one or two glasses each day. This will provide the good bacteria in yogurt with lactose, one of their favorite foods.

If you opt for supplements, just be aware that not all supplements supply what they say they do. Some helpful guidelines:

❦ Look for powdered supplements packaged in dark brown glass bottles.

❧ Choose supplements that need to be refrigerated. Capsules and tablets stored at room temperature will keep their strength for about six months, even less if they're exposed to moisture.

THE WISE YOGURT CONSUMER

Not all yogurts are created equal. Yogurt may contain high levels of fat or be fat free. It may be swimming with live bacteria or have none at all. It may be plain or sweetened with natural or artificial flavors.

In any case, the Federal Drug Administration (FDA) requires all these facts to appear on the label. And all yogurt products must meet certain FDA requirements before they can be labeled with standardized terms. For example, all yogurt must be cultured with *L. bulgaricus* and *S. thermophilus* bacteria. Certain other cultures, such as *acidophilus*, also may be included.

All yogurt offers calcium and protein health benefits, whether it is pasteurized or nonpasteurized, fat or nonfat. If you hope to reap some other benefits, such as warding off yeast

---

FEASTING ON FROZEN YOGURT

Frozen yogurts contain the same two bacteria as regular yogurt. However, you'll likely find frozen yogurts much sweeter than the regular kind. Today's frozen yogurts taste more like desserts, because they're not fermented as long as non-frozen yogurt. This makes them less acidic and gives them a sweeter taste.

Frozen yogurts also may not have the same amount of living bacteria as their non-frozen counterparts. Some manufacturers make frozen yogurt by fermenting milk the traditional way, then freezing the mixture. Others make a kind of ice-milk mixture and add the bacteria later. As a result, the number of live culture organisms in frozen yogurt varies greatly between brands. If you want to be sure your frozen yogurt contains live and active cultures, look for the National Yogurt Association's "Live and Active Cultures" seal on the carton.

---

infections or protecting yourself against diarrhea, look for the words "active cultures," "live active cultures," or "contains viable cultures" on the yogurt label.

Don't buy heat-treated yogurt. This treatment makes the yogurt last longer but also kills the bacteria. Be sure to buy only refrigerated yogurt, and keep it cold. Cultures stored at room temperature die sooner, and the more live cultures in the yogurt, the better it is for you.

Don't be confused by labels that say "made with active cultures" or "made with viable cultures." All yogurts are made this way. Only the brands that are not heat treated keep their live active cultures.

Certain brands of yogurt will say "contains *acidophilus.*" Don't let yogurt with acidophilus linger too long in your refrigerator. If you do, the bacteria may die or be squeezed out by the *bulgaricus* bacteria before the yogurt expires.

Yogurt lasts about two weeks in the refrigerator. Mold and gas bubbles are signs of spoilage. But don't be concerned about the greenish or clear liquid floating on top. It's just the whey, a harmless liquid. Simply mix it in with the yogurt before enjoying your first creamy bite.

YOGURT CAUTIONS

If you're watching your waistline, be sure to check yogurt labels for fat and sugar content. Eight ounces of yogurt provides between 110 and 300 calories, depending on the milk-fat content and flavorings.

Fatwise, yogurt is available in three different forms:

❦ Regular. This yogurt is made from whole milk and contains at least 3.25 percent milk fat.

❦ Low-fat. It's made from low-fat or part-skim milk and has between 2 and .5 percent milk fat.

❦ Nonfat. This yogurt is made from skim milk and contains less than .5 percent milk fat.

If you're trying to skimp on sugar, remember that fruit-flavored yogurts tend to have more sugar than other types.

Flavors that usually contain less sugar include coffee, lemon, and vanilla.

One quick and easy way to limit calories and fat is to buy plain, unsweetened nonfat yogurt and add your own fresh or unsweetened canned or frozen fruit. Let your imagination lead you to your own culinary creation. If you can let your concoction stand for several hours or sit overnight, the flavors will blend better.

EASY WAYS TO ADD YOGURT TO YOUR LIFE SO YOGURT CAN ADD LIFE TO YOUR YEARS

❦ Substitute yogurt for milk, sweet cream, or sour cream to thicken meat gravy or vegetable soup. If possible, add yogurt to food after it has been cooked since heat causes yogurt to separate. Or mix one tablespoon of cornstarch with one tablespoon of yogurt, then stir it into the remaining yogurt. Warm this yogurt mixture over medium heat before adding it to the food. Another method is to mix a few teaspoons of cooked food into the yogurt before adding it to the rest of the food. Just remember that heating yogurt will kill the active cultures.

❦ Use low-fat or nonfat yogurt as a substitute in recipes calling for mayonnaise, sour cream, cream cheese, or buttermilk. Make sure you fold in the yogurt and any ingredients you add later. Beating or stirring yogurt makes it mushy.

❦ Brighten broccoli, brussels sprouts, and asparagus with a topping of plain low-fat yogurt and fresh minced dill. Sprinkle on some slivers of unsalted almonds if desired.

❦ Make a pretty and tasty baked-potato topper by adding dill, curry powder, garlic, onion, or parsley to plain nonfat yogurt. This also makes a good veggie dip.

❦ Whip up a flavorful, fat-free topping for a pound cake or other dessert by folding two tablespoons of unsweetened frozen juice concentrate into eight ounces of nonfat yogurt. Sprinkle with cinnamon if desired.

It's hard to believe, but more than 90 percent of healthy elderly people don't get the minimum daily requirement of zinc. Even if you feel healthy, increasing your zinc intake could improve your sense of sight, smell, and taste; boost your immune system; and help you heal faster after accidents or surgery. It's even been shown to help the common cold. Just a little zinc can help you live a longer, zestier life.

ZINC

You may not even be aware of a quiet gland that stands guard in your body, protecting you from disease. Your thymus gland, which is part of your immune system, may not attract much attention, but it performs a valuable role in keeping you healthy and disease free.

Located in your upper chest, your thymus consists of fat, epithelium (membranes), and lymphocytes (white blood cells). The thymus' job is to turn these lymphocytes into special kinds of cells, called T cells, which help your immune system fight off disease.

Helper T cells identify harmful substances in your body, like bacteria and viruses. They then alert the killer T cells, which latch onto and destroy any cells these substances have invaded. Without T-cell protection, you would soon fall prey to every infectious disease you encountered. Aren't you lucky your thymus sends out these good guys to help guard your health?

Your thymus gland grows until late puberty, then begins to shrink, and fat cells slowly replace all your wonderful protective lymphocytes. It also can shrivel up within hours if you become seriously ill. What if you could preserve the immunity boosting power of a younger, bigger, stronger thymus? You'd probably stay healthier and live longer because you'd be better able to fight off infections and disease.

Evidence for the anti-aging powers of a strong thymus comes from Dr. Gregory Fahy, a leading researcher on aging. According to Dr. Fahy, transplanting the thymus of a young animal into an old animal actually reverses age-related changes. If a younger thymus can make an old rat young again, could it do the same for you? Unfortunately, you can't go out and replace your thymus every 10 years. But you can keep this incredible gland working at peak production to help you stay young.

What's the secret? A little-noticed mineral called zinc. This critical mineral helps restore your thymus, enabling it to produce those incredible T-cell warriors. Studies show that people with low zinc levels have fewer T cells, and tend to be more susceptible to infectious disease. When they raise their zinc levels, T-cell levels shoot up as well.

8 WAYS ZINC FIGHTS AGING

Restores your senses. Have you ever told someone they've lost their senses? You probably didn't mean it literally, but this actually could happen. As people get older, they often experience a loss of certain senses, such as taste and smell. Good nutrition is essential to staying young, but if something doesn't smell good or taste good, you may not want to eat it. This can lead to poor eating habits at a time when proper nutrition is especially important. Some people even develop anorexia, a severe eating disorder.

Zinc helps put the zip back into your sense of smell and the zing back in your taste buds. Many elderly people who begin zinc supplementation are amazed at the return of these senses, because the losses occurred so gradually they didn't realize they had a problem.

Speedy healing. No matter how lucky you are, you'll probably get injured or have surgery sometime in your life. The less time you spend healing, the more time you will have to enjoy life. How can you decrease the time you spend recuperating? Studies show that zinc increases the rate of healing when given to people before and after surgery. People who are zinc deficient heal more slowly than others, so make sure you get enough zinc in your diet to enjoy a speedy recovery.

Controls complications of diabetes. Diabetes can cause lots of complications, and the loss of your sight may be the one you fear most. However, zinc just may come to the rescue and save your precious vision.

Studies show that diabetics with retina damage have even lower levels of zinc than usual. Researchers believe zinc protects your eye from free radicals, and when you don't have enough, it leaves you open to free-radical attack and possible eye disease. One small study found that a daily 30-mg supplement of zinc raised diabetics' zinc levels while lowering their free radical levels.

Studies also show that if you lack zinc you may not be able to keep your blood sugar level normal after eating. This is partly due to lower concentrations of insulin in your blood. A survey found that only 6 percent of diabetics were getting their Recommended Dietary Allowance (RDA) of zinc, so supplementing might be good insurance against diabetes.

Aids vision. Zinc also may help protect vision in people who don't have diabetes. Your eye contains more zinc than any other part of your body. In macular degeneration, an age-related disease of the eye, injury caused by light may set off free radical damage that can slowly rob you of your sight. Zinc supplementation may protect against this damage or even reverse damage that has already occurred.

Zinc plays a role in keeping your night vision sharp, possibly because it helps activate vitamin A in your eye. Vitamin A is well known for its eye-protecting abilities, but zinc may be its silent, helpful partner.

Curtails cold symptoms. The common cold may not make you older, but it sure can make you feel older. It is probably the most frequently occurring illness in the world, and scientists have been searching for centuries to find a cure. Zinc may not be the miracle cure for the common cold, but it may provide quicker relief from the symptoms. One study found that people who used zinc lozenges spent half as many days with coughing, nasal drainage, and sore throat as those who didn't. The lozenges also reduced the number of days they experienced headache, hoarseness, and nasal congestion.

However, the zinc also produced some side effects, such as nausea and an unpleasant taste, so the lozenges may not work for everyone. The flavorings in some lozenges also may interfere with the zinc so it can't work. Look for a form of zinc called zinc gluconate-glycine, which is easily released when you suck on the lozenges.

Axes anemia. Do you feel older than you are because you're tired all the time? Anemia is a condition in which your blood loses some of its ability to carry oxygen. The result is fatigue, dizziness, and breathing difficulty. You may even experience heart palpitations because your heart isn't getting enough oxygen. Iron deficient anemia is the most common form of anemia, but surprisingly, you may need to treat it with zinc in addition to iron supplements. Studies show that zinc helps return your blood to its proper oxygen pumping potential.

Sizzling sexual function. Have you ever heard that oysters are an aphrodisiac? They actually may boost a man's sex drive because of their rich supply of zinc. Since zinc is necessary for production of testosterone, sperm, and semen, it could help put some zip back into your sex life.

Fights cancer. Low zinc levels are common in people with many different types of cancer. This is probably because the T cells that zinc helps stimulate are some of your body's leading weapons in the battle against cancer. Zinc levels may quickly become exhausted while trying to help produce enough T cells to fight this serious disease.

Although zinc has not been proven to help treat or prevent cancer, it is being used as an additional treatment in precancerous conditions of the esophagus. One study found that people with a certain type of lung cancer lived longer if they had high levels of zinc.

YOUR ACTION PLAN

HOW MUCH IS ENOUGH?

The current RDA for zinc is 11 mg for men, 8 mg for women, 11 mg for pregnant women, and 12 mg for lactating women. However, some experts recommend taking from 30 to 50 mg a day, particularly if you have a condition like poor night vision, or a decreased sense of taste and smell.

HOW TO GET MORE ZINC NATURALLY

If you like to eat oysters, you should be getting plenty of zinc. A three and a half ounce serving of steamed oysters contains 182 mg of this important mineral — more than 15 times the RDA. However, if you don't eat oysters, you can still get plenty of natural zinc. Zinc is found in other seafood, and in red meat, poultry, legumes, and whole grains.

Fiber reduces the amount of zinc your body can absorb, so you don't use the zinc in grains, legumes, and other plant sources as well as the zinc from animal sources like beef. In fact, if you like to dig into a juicy steak every once in a while, you're doing your body some good. Beef is the most important source of zinc in the U.S. food supply.

DO YOU NEED SUPPLEMENTS?

Zinc supplements probably aren't necessary for most people. It's not difficult to get enough zinc from the food you eat. However, if you're one of the estimated 90 percent of healthy elderly people who don't get enough zinc, supplements may be the answer. Before deciding to supplement with zinc, consider how much you are getting in your diet. If you think you take in 20 mg a day, don't go overboard with a 50-mg supplement. You can get too much zinc. Always tell your doctor about any supplements you are taking.

THE WISE ZINC CONSUMER

You can buy zinc supplements alone or as part of a multi-vitamin or multi-mineral supplement. It is probably cheapest to buy a combination tablet if you plan to use other supplements, rather than buying each one separately.

Zinc supplements combine elemental zinc with other substances. Zinc picolinate or zinc orotate may be the most easily absorbed, but they are also more expensive. Zinc sulfate is cheaper but may cause stomach problems. Zinc gluconate, also called chelated zinc, may be the best choice. When choosing a zinc supplement, check the amount of elemental zinc listed on the label, since that's what your body uses. An 80-mg supplement of zinc gluconate may contain only 10 mg of elemental zinc.

ZINC CAUTIONS

As beneficial as zinc is, too much zinc can irritate your stomach and cause vomiting. However, this toxic reaction usually only occurs with extremely high doses (2,000 mg or more).

Even at lower doses, zinc may give you problems. It may lower your ability to absorb copper and raise your "bad" cholesterol levels. Because of this, some experts recommend no more than 9 mg of zinc a day. However, other experts say that most people get too much copper anyway. You will have to use your own judgment on how much you should take, but it probably isn't a good idea to exceed 50 mg a day. Of course, that means if you pig out on zinc-rich oysters, you will have to avoid zinc in any other foods for a while!

SUBSTANCES THAT CAN INTERFERE
WITH ZINC ABSORPTION

- ❦ Alcohol
- ❦ Coffee
- ❦ Diuretics
- ❦ Oral contraceptives
- ❦ Soy protein
- ❦ Tea
- ❦ Wheat and corn flour

SUPER HEALTH SECRETS

A tiny, common pill could defend your heart against the ravages of time. You may already have this potent and inexpensive heart protector right in your medicine cabinet. Aspirin has been shown to prevent heart attacks and speed healing following a heart attack.

ASPIRIN

Have you learned CPR so you can help a loved one or even a stranger who may suffer a heart attack? If so, you're a responsible and caring person, but you also need to know how aspirin can help save lives. Keeping aspirin in your purse or backpack could save someone's life, perhaps even your own.

You might think that aspirin in your first aid kit is just for headaches or fevers, but it may play a much more important role than that. A huge international study found that aspirin given to heart attack victims when admitted to the hospital decreased deaths significantly. It also reduced subsequent non-fatal heart attacks and strokes by almost half. The sooner the aspirin was given, the greater the chances of recovery.

6 WAYS ASPIRIN FIGHTS AGING

Heads off heart disease. The smoother your blood flows, the better for your heart. Aspirin helps prevent platelets in your blood from clumping together, forming clots. There is an overwhelming amount of evidence that daily aspirin helps prevent heart attack, and recent studies find that it reduces risk of death after a heart attack by even more than was previously thought, up to 70 percent. However, not all hospitals have taken notice of these exciting studies. About one-third of heart attack patients are still not given aspirin in the hospital. According to one estimate, this results in over 5,000 deaths a year that could be prevented by aspirin therapy.

Slashes stroke risk. Aspirin protects against *ischemic* stroke, which is caused by a blood clot forming in your blood vessels and traveling to your brain. But because aspirin causes the blood to be thinner, some doctors were concerned that it might increase the risk of *hemorrhagic* stroke, which is caused by vessels that rupture and bleed. However, since hemorrhagic stroke is very rare, the risk is overshadowed by the protective benefits of aspirin for the more common ischemic stroke. And one of the largest heart attack studies so far found no increase in the risk of hemorrhagic stroke associated with aspirin.

Clobbers cataracts. Regular use of aspirin may save your eyesight. Studies show that aspirin may help prevent cataracts by neutralizing proteins that can damage your eyes.

Cuts cancer risk. Aspirin slows your body's production of prostaglandins. Prostaglandins are hormone-like chemicals that increase blood clotting, set off menstrual cramps, trigger inflammation, and promote cell division, including cancer cells.

❦ **Colorectal cancer.** If you have a history of colorectal cancer in your family, taking aspirin for preventive purposes could save your life. Although the benefits are greatest with long-term aspirin use (10 years or more), if you are at risk, aspirin is easy and inexpensive protection against a terrible disease. One large study found that taking aspirin regularly for 20 years cut the risk of colon and rectal cancer almost in half.

❦ **Breast cancer.** The drug most commonly used to treat breast cancer, tamoxifen, causes an increase in the risk of uterine cancer. Perhaps aspirin is a safer alternative. However, studies conducted on aspirin's effect on breast cancer give confusing and conflicting results. Aspirin has shown a preventive effect in animal studies and in some human studies, but other human studies show no protective benefits. But because of aspirin's importance in preventing other cancers, scientists continue to conduct studies on its effect on breast cancer.

❦ **Esophageal cancer.** Regular use of aspirin has been shown to cut the risk of esophageal cancer by a whopping 90 percent.

❦ **Lung cancer.** Studies on mice indicate that aspirin may keep lung cancer cells from growing by cutting the production of prostaglandins, but more studies need to be done on humans.

Helps you avoid Alzheimer's. Several studies have found that aspirin may protect you from this mind-robbing disease. For example, one study found that among pairs of elderly twins, those taking anti-inflammatory drugs, like aspirin or ibuprofen, on a regular basis were 10 times less likely to develop Alzheimer's. Since Alzheimer's is very likely to run in families, that's pretty impressive. Researchers think that regular use of anti-inflammatories may delay the disease by reducing inflammation in the brain that could cause brain cell damage. Aspirin may also help because it keeps your blood flowing steadily to your brain.

Eases arthritis pain. The pain and aching of arthritis can slow you down and make you feel as old as Methuselah. Aspirin has been used to treat the symptoms of arthritis perhaps since Methuselah's days. It can help put a youthful and pain-free bounce back into your step.

YOUR ACTION PLAN

HOW MUCH IS ENOUGH?

Most studies on aspirin used a daily dosage of either 160 milligrams (mg) or 325 mg. A standard aspirin contains 325 mg.

HOW TO GET ASPIRIN'S BENEFITS NATURALLY

In the fifth century B.C., Hippocrates, the father of modern medicine, used willow bark to create a pain relieving medicine. The ingredient in willow bark that made it such a powerful pain reliever, salicylate, is the same active ingredient in modern aspirin. You can still buy willow bark extracts in health food stores, but salicylate is also found in many foods, beverages, and flavorings. The main sources include fruits, vegetables, teas, and spices. Peppermint and wintergreen flavored foods and candies may contain relatively high amounts of salicylates.

DO YOU NEED DAILY ASPIRIN?

The decision to take aspirin daily should be made with your doctor's assistance. However, you are more likely to need aspirin's benefits if:

❦ you have a history of heart attack or stroke.
❦ colorectal cancer runs in your family.
❦ you have a high cholesterol level.

THE WISE ASPIRIN CONSUMER

If aspirin causes you stomach discomfort, try enteric aspirin, which is coated with a substance that resists the acid in your stomach, but dissolves in your intestines, where the aspirin can then be absorbed. You can also reduce side effects by taking it with food or antacids.

Researchers are working on an aspirin skin patch that provides aspirin's benefits without the stomach upset.

Aspirin Cautions

❦ Aspirin can cause stomach problems.

❦ Don't take those aspirin that have been sitting in your medicine cabinet for years. Aspirin slowly reverts back to salicylic acid, which is even tougher on your tummy.

❦ You can overdose on aspirin. A single dose of 30 tablets can be life-threatening for an adult because it makes the blood too acidic.

❦ Because aspirin helps thin your blood, don't take it if you are already taking blood thinning medication.

The Chinese have believed in the healing power of shark cartilage for over a hundred years. Shark fin soup was, and still is, consumed not only for its taste but to cure a wide assortment of ailments. Perhaps the Chinese are onto something. Modern research indicates that shark cartilage may contain a key to curing cancer.

CARTILAGE

Despite the seemingly sudden interest in cartilage as a healing, life-prolonging agent, cartilage research has been going on longer than you may think. The step-by-step research process has already taken years, and it is far from over.

❦ Over 40 years ago, Dr. John F. Prudden theorized that cattle cartilage was a natural healing agent for wounds and maybe even for cancer. After decades of cartilage research, he was awarded the Linus Pauling Scientist of the Year Award in 1995 for his efforts.

Dr. Prudden began by placing cattle cartilage into the wounds of rats. He claimed that the wounds healed very quickly with little swelling. Since then, he's given cartilage to over 100 people with cancer, and he believes he's seen some miraculous recoveries.

❦ In the 1960s, Judah Folkman of Harvard Medical School theorized that the growth of a tumor could be prevented if the growth of new blood vessels that nourish the tumor could be stopped. Since cartilage usually contains no blood vessels, he experimented with it and found that calf cartilage did stop tumor growth.

❦ In 1990, Robert Langer, a doctor of science at the Massachusetts Institute of Technology, identified a specific protein in cattle cartilage that prevents the growth of the tiny blood vessels that provide nourishment to tumors. He called this substance CDI (cartilage-derived inhibitor). Langer is still trying to get at and make usable the substance that interferes with blood vessel growth in shark cartilage.

Although cattle cartilage was the first to be identified as a potential cancer fighter, most research has focused on shark cartilage. That's mainly because shark cartilage is so plentiful. The shark's skeleton is made up entirely of cartilage.

3 WAYS CARTILAGE FIGHTS AGING

Chomps cancer? It's almost impossible to give cancer to a shark, no matter what you expose it to. But it's highly unlikely that a shark's good health has anything to do with its cartilage. For starters, sharks have powerful immune systems. Unlike humans, they have certain infection-fighting molecules that constantly course through their bloodstreams.

If shark, or cattle, cartilage does fight cancer in humans, it probably works by interfering with blood vessel growth. For a cancerous tumor to grow, it needs new blood vessels to grow toward it. That's how the tumor gets nourishment. This process is called angiogenesis. Cartilage contains a protein that is supposedly anti-angiogenic, which means it inhibits the growth of blood vessels.

According to MIT's Dr. Langer, shark cartilage has 1,000 times more of this anti-angiogenic substance than cartilage from other animals. Since cancer tumors need blood vessels to bring them nourishment, a substance that stops blood vessel growth can, theoretically, stop tumor growth. Scientists have identified more than two dozen substances in cartilage that interfere with the growth of blood vessels.

Shark cartilage as a cancer cure may seem crazy, but penicillin once seemed like a flaky idea, too. Many people found it hard to believe that a substance found in mold could fight deadly infections and help prolong life.

On the other hand, shark cartilage may just be the current flash-in-the-pan medical "miracle" of the day. Only time will tell.

Takes the ache out of arthritis. The collagen found in cartilage may help with the symptoms of rheumatoid arthritis. In one small study, people with rheumatoid arthritis stopped taking their medicine and started taking collagen derived from chicken cartilage. Most people reported a decrease in the number of swollen and tender joints. In fact, almost a quarter of the study participants experienced a total remission of the disease.

Arthritis researchers have experimented with cattle cartilage, too. They've had good results in a number of clinical trials.

Speeds wound healing. Studies have found that cattle cartilage may help wounds heal faster.

YOUR ACTION PLAN

DO YOU NEED SUPPLEMENTS?

While some researchers think cartilage is a natural healer, most think taking a shark cartilage pill won't do you any good.

Arthritis sufferers who want to experiment with bovine tracheal cartilage tablets can find them at health food stores.

These tablets, derived from cows, may or may not help you, but they do seem to be safe and without side effects. Just be sure to tell your doctor that you are trying a new treatment.

If you have been diagnosed with cancer, please don't expect shark cartilage, or any other type of cartilage, to bring about a miracle cure. Harvard's Dr. Folkman, who has spent a lifetime studying cartilage, believes that the shark cartilage pills you can buy in a health food store won't fight cancer. In fact, he says he has "solid scientific evidence" that they can't work. Here's why:

❦ Shark cartilage does contain a substance that stops blood vessel growth and, therefore, could stop tumor growth, he says, but it also contains another substance that stimulates blood vessel growth.

❦ Stomach acid totally destroys the helpful substance that stops blood vessel growth. Fortunately, it also destroys the substance that stimulates blood vessel growth.

❦ Even if the helpful substance could survive the stomach acid, the protein molecules are too large to get into the bloodstream without being broken down first. That's not unusual. You can't drink insulin, either, because its molecules are too large to pass into your bloodstream.

❦ Finally, even if the cancer-fighting substance could make it into your bloodstream, you would have to eat pounds of shark cartilage to get any benefit. A shark cartilage pill contains such a tiny amount of the helpful protein that it has no effect.

What researchers like MIT's Dr. Langer are trying to do is to isolate the helpful protein in the cartilage. If they can get a handle on that substance, they may be able to use it to make a powerful cancer-fighting medicine.

In spite of all this negativity, at least one National Cancer Institute-sponsored clinical trial on shark cartilage as a cancer treatment is now underway. The brand of cartilage being tested is Benefin. The result of this trial may finally provide some answers about the possible benefits of cartilage.

CARTILAGE CAUTIONS

Remember, there is no solid proof that cartilage fights cancer. And because of the high level of calcium in shark cartilage, there is a danger of hypercalcemia — too much calcium in your bloodstream.

Since cartilage products are meant to stop the growth of new blood vessels, they should never be taken by pregnant women or women trying to become pregnant, people with heart disease, or people recovering from surgery.

Always consult with your doctor before taking any type of supplement.

If your heart is the motor that keeps your body running, Coenzyme Q10 is the spark plug that keeps your heart running. Studies show that this energy producer is essential to life, and it's particularly important to organs that require lots of energy, like your heart and brain.

COENZYME Q10

One of your body's most energetic watchdogs against aging is a compound called Coenzyme Q10. Coenzymes cooperate with enzymes to perform the chemical reactions needed to keep your body running. Coenzymes either contain vitamins, or vitamins themselves act as coenzymes. Some experts think that CoQ10 should be named vitamin Q because it is actually a fat-soluble vitamin or vitamin-like substance.

Coenzyme Q-10 is also known as ubiquinone, which comes from the word ubiquitous, meaning "to be everywhere." This is because CoQ10 is present in every cell of your body. It works in each of those cells to produce energy. Without energy, those cells would soon die, and you would age more rapidly.

Coenzyme Q10 is produced naturally in your body, but in order for it to work its magic, it requires lots of cooperation.

Your body makes CoQ10 in a complicated 17-step process involving several other substances, especially B vitamins like riboflavin and folic acid. If your body doesn't have enough of these other substances, it won't produce enough CoQ10 either.

CoQ10 provides plenty of antioxidant protection. It may be an especially important antioxidant, since it is present in every cell of your body. It may also help regenerate another antioxidant, vitamin E, allowing it to function as an antioxidant over and over.

3 WAYS COENZYME Q10 FIGHTS AGING

Halts heart disease. Your heart is one of the driving forces of your body. As it ages, you age. Numerous studies have found that CoQ10 improves heart function, even restoring normal function to hearts that have already been damaged by disease.

The most exciting studies on CoQ10 have involved its effect on people with congestive heart failure. Heart failure does not mean that your heart stops, as it does in cardiac arrest. It just means that your heart cannot pump enough blood to supply all the parts of your body it should. In other words, it is not doing its job properly. Your body tries to compensate for your heart's job deficiency by retaining salt and water, forcing your blood volume to increase. However, this can result in a buildup of dangerous fluid in your lungs, which can cause pneumonia, or swelling in your legs. About half the people diagnosed with heart failure die within four years, and if the disease is advanced when diagnosed, about half die within one year.

The cells of your heart contain high levels of CoQ10, probably because those cells require so much energy. People with congestive heart failure, however, have CoQ10 levels lower than normal. In fact, the lower the CoQ10 levels, the more severe the heart disease, or vice versa. Several studies have found that supplements of CoQ10 improved heart function, allowed the heart to pump more blood, and decreased heart disease symptoms like breathlessness, fatigue, and chest pain. In some cases, the size and function of the heart returned to normal on CoQ10 alone.

Enhances exercise. Do you want to remain young and vigorous? Walk an extra block. Run an extra mile. Play another set of tennis. Regular exercise makes you feel better, look better, and live longer, but it also increases free radicals in your body. That's right. Exercise helps to create free radicals because it makes you take in more oxygen. Does this mean you're trapped in a no-win situation? Not according to the latest research. Studies have found that CoQ10 can help repair exercise-induced cell damage.

Clobbers cancer? The effect of CoQ10 on cancer has been examined in a few experimental studies. One study found that people with cancer may survive longer on CoQ10 therapy. Another study shows that CoQ10 might protect your cells from cancer-causing free radical damage.

YOUR ACTION PLAN

HOW MUCH IS ENOUGH?

Most studies used doses from 30 to 200 milligrams (mg) per day. One of the leading researchers of CoQ10 recommends therapeutic doses of 120 to 160 mg a day for people with heart disease and doses of just 10 to 30 mg a day for healthy people who want to increase their energy levels.

HOW TO GET MORE COENZYME Q10 NATURALLY

Your body can manufacture its own CoQ10 provided you take in enough B vitamins and vitamin C. Good food sources of CoQ10 include beef, mackerel, bran, sesame, beans, sardines, spinach, soy, and peanuts.

DO YOU NEED SUPPLEMENTS?

❦ If you have heart disease, you may benefit from CoQ10 supplements. Ask your doctor.

❦ If you are taking a cholesterol-lowering drug, you may need supplements because many of these drugs inhibit your body's production of CoQ10.

THE WISE COENZYME Q10 CONSUMER

Coenzyme Q10 is available at health food stores. Because it is fat-soluble, you should either buy an oil-based gel cap or take it with food that contains fat. As with most supplements, it is better to take it with meals.

COENZYME Q10 CAUTIONS

Very few side effects have been reported with CoQ10, even in high doses. However, if you are taking Coumadin, a blood-thinning drug, CoQ10 could make it ineffective and increase your risk of blood clots.

The search for a magical anti-aging potion may have ended with the discovery of DHEA ... at least that's what some people think. Others think of it as a modern day "snake oil" that claims to cure everything with no real evidence that it works. Some experts think it may significantly lengthen your lifespan. One of the first studies on DHEA claimed that men who increased their DHEA levels reduced their risks of death from any cause by 36 percent and their risks of death from heart disease by 48 percent.

DHEA

DHEA (dehydroepiandrosterone) is a hormone that acts like a chemical chameleon in your body, changing according to your needs. It is sometimes called the "mother hormone" because your body converts it into whatever hormone it needs most at the moment, like testosterone, estrogen, or adrenaline.

DHEA also shows its versatile nature by producing different results under different circumstances. For example, men who take it seem to lose weight while increasing muscle, but women don't, at least not in the studies so far.

Levels of DHEA peak around age 20 and then decline steadily throughout the rest of your life. In fact, DHEA levels are known to be one of the most reliable measures of aging. Many scientists think that older people may be able to bring back their youthful vitality by increasing the amount of DHEA in their bodies.

7 WAYS DHEA FIGHTS AGING

Softens the blow of "male menopause." At a certain age, a woman's reproductive system shuts down, sending her hormones into a tailspin. Although men don't experience a crash in hormone levels like menopausal women, their hormone levels do decline with age. They also lose muscle mass and bone mass. Their testicles shrink, their sperm production slows, and most men begin to experience at least occasional impotence. Many experts call this period "andropause" or "viropause." Some doctors prescribe testosterone replacement therapy for men experiencing viropause, but testosterone is expensive and requires a prescription. DHEA may provide an alternative to drug therapy.

Although both men and women produce DHEA, like testosterone, it is considered mostly a male hormone. Because DHEA helps your body produce hormones, particularly testosterone, it can have similar, although milder, effects. It supposedly helps improve mood, boost sex drive, increase muscle mass, and strengthen your immune system. Not all of these benefits have been proven, however, and the long-term effects of DHEA supplementation are not known. One study found that DHEA caused severe liver damage in laboratory rats. Whether it would have the same effect on humans is not known, but this should be considered when making the decision to take supplements.

Controversy over DHEA can be compared to the controversy over estrogen replacement therapy. Estrogen replacement has many benefits for women trying to get through menopause, but it also has proven risks. Women and their doctors must weigh the benefits against the risks when deciding whether to begin estrogen therapy. Perhaps men will now have to face those same difficult decisions when considering supplementing with DHEA.

Stops heart disease cold ... for men. Heart disease cuts short the lives of more men than any other disease. According to the

American Heart Association, almost half a million men die from heart disease each year in the United States alone, accounting for over 40 percent of deaths. Cancer, which is the second leading cause of death, accounts for only about 25 percent of deaths in men. DHEA may be able to cut heart disease risk in half, allowing more men to enjoy life a little while longer.

Several studies have found that DHEA can reduce the risk of death from heart attack. A 12-year study among men ages 50 to 79 found that an increase in DHEA reduced the risk of death from heart disease by almost half. Another study that followed men ages 30 to 82 for 19 years resulted in similar findings. However, this same study found that high levels of DHEA resulted in a small *increase* in risk of heart disease death in women.

Battles breast cancer ... sometimes. In keeping with its chameleon-like qualities, DHEA may either increase or decrease the risk of breast cancer. According to researchers, high levels of DHEA may protect against breast cancer in premenopausal women, but after menopause, high levels of DHEA can increase a woman's risk of breast cancer.

Obliterates obesity? DHEA may help keep your pet rat or dog from putting on excess pounds, but can it help you? Animal studies have discovered that DHEA reduces body fat, and many people who take it agree, even though the evidence for this reported benefit is skimpy. The few studies that suggest DHEA reduces fat while preserving lean body mass are more favorable to men than women.

Ditches diabetes? DHEA may help treat non-insulin-dependent diabetes. People with non-insulin-dependent diabetes have increased insulin resistance. This means their bodies are insensitive to insulin, and the insulin can't do its job properly, which is to move glucose from your blood into your body's cells to be used as energy. One study on the effect of DHEA in diabetics found that it improved insulin sensitivity by about 30 percent.

Builds better brains. Quick! Can you remember what you had for lunch last Tuesday? If you can't remember, maybe you need more DHEA. Research has found that DHEA improves memory in mice and increases the speed of brain functions. This could indicate that DHEA may help you think faster and remember longer. Brain tissue contains more DHEA than any other part of your body, so adequate levels of DHEA may be particularly important to your brain. Studies also show that people with Alzheimer's may have almost 50 percent less DHEA than people who don't have Alzheimer's.

Enhances immune system. As you age, you become increasingly susceptible to infectious diseases. Studies show that DHEA may strengthen your immune system by controlling stress hormones. Other studies find that DHEA may increase the effectiveness of vaccines for diseases like influenza in elderly people.

Your action plan

How much is enough?

There is no Recommended Dietary Allowance (RDA) for DHEA like there is for vitamins and minerals, but most people take between 10 and 25 milligrams (mg) daily. You should not exceed 50 mg a day.

How to get more DHEA naturally

Relax! One study found that behavior modification therapy led to increased levels of DHEA in the body. Reducing your stress level may be the only way to boost your DHEA level naturally.

Do you need supplements?

Obviously, young people don't need to take DHEA supplements, since their levels are still high, but middle-aged men may want to take it to combat the effects of aging. Since the long-term effects of supplementing with DHEA are unknown, talk with your doctor before making the decision to take supplements.

THE WISE DHEA CONSUMER

DHEA is available in health food stores. According to law, it is legal to sell a supplement over the counter as long as the label doesn't make unsubstantiated health claims. Although DHEA is available, the quality may be questionable since it isn't subject to regulation.

Some people say an extract of the herb known as Mexican yam can be converted to DHEA in your body. However, Dr. Arthur Schwartz, one of the leading experts on DHEA, says that Mexican yam or wild yam does not help create more DHEA in your body.

DHEA CAUTIONS

The long-term effects of DHEA supplements aren't clear yet, and studies are still underway. DHEA has been known to cause excess growth of body hair in women, acne, mood swings, and fatigue. It may also cause damage to the liver, ovaries, prostate, or uterus. Because it isn't regulated by the Federal Drug Administration, it is possible that poor quality could prove dangerous. Impurities in tryptophan, another trendy supplement, led to illness and several deaths a few years ago.

If you decide to take DHEA, consult your doctor first. To protect yourself in case of liability, one doctor recommends that you save the bottle your DHEA came in, along with the last five pills, and store it in a cool, dark place.

Before antibiotics came along in the 1930s, one of the most popular products a drug company could sell was echinacea, a native North American flower often called Purple Coneflower. Sold as creams and pills, echinacea products were used to fight both minor infections as well as killers like typhoid, malaria, meningitis, and diphtheria.

ECHINACEA

Although it might be considered "folk medicine" by many people, echinacea is in the realm of serious medicine in Germany. Companies there extract medicine and squeeze juice from both the roots and leaves of the flower, and they market more than 180 echinacea products.

The German government has approved echinacea to stimulate the immune system and to treat respiratory and urinary infections, connective tissue diseases such as rheumatoid arthritis and lupus, abnormal growth of white blood cells, tuberculosis, and multiple sclerosis. Echinacea creams and ointments are used to treat hard-to-heal wounds. Sold without a prescription, echinacea is also a favorite remedy in Germany for colds and flu.

American Indians used echinacea, and they brought the member of the daisy family to the attention of European settlers.

In fact, echinacea was one of the most popular herbs among at least 14 tribes of Native Americans. It was used for toothaches, colds, coughs, sore throats, tonsillitis, syphilis, and even snakebites — hence an Indian name for the plant, snakeroot. Other tribes called it "toothache" plant for the numbing effect the herb produces when chewed. Indian medicine men worked wonders with this anesthetic effect. They would rub the mashed root juice on their hands and then handle fire.

A German lay doctor living in Nebraska introduced echinacea into mainstream medicine in 1871. He learned of its healing virtues from Native Americans and began making a patent medicine from it. Echinacea remained a popular remedy until the 1930s when it was displaced by the new antibiotic wonder drug, sulfa.

Today we know this flower as the Purple Kansas Coneflower, Black Sampson, Red Sunflower, the Comb Flower, and, its most widely known moniker, the Purple Coneflower. The perennial plant is native to Kansas, Nebraska, and Missouri. It has narrow leaves; a stout stem up to 3 feet high; and a single, large, purplish, spiny flower. Nine species of echinacea grow in the United States. *Echinacea purpurea* is the most commonly used medicinal species, followed by *Echinacea angustifolia*.

5 WAYS ECHINACEA FIGHTS AGING

From allergies to arthritis, it keeps swelling down. When one of your body parts swells angrily because of an infection or arthritis, much of the blame can be put on the enzyme hyaluronidase, which destroys cell barriers and allows invaders in. By neutralizing this enzyme, echinacea keeps inflammation down.

Echinacea reduced inflammation by 22 percent in arthritis sufferers, according to one research study. While it is only half as effective as steroids, those drugs frequently have serious side effects such as mood swings, rapid weight gain, swelling, and fatigue while echinacea has virtually none. What's more, steroids suppress the immune system so they increase your risk of infection and illness. Echinacea, on the other hand, supports the immune system and aids the body in healing.

Growing echinacea yourself isn't practical because it takes a concentrated extract to do any good, but you may find the flower growing wild in your backyard, especially if you live in Kansas, Nebraska, or Missouri. It has narrow leaves, a single purple flower, and a sturdy stem that can be 3 feet tall. Chewing the strong, bitter plant makes your lips and tongue tingle.

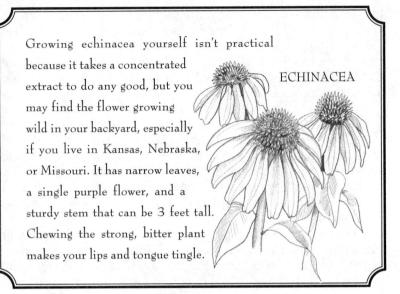

ECHINACEA

Echinacea may even halt the progress of degenerative inflammatory diseases such as rheumatoid arthritis. The Purple Coneflower heals inflammatory skin conditions like poison ivy, eczema, impetigo, and psoriasis. Other studies show it reduces or prevents the redness and swelling of allergic skin reactions.

Its anti-inflammatory properties may be the reason echinacea is effective in treating chronic enlarged prostate gland, pelvic inflammatory disease, and respiratory allergies.

Immune system enhancer. In 1978, German scientists put human cells in test tubes; treated the cells with echinacea; then infected them with flu, herpes, and canker sore viruses. The echinacea increased the cells' resistance to infection by 50 to 80 percent — exactly the same as treatment with interferon, a key protein in your body's natural defense system.

Interferon keeps viruses from multiplying and ties up receptors on cells that viruses would normally attach to. Researchers aren't sure whether echinacea actually works like interferon or whether it stimulates the immune system to produce more interferon. Or both. Either way the results are the same — reduced infection.

A strong immune system becomes vitally important as time subjects us more and more to the ravages of free radicals. The better your immune system works, the better you can fight off illness and remain healthy and "young." Scientific studies clearly show how echinacea boosts immune function:

❦ Echinacea stimulates the lymph system to clean up waste material, bacteria, and other invaders and toxins from the blood. The flower puts several of our natural infection-killers to work. Macrophages, specialized white blood cells that engulf bacteria and viruses at the site of an infection, get more active in the presence of echinacea. And echinacea seems to increase production of white blood cells called T lymphocytes (T cells), which are the body's main defense against acute bacterial infection as well as cancerous cells. T cells are also important in producing B lymphocytes (B cells), which make antibodies targeted to specific enemies. And third, echinacea stimulates two proteins that help prevent or diminish infection — interferon and properdin. Properdin actually attaches to the surface of invaders and causes them to explode.

❦ Echinacea also helps cells set up a barrier against invading bacteria. It neutralizes an enzyme called hyaluronidase that invites infecting invaders into cells, and echinacea increases the strength of the cell wall to keep out invading germs.

❦ The flower even helps regenerate cell-connecting tissue destroyed during an infection.

Cancer treatment. Because it enhances the immune system, echinacea may be a weapon against cancer. In studies, oil extracted from echinacea fought the growth of two types of cancer — lymphatic leukemia and Walker's carcinosarcoma.

Echinacea could especially benefit people with cancer who are getting radiation and chemotherapy treatments because it naturally stimulates your own defenses\— particularly important when your immune system is suppressed by those standard cancer treatments. Studies found the flower increased the number of white blood cells in people undergoing radiation.

Fights cold and flu. In Germany, echinacea is listed by the government as a standard, accepted treatment for colds, coughs, sore throats, and flu. Echinacea's antiviral role is especially important because antibiotics are ineffective against viruses.

You might consider taking it during cold and flu season. After symptoms appear, the herb also seems to relieve symptoms and help you get over colds, flu, chronic upper respiratory tract infections, and ear infections faster.

Commonly, people report they begin taking echinacea extract at the first sign of a cold and often, to their surprise, they find the cold disappears within 24 hours, sometimes after taking the extract only once.

Skin problems. Echinacea's capacity to stop bacteria from entering cells makes it an excellent treatment for skin conditions such as cuts, burns, scrapes, mouth and gum infections, vaginal infections, and even acne. Echinacea acts as an antibiotic against the bacteria *staph* and *strep,* which commonly cause skin infections. This makes it an effective treatment for strep throat, too.

Echinacea actually aids blood clotting — essential to healing open wounds — and stimulates the growth of new tissue. All of these qualities make echinacea particularly valuable in treating wounds that are slow to heal.

Echinacea has proved useful against other skin conditions such as warts, chronic skin ulcers, boils and abscesses, and frostbite, as well as insect bites.

YOUR ACTION PLAN

Liquid extracts of echinacea that you take by mouth are the most common. Some researchers think that the liquid begins stimulating your immune system as soon as you put it in your mouth, making it preferable to dried herb capsules.

The form is less important than the herb's quality and the care taken in the manufacturing process. The U.S. Pharmacopeia (USP) is a non-government, not-for-profit organization that establishes standards for medicines and other health care products. Because there is no government program in place to ensure the quality of dietary supplements, the USP developed a Dietary Supplement Verification Program (DSVP). It tests and reviews supplements for safety and quality.

If you see the USP "Mark of Quality" on the label — which says the dietary supplement has been verified — that product has passed five quality tests and:

❦ contains the ingredients stated on the label.

❦ has the declared amount of ingredients.

❦ will dissolve as needed to release nutrients.

❦ has been screened for harmful contaminants such as pesticides, bacteria, etc.

❦ has been manufactured using safe, sanitary, and well-controlled procedures.

How much is enough?

Tests show echinacea is "dose-dependent" — that is, less than the ideal amount doesn't have any effect and more than the ideal amount doesn't give you more immunity. One study showed that 180 drops of extract really helped relieve flu symptoms and helped people get well faster, but 90 drops were no more effective than a fake echinacea mixture of water and alcohol.

A dose of 10 to 25 drops per day of liquid or one to two capsules or tablets per day seems to be the best for boosting the immune system to ward off colds, flu, and other infections.

If you do get sick, take about 50 drops (about one dropperful) of the liquid or 300 to 400 milligrams (mg) of the dry extract in capsules or tablets. Take this dose three times a day for the first two days of an illness. In the case of acute infections, inflammation, or fever, you may take up to eight capsules or two dropperfuls, two to three times a day.

The wise echinacea consumer

Because of its cold and flu fighting properties, echinacea is one of the most popular herbal remedies in the United States.

HOW TO USE ECHINACEA ON YOUR SKIN

- **Wounds, burns, scrapes, and cuts** — make sure the skin is clean, then apply a few drops of the extract. After this has dried, apply zinc oxide or another nonmedicinal ointment. Change dressings often and apply more echinacea.

- **Toothache, gum, and mouth infections** — apply undiluted extract to the area, use extract diluted with water as a mouthwash, or take the extract internally as directed earlier in the chapter for colds and flu.

- **Bites, stings** — apply full-strength to the affected area.

- **Boils, carbuncles, abscesses, and ulcers** — apply full strength and dress as for wounds.

Some conditions, such as vaginitis, have been shown in studies to respond better to treatment with both oral echinacea and a cream made from the plant.

As a result, a wide variety of preparations are sold at nearly every health food store and even at some drugstores. Liquid extracts using both alcohol and glycerine as bases are common, as are tablets and capsules. Creams and ointments using echinacea are not as readily available.

Because there are no government standards for herbal preparations, read labels carefully to be sure you're getting a quality product. The market is flooded with questionable products, according to herbal medicine experts.

Two brands that have passed the USP testing criteria are Kirkland Signature and Nature Made. They come in softgel capsules, time-release formulas, and lozenges.

In addition, ConsumerLab.com, a national consumer testing organization, lists products that actually contain the ingredients they claim on their label. Visit their site on the Internet at <www.consumerlab.com>.

You can find echinacea supplements at almost any drug or natural foods store. Expect to pay $5 to over $20 for a bottle, depending on the product.

ECHINACEA CAUTIONS

Don't take echinacea for long periods of time without a break. It quits working well after taking it for about five days in a row. Using it every day for weeks may actually weaken your immune system. Either alternate three days on/three days off, or take it for a few weeks then stop for a few weeks.

Even at very large doses, echinacea doesn't seem to be toxic, and allergic reactions to the plant are rare. Prolonged use may increase your need for certain vitamins such as vitamin E, so take a multivitamin supplement as well. Also, heavy use of the herb may result in temporary male infertility as echinacea inhibits an enzyme necessary for fertilization.

If you suffer from an immune system disorder, like rheumatoid arthritis, multiple sclerosis, or hypothyroidism; or have a weakened immune system, during cancer or leukemia treatment, for instance, experts say you shouldn't take echinacea.

One of the oldest surviving tree species can turn your brain cells into survivors, too. Recently, people ages 50 to 70 took part in a study which showed that the fan-shaped leaves of the gingko tree increased blood flow to their brains by 70 percent. Better blood flow boosts brain power, improves short-term memory, and may fend off Alzheimer's disease.

GINGKO

Think you've lost a little spring in your step? What about a little bounce in your brain? As long as you don't have any serious medical problems, exercising and eating right will ward off some of the physical signs of aging. Mental fitness is much more difficult to maintain — unless you know the secret of the gingko.

In China, the gingko (correctly spelled either gingko or ginkgo) tree is considered sacred, and it's easy to see why. The tree has survived in that part of the world for 200 million years. A single tree can live for more than 1,000 years, surviving even on the side of a traffic-jammed city street. It seems only natural that anything that's survived so long holds some secrets to longevity.

Traditional Chinese doctors have been unlocking the mysteries of the gingko in the Orient for more than a millennium.

The Chinese use gingko to relieve chilblains — the swelling of hands and feet after exposure to moist, cold weather. They also use gingko as a digestive aid and a preventive for drunkenness. Skin and head sores have been treated with gingko, as have diarrhea, urinary incontinence, a type of vaginal discharge, and infections.

But it's only been in the past 20 years that Western studies have proven what the Chinese have known all along — gingko offers significant health benefits that can help you live longer and better.

One way gingko increases longevity is by helping your body get rid of cell-destroying free radicals. The herbal extract from the gingko tree is a "free radical scavenger" or natural antioxidant. Gingko inactivates free radicals, protects the genetic material in cells, and helps slow down aging. One study showed that gingko supplements were more effective than either beta carotene or vitamin E in reducing free radicals in the body.

Inspired by a Gingko Leaf

My garden grows an ancient tree,
That comes from old Cathay
Its leaf holds secrets you can't see,
Unless you know the way.

Excerpt from poem by Johann Wolfgang von Goethe   1815
Translated by Varro E. Tyler, Ph.D.

15 WAYS GINGKO FIGHTS AGING

Improves circulation. Gingko gets your juices flowing better in four ways.

First, it widens your blood vessels so more blood can get through. Scientists have isolated a group of compounds called flavonoids in gingko extract. These flavonoids force the blood vessels to relax, which allows them to carry more blood.

Gingko also makes the blood less sticky by keeping platelets separated. Platelets normally help blood clot by clumping

Even the Royal Swedish Academy of Sciences in Stockholm has recognized the importance of gingko. The distinguished group awarded the 1990 Nobel Prize in chemistry to Dr. Elias J. Corey of Harvard University. Dr. Corey and his research group have recreated in the laboratory hundreds of complex molecules ordinarily found in nature. One of the molecules Corey recreated was Gingkolide B, a very complex molecule found only in the leaves and roots of the gingko tree. The Academy said Corey's work has contributed to "the high standard of living and health, and the longevity enjoyed at least in the Western world."

together at the site of a cut or scrape. The clotting is triggered by a substance called platelet activating factor, or PAF. While PAF is a good thing to have in your body when you have an injury, it can also cause the platelets to clump within your blood vessels. Normally, there isn't enough clumping to cause a problem. But if you already have reduced blood flow, this platelet clumping can gum up the works even further. Gingko makes the platelets keep their distance by blocking PAF. Doctors often prescribe blood thinning drugs for people as they get older, but by blocking PAF, gingko is a natural blood thinner.

Third, gingko strengthens tiny blood vessels known as capillaries so they don't leak. The flavonoid rutin, contained in gingko extract, makes capillaries less fragile.

Finally, gingko keeps LDL cholesterol from clumping up on blood vessel walls, keeping the veins and arteries wide open for maximum blood flow.

Boosts brain power. Like any other part of the body, the brain needs adequate blood flow, or it can't function properly. Unfortunately, your body has a hard time sending the brain all the blood it needs as you get older.

Imagine the drain pipe from your kitchen sink. Over time, water begins to drain through the pipe a little slower. It happens in everybody's kitchen. If you pour a little drain opener down the sink, the water starts to flow faster. That's what gingko can do for blood flow to your brain.

Clinical studies show that extracts of the gingko tree can increase blood flow to the brain. What's more, the older you are, the better gingko appears to work. One study found that blood flow to the brain was increased by about 20 percent for people ages 30 to 50, but for people ages 50 to 70, the increase was 70 percent. In another study, a group of elderly men with age-related memory loss took gingko supplements. The gingko actually sped up how fast their brains could process information taken in by their eyes.

More blood flow means more brain power and better short-term memory. It specifically means protection against what doctors call "cerebral insufficiency" or "dementia." Most people have some degree of dementia in their later years.

The 12 symptoms of cerebral insufficiency which gingko may improve are:

- ❦ difficulty concentrating
- ❦ absentmindedness
- ❦ confusion
- ❦ lack of energy
- ❦ tiredness
- ❦ decreased physical performance
- ❦ sadness or depression
- ❦ anxiety
- ❦ dizziness
- ❦ tinnitus (ringing in the ears)
- ❦ headaches

Alzheimer's disease. Though it remains controversial, evidence points toward gingko as prevention or early therapy for Alzheimer's disease. One study followed 40 people with Alzheimer's. Some took 80 milligrams (mg) of gingko extract three times a day, while some took a placebo, a harmless, unmedicated pill. The people who took the gingko had improved memory and were able to pay attention more than those who took the placebo. Some researchers speculate that gingko actually increases the number of brain receptors responsible for memory.

People who are just beginning to experience symptoms of Alzheimer's might consider taking gingko to boost brain power and delay further loss of memory.

Intermittent claudication. Do you have leg pain or constant cramping in your calf muscles after even a short walk? As many people get older, their legs don't get an adequate blood supply because of hardened or blocked blood vessels. This painful condition is called intermittent claudication. Fifteen clinical studies show that gingko extract relieves the symptoms of intermittent claudication.

Raynaud's disease. People who have this disease of the blood vessels react very strongly to colder temperatures. Even moderately cold temperatures can trigger spasms in the blood vessels of their fingers, which prevent proper blood flow. The fingers can turn blue or white and be very painful. By dilating the blood vessels, gingko helps get blood to the tips of the fingers to relieve the pain and restore the normal color to the skin.

Varicose veins. One of the compounds in gingko extract, tebonin, is particularly helpful in relieving the unsightly, and sometimes painful, varicose veins that plague people in their prime.

Lowers cholesterol. Gingko can cut some of the guilt out of Thanksgiving dinner. In one study, researchers tested people's blood levels of fat and cholesterol before the holiday season. They tested again a few weeks later after everyone had enjoyed all of the rich holiday meals and snacks. The people who took gingko had lower cholesterol levels after the holidays than those who didn't take gingko. Other studies confirm that gingko can lower blood cholesterol levels. If you have high cholesterol, gingko may help you bring it under control.

Heart disease. Like other flavonoids, gingko can reduce the risk of heart disease. One study showed that people who get the most flavonoids have about one-third the risk of heart disease compared with people who get the least flavonoids. Flavonoids are helpful, natural compounds found in citrus fruits, onions, apples, and tea, as well as in supplements like gingko, grape seed extract, bilberry, and others.

Plantations of gingko trees (also known as maidenhair trees) supply the booming herbal market. A Sumter, S.C., plantation grows 10 million gingkoes on 1,000 acres. The leaves are harvested green, then dried and shipped to Europe for processing into gingko biloba extract. Male trees over 20 years old blossom in the spring, while adult female trees produce a fruit that falls in late autumn.

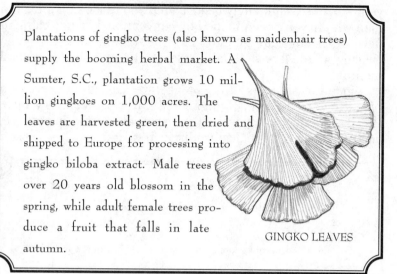

GINGKO LEAVES

Dizziness. Dizziness is a natural side effect of reduced blood flow to the brain. That's why it's so common among older people. Dizziness can lead to falls, and that's especially dangerous if you have osteoporosis. It doesn't take much of a fall to break a hip or crack a vertebra if you have brittle bones. While gingko won't strengthen your bones, it can increase your blood flow, reduce the dizziness, and return you to your sure-footed self.

Prevents blindness. When the eyes don't receive enough oxygen from the blood, the retina can be damaged, often robbing people of their sight as they get older. Since gingko increases blood flow, more oxygen can get to the eyes.

Headaches. You don't have to be old to have headaches, but the reduced blood flow associated with aging can certainly make headaches more common. Gingko can help alleviate this type of headache.

Impotence. It may be comforting to know that many men experience impotence or decreased rigidity as they age, but the only real comfort is something that restores the vigor to your sex life. Gingko may be just what you're looking for. Even men who haven't been helped by conventional drug treatment have responded to gingko, but the results didn't happen overnight. You'll have to take at least 240 mg daily for several months.

Since not all cases of impotence are caused by decreased blood flow to the penis, gingko will not work for every man. But if your doctor says you have arterial erectile impotence, you may discover a real aphrodisiac in gingko.

If gingko has so many proven health benefits, why isn't it sold in the United States as a drug? It's a good question without a very good answer.

One noted herbal expert, Dr. Varro E. Tyler, had a few ideas. First, Dr. Tyler pointed out that in Europe, a drug only has to meet a test of "reasonable certainty" to be approved. In the United States, a drug must have absolute proof of being safe and effective.

Though there have been nearly 50 tests on gingko in Europe, some experts have charged that the tests were not scientifically valid. In Dr. Tyler's opinion, the fact that all the tests showed the same positive results is proof in itself. He also maintained that there is no perfectly designed scientific study and virtually all studies are open to some criticism.

Nevertheless, this criticism has likely kept the world's largest supplier of gingko, the Schwabe Company of Germany, from seeking approval for gingko as a drug in the United States. It would be costly to seek approval, and it might be difficult to secure patent protection, since the extract dates back to ancient China. Instead, as Dr. Tyler put it, "in this country, it falls in the present never-never land of unproven herbal remedies, a category in which it probably does not belong."

Tinnitus and hearing disorders. Tinnitus, or ringing in the ears that won't go away, is an annoying problem that doctors sometimes find difficult to treat with traditional medicine. That's why some doctors are turning to gingko to help their patients.

One doctor in Texas, who treats a fair number of people with tinnitus, was dead set against "alternative" medicine until his son, a distributor of herbal products, convinced him to prescribe gingko tablets. The son cited a European study that showed good results in relieving tinnitus. The doctor began recommending gingko, and many of his patients found complete relief. Others may still have some ringing, but it's much less than they had before they began taking gingko.

People who have hearing disorders related to low blood flow to the ears can also find relief after taking gingko for several months. Vertigo, a type of dizziness sometimes related to problems in the inner ear, might also be relieved by gingko.

Diabetes. Though there's no evidence that gingko can cure diabetes, it can be useful in treating a heart problem called diabetic angiopathy that is often associated with diabetes. And it can help prevent one of the most common problems faced by people with diabetes — poor circulation. In some cases, poor circulation can lead to amputation of limbs. Gingko has been shown to increase blood flow to the arms and legs of people with diabetes by 45 percent.

Asthma relief. The same substance that causes platelets to clot, PAF, can also trigger asthma. PAF causes spasms in the sacs that make up the lungs. By blocking PAF, gingko can prevent these spasms and make it easier to breathe.

YOUR ACTION PLAN

If you were in Europe, you could buy gingko extract as an over-the-counter drug, or your doctor might prescribe it. In fact, it is one of the most prescribed drugs in Germany.

In the United States, you'll have to make a trip to your local health food store or herb shop to find gingko. Even if you have a gingko tree nearby, don't even think about harvesting the leaves to make a tea. The extract has to be far more concentrated than the amount you would get in tea, and the leaves contain substances called tannins, which could be toxic.

HOW MUCH IS ENOUGH?

In the health studies on gingko, researchers most often used 40 mg three times a day. You might need a higher dosage for some disorders, like impotence.

Gingko is a supplement you can add to your list of daily vitamins and herbs, but don't wait until you feel bad to take it. You will probably have to take the supplements for four to six weeks before you notice any difference in your health.

THE WISE GINGKO CONSUMER

When you shop for gingko, keep in mind that all extracts are not the same. What you should look for is gingko biloba extract (gingko biloba is the scientific name for the tree, referring to the two parts or lobes of the leaf). Gingko biloba extract is sometimes referred to as GBE or GBX.

The extract should be 24 percent flavoglycosides, 10 percent of which should be quercetin. It should also contain 6 percent terpenoids. Here are some supplements that are best bets for getting what you pay for.

❦ Maxi Ginkgo Biloba Standardized Extract

❦ Nature's Resource Premium Herb Extra Strength Ginkgo Biloba

❦ Nature's Way Ginkgold

❦ Nutrilite Ginkgo Biloba and DHA Dietary Supplement

These all contain the expected amounts of flavonol glycosides and terpene lactones.

If you get confused, look for ConsumerLab.com's Seal of Approval on the product label. It should read "Approved Quality - Ginkgo Biloba."

GINGKO CAUTIONS

Overall, gingko is safe. At the normal doses, there haven't been any reports of severe side effects. In a few people, gingko extract has caused headaches or mild stomach upset.

However, talk to your doctor before taking this — or any — supplement. Gingko can interact with other nutrients or drugs, especially blood-thinners like coumadin or aspirin.

Also, stay away from the fruit of the female gingko. Touching the pulp can cause severe itching, similar to what you'd expect from poison ivy. Eating as little as two pieces of the pulp can cause serious intestinal problems.

Revered by many Korean and Japanese people and eagerly sought after by millions of others, ginseng is often called the "root of immortality." Although 2,000 years of continuous use have given ginseng its own bit of immortality, its effect on the mortality of man is a little less certain. Even enthusiastic Eastern advocates of the root can't claim that ginseng will give you everlasting life. However, it is possible that ginseng will give you a longer life ... and a more lively one as well.

GINSENG

For centuries, ginseng has been one of the world's most popular herbs, consumed by people from hundreds of different generations for thousands of years. Today, millions of people around the world still take ginseng, including some of the world's foremost aging and longevity researchers.

Because ginseng supposedly strengthens all the body's organs and makes them more resistant to disease, it has been given credit for curing almost every illness under the sun, from cancer to impotence. While you have the testimony of millions of people who've trusted ginseng with their health for several thousand years, scientists still have trouble nailing down exactly what, if anything, ginseng does.

Precisely because so many health claims are made for ginseng, it's hard for Western science to take the herb seriously. In fact, many Western researchers still insist that there is very little credible research to back up the claims despite the 3,000 scientific studies that have been done on ginseng in the past 50 years.

Many researchers are also skeptical because ginseng seems to produce no specific effects, treating instead a wide range of conditions. For the most part, Western doctors still believe that any benefits of ginseng come from the placebo effect. In other words, they think it works wonders because the person taking it believes it will.

In contrast, Chinese medicine rates ginseng as one of its most potent healers. Traditionally, the Chinese classify their drugs into three categories: inferior, middle, and superior. Inferior drugs have specific effects for specific conditions. This is exactly the type of drug Western researchers dream about and love to discover or invent. In the Chinese system, middle drugs strengthen body function. Superior drugs work for everything, and it is into this category that Chinese doctors place ginseng.

In Eastern medicine, ginseng is considered an adaptogen. This means it works to keep the body in balance in all circumstances, bad or good. An adaptogen also increases the body's resistance to unhealthy influences. It works only when needed or when the body has a deficiency. Since ginseng does contain antioxidants, it may be those compounds that give ginseng its body-balancing abilities. Researchers also suspect it's ginseng's antioxidant activities that can help protect your heart, liver, and lungs.

Recently, United States Department of Agriculture scientists discovered that the mineral chromium works in a way similar to an adaptogen, by raising and lowering blood sugar as needed. It's very possible a number of foods and nutrients work only as needed, which gives 20th-century credibility to the ancient health claims made for ginseng.

10 WAYS GINSENG FIGHTS AGING

In the late 1980s, a Chinese study suggested that ginseng's antioxidant status might make it a potent anti-aging drug. A recent Chinese study offered support for this theory when it

GINSENG: THE MAN-ROOT

The word ginseng comes from the original Chinese character for the root, pronounced "schin-seng," which means "essence of the earth in the form of a man," or more simply, "man-root."

No doubt early Chinese healers were influenced in their choice of a name by ginseng's thick root trunk and various little roots growing off the trunk that looked like arms or legs.

As little as you may think that ginseng resembles the human figure, it wasn't unusual for early healers to stretch their imaginations to designate a healing plant as having some human shape or characteristic. Plants or roots like ginseng that resembled the whole body were called whole body tonics.

For some healers, identifying certain plants with certain body parts may have simply helped them remember the specific healing properties of that plant. Others, however, felt that the Creator made man's eternal search for health easier by stamping all beneficial plants with a so-called "signature," such as a resemblance to the body part it could help heal, to indicate how the plant was to be used.

Thus, the term "doctrine of signatures," came to be applied to plants used for healing. Originally, the doctrine of signatures was solely a spiritual philosophy based on the notion that God marked everything he created with a sign to indicate its purpose.

In ginseng's case, the early healers may not have been too far off base to classify ginseng as a whole-body tonic as today's scientific studies continue to provide evidence for ginseng's body-balancing activities.

However, as time and other scientific tests have proven, the doctrine of signatures system of plant classification had about as much success as you might have at any other game of chance. When it comes to your health, hard science is a much safer and healthier bet than gambling on the doctrine of signatures.

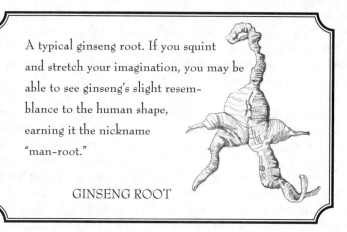

A typical ginseng root. If you squint and stretch your imagination, you may be able to see ginseng's slight resemblance to the human shape, earning it the nickname "man-root."

GINSENG ROOT

found that ginseng actually slowed the aging process of 71 people over age 60.

Other antioxidants may help you live longer, but with ginseng, you get the double advantage of living longer and feeling like enjoying all those extra years.

Better blood sugar control. Both animal and human studies indicate that ginseng improves blood sugar control. In animals, ginseng improves the release of insulin from the pancreas. For diabetics, this means an improved ability to keep blood sugar levels normal.

Two recent human studies also reported that ginseng significantly lowers blood glucose levels. Lower blood glucose levels mean less work for your kidneys and less risk of developing ketoacidosis, a toxic buildup of ketones (substances produced when the body breaks down fat for fuel) that can be fatal.

In addition, one of those studies found that 100 to 200 milligrams (mg) of ginseng a day significantly improved mood, vigor, well-being, and mental and physical performance in newly diagnosed diabetics.

Boosts brain power. At least four different human studies indicate that ginseng can improve memory and concentration.

In 1990, a two-month study conducted in China of 358 people ages 50 to 85 revealed that 50 mg of ginseng given three times a day for two months significantly improved memory and overall health.

An experiment conducted by Dr. Israel Brekhman, the Soviet researcher who pioneered much of the research on East Asian ginseng, revealed that radio operators who received a ginseng extract transmitted text faster and made fewer mistakes than radio operators not given ginseng.

Cans cancer. Several recent studies suggest that various components of ginseng may be protective against a variety of cancers, including skin cancer; liver cancer; ovarian cancer; and cancers of the larynx, esophagus, pancreas, and stomach.

In fact, in laboratory studies of ginseng's effect on liver cancer cells, researchers were astonished to find that ginseng turned tumor cells into normal-functioning cells. Researchers noted that ginseng had a similar effect on skin cancer cells. According to cancer researchers, the ability of any substance, natural or man-made, to turn cancer cells into normal-functioning cells without damaging other cells is a pretty rare occurrence. As promising as the studies are, researchers hasten to point out that they do not know if the active ginseng components would have any effect on an actual tumor site in a human.

Another study conducted at the Korea Cancer Center Hospital in Seoul revealed that people who regularly consumed ginseng had only half the risk of developing cancers of the mouth, pharynx, esophagus, stomach, colon, rectum, liver, pancreas, larynx, lung, and ovaries as people who never consumed ginseng. In fact, the longer a person had used ginseng, the lower his risk. A person who had taken ginseng for one year had a 36 percent lower risk of cancer, while a person who had used ginseng for five years or more had a 69 percent lower risk of cancer.

Most ginseng products, except fresh ginseng slices, fresh ginseng juice, and white ginseng tea, were associated with a lower risk of cancer.

Invigorates the immune system. More and more studies suggest that ginseng's anti-cancer activity may be due to its effect on the immune system. Ginseng revs up your immune system by stimulating the production of T lymphocytes and natural killer cells, which help your body combat infections.

Could control cholesterol and help keep heart healthy. There is some speculation among researchers that ginseng may help

THE GINSENGS AND THEIR IMITATORS

When purchasing ginseng products, it's helpful to be familiar with scientific and popular names for the true ginsengs as well as the ginseng imitators.

❦ Asian ginseng. Scientific name: *Panax ginseng* C.A. Meyer. May also be called *Panax ginseng*, Oriental ginseng, or rarely *P. schinseng* Nees. Commonly grown in China, Korea, Russia, and Japan. Of the three true ginsengs, Asian ginseng has been most completely investigated.

❦ American ginseng. Scientific name: *Panax quinquefolius* L. A native American species, this ginseng grows in wooded areas from Quebec to Minnesota to Oklahoma and Georgia. American ginseng is generally considered milder than Asian ginseng.

❦ San qui ginseng. Scientific name: *Panax pseudo-ginseng* Wallich. Also known as sanchi or tienchi ginseng. This ginseng is widely cultivated in China. Although studies show san qui ginseng contains ginsenosides identical to the ones found in Asian ginseng, more studies need to be done to determine its safety and effectiveness.

❦ Siberian ginseng. Scientific name: *Eleutherococcus senticosus* Maxim. Also called eleuthero, eleuthero-ginseng, touch-me-not, devil's bush or shrub, eleutherococc, spiny eleutherococc, and wild pepper. Although commonly called a ginseng and sold as a substitute for true ginseng, *Eleutherococcus* is not a true ginseng.

❦ Brazilian ginseng. Scientific name: *Pfaffia paniculata*. Although sometimes called Brazilian ginseng, pfaffia is not related to the true ginsengs.

control cholesterol. A component called sitosterol, which is absorbed by your intestines and lowers cholesterol, has been isolated from ginseng.

In fact, animal studies provide support for the theory. These studies show that long-term use of several ginseng components does decrease cholesterol and triglyceride levels. To ginseng users, this may mean a lower risk of clogged arteries and heart disease.

In addition, another study of 358 people ages 50 to 85 found that 50 mg of ginseng three times a day provided effective treatment of coronary heart disease.

Energizes you to help you keep going and going and going ... Ginseng can help you keep going just when you think you can't go any more. It may be especially helpful for people lamenting the lost energy of their youth.

In a study of 120 people ages 30 to 60, researchers found that ginseng significantly improved lung performance and responses to reaction tests in people ages 40 to 60, but not in the younger adults.

Even though ginseng may provide the most benefits to older people, it can even improve the performance of top athletes. It boosts performance by increasing the body's uptake of oxygen, lowering the heart rate, and maintaining glycogen (a storage form of carbohydrate energy) more efficiently, which enables your muscles to work longer before they reach exhaustion.

Dr. Brekhman found that runners in a 2-mile race who took ginseng finished an average of 53 seconds faster than runners who didn't take ginseng. Another study of 12 student nurses found that ginseng slightly improved their speed and coordination while working the night shift.

Stops stress. Some researchers suggest that ginseng's ability to fight off fatigue is connected to ginseng's general ability to relieve stress.

Researchers theorize that ginseng stops stress by indirectly recharging rundown adrenal glands, which sit on top of your kidneys and help your body react and adapt in times of stress. When constant stress has left your adrenals run down and worn out, ginseng gets them going again. Once the adrenals are recharged, they can continue to help your body rebound from stress.

Many animal studies support the theory that ginseng helps the body cope more effectively with stress, preventing illnesses that stress can cause. Early research suggests that ginseng may have a similar effect in humans.

Usurps ulcers. Animal studies have indicated that ginseng may help prevent stress-induced ulcers. Several studies also indicate that ginseng can help prevent stomach damage caused by drinking alcohol. In this case, whole ginseng seems to be more effective than other ginseng products.

May lick liver disease. One study found that ginsenosides, the active components in ginseng, appear to be protective against liver disease. Red ginseng appears to be more potent than white ginseng. Another study conducted at Kurume University School of Medicine in Japan found that ginseng combined with several herbs into a formula the Japanese call *Sho-saiko-to* provides powerful healing for chronic liver diseases, as well as being protective against cancer.

Acts like an aphrodisiac. Ginseng's most famous claim to fame is its reputed ability to help men overcome impotence. Thus far, there's been very little scientific support for the super sex claims made for ginseng.

Recently, however, Dr. Tony Lee, professor of pharmacology at Southern Illinois School of Medicine, uncovered information that gives some credibility to this age-old claim. According to Dr. Lee, ginseng contains compounds that stimulate nerve cells in the penis, which may help men maintain an erection.

But that's not all ... In addition, some research has indicated that ginseng may be helpful in preventing blood clots, anemia, and swelling caused by fluid retention. It may also help relieve depression.

YOUR ACTION PLAN

Although there are at least eight different types of true ginseng and a number of ginseng wanna-be's, most of the studies have been done on Asian ginseng.

Based on their studies, researchers believe that ginseng's healing powers come from its ginsenosides, steroid-like compounds found in the bark, or outer layer, of the root. In addition, ginseng also contains vitamins B1 and B2, manganese, phosphorus, iron, copper, cobalt, sulfur, and germanium, which probably contribute to the root's body-balancing effects.

Generally, the more ginsenosides a root contains, the more valuable it is. Because ginsenoside content of the root increases with age, normally only plants six years or older have roots with therapeutic value.

Ginseng roots contain at least six primary ginsenosides and seven secondary ginsenosides. Some of the ginsenosides have an exact opposite effect of others. For example, some ginsenosides may stimulate your central nervous system and get you raring to go, while others have a calming, relaxing effect, making you feel peaceful and tranquil.

For this reason, only the whole ginseng root, and not individual ginsenoside extracts, are used in supplements. Also, according to traditional Chinese custom, Oriental healers maintain that the whole root is more beneficial than any of its parts.

HOW MUCH IS ENOUGH?

If you use the raw root, Varro Tyler, herbal expert and Lilly Distinguished Professor of Pharmacognosy in the School of Pharmacy and Pharmacal Sciences at Purdue University, recommends using 1/2 teaspoonful of the root to make a cup of tea, which can be taken one or two times a day.

For people who prefer supplements, look for supplements standardized to 4 to 7 percent ginsenosides. Seven European studies of ginseng extracts with 4 to 7 percent ginsenosides found those supplements significantly improved the reaction time, alertness, and concentration powers of study participants.

Donald J. Brown, N.D., and author of *Herbal Prescriptions for Better Health: Your Everyday Guide to Prevention, Treatment, and Cure* recommends taking 100 mg once or twice daily. If you use supplements of nonstandardized extracts, he recommends 1 to 2 grams daily.

He also suggests using ginseng for two to three weeks continuously, followed by a one to two week rest period before beginning to take ginseng again. He does not recommend highly extracted ginseng products of more than 7 percent ginsenosides because he feels they may lack other important components that can improve blood sugar and boost immune functioning.

How to get more ginseng naturally

Buy ginseng roots, which you can find at Oriental markets and in some specialty grocery stores, or grow your own ginseng. If you decide to grow your own, keep in mind that it will be at least six years from the time you plant until you can harvest your roots.

You can either chew ginseng roots or make a tea from them. To make chewing easier on your teeth, steam the roots about 10 minutes to soften. Chew small pieces of ginseng slowly and completely.

To make tea, simmer a small chunk of root in a glass or ceramic pot — don't use metal pots or utensils — for about 30 minutes. Use 1/2 teaspoon of ginseng for each cup of water. You may want to experiment with the amount of ginseng you use and simmering times to find out what tea strength gives you the best results.

Do you need supplements?

If you don't want to buy ginseng roots or grow your own, you will have to use supplements. However, you do have a wide variety of ginseng products to choose from, such as teas, capsules, extracts, tablets, wine, chewing gum, cola, and candy.

The wise ginseng consumer

What you need to know about buying ginseng depends on whether you're buying whole roots or supplements. To assure quality, Dr. Varro Tyler recommends that you buy ginseng in the root form. Older roots are more expensive because they're believed to have more healing power. Even among roots, however, potency can vary depending on the type of ginseng, where and how it was grown, and how it was stored and prepared.

When buying roots, be prepared to choose between red and white ginseng. The difference between the two types is the way they are prepared. Red ginseng is processed with steam and heat, which turns the traditionally tan roots red. White ginseng has not undergone any processing other than being washed and dried. Traditionally, red ginseng is considered more stimulating than white.

At this point, it will be helpful to know about the different varieties of ginseng commercially available. (For a more complete description of the different ginsengs and similar products, see the article *The ginsengs and their imitators* on page 249.) The most popular commercial ginseng products are Asian ginseng, American ginseng, and Siberian ginseng.

Although most of the studies have been done on Asian ginseng, the few studies done on American ginseng suggest it has a similar effect to the Asian variety. American ginseng appears to be milder than Asian, so it may be just the thing if you find you are overstimulated by Asian ginseng. Siberian ginseng is not a true ginseng at all, although some research suggests it may have some of the same effects as the true Asian or American ginsengs.

If you choose to buy supplements instead of roots, be sure you choose a ginseng manufacturer with a good reputation. Some products will have very little, if any, ginseng. A quality ginseng product will contain ginsenosides. The more ginsenosides a product has, the more likely you'll benefit from it. Look for products containing 4 to 7 percent ginsenosides.

Your best bet is to buy only products that are standardized for ginsenoside content. Herbs or herbal formulations labeled as "standardized" are guaranteed by the manufacturer to contain a specific amount of a certain active ingredient in the product.

To store ginseng, keep it cool and dry, but don't freeze.

GINSENG CAUTIONS

Most studies report very few, if any, side effects from taking ginseng. Generally, the most common side effects of ginseng are nervousness and excitability. These usually go away after a few days of use. Other reported side effects include insomnia, skin rashes, diarrhea, nausea, and vomiting.

Don't take ginseng on an empty stomach or with caffeine. This will increase the likelihood you'll feel nervous or develop an upset stomach.

Occasionally, individual preparations of ginseng may contain compounds capable of producing symptoms such as sore throat, conjunctivitis, dry cough, rash, mouth sores, and corneal ulcers. This is another reason why it's generally best to stick with roots or standardized products.

People with high blood pressure should also be aware that ginseng may raise blood pressure. You may be able to eliminate this side effect by lowering the dose or switching to American ginseng. If you have high blood pressure, work with your doctor if you want to take ginseng.

Diabetics should also use ginseng with caution. Although no serious reactions have been reported, ginseng can lower blood sugar, so you should only use ginseng under the supervision of your doctor.

Some studies have reported that ginseng has estrogen-like effects on women. Although one analyst of these studies concluded that none of them offered substantial evidence to support such conclusions, women with hormone imbalances, fibrocystic breast disease, uterine fibroids, and breast cancer may want to avoid ginseng.

Red ginseng, supposedly the most stimulating of the ginsengs, may also worsen symptoms of premenstrual syndrome, increase menstrual flow, or alter menstrual cycles.

In addition, there are certain times when even completely healthy people should not take ginseng, according to herbal expert Dr. Tei Fu Chen. He recommends avoiding ginseng if you have a fever or are fighting off a cold, the flu, or bronchitis. In addition, you should probably avoid ginseng if you are constipated or very overweight. Oriental medicine considers constipation and obesity congestive symptoms, which traditional Eastern doctors say don't respond well to ginseng.

Fortune tellers may claim they can predict how long you'll live, but scientists have found a better way, and it doesn't require a crystal ball. According to research, a high glutathione level is one of the most reliable indicators of health and longevity.

GLUTATHIONE

If you've ever lived in a really old house, you know it helps to have a handyman around for things like patching plaster and repairing leaky pipes. Your body has the same kind of handyman — glutathione. This amino acid is involved directly or indirectly in many handy activities. It helps build proteins and DNA, which contains your genetic code and is found in all your cells; assists in metabolism; fights free radicals; helps keep red blood cells healthy; and protects cells from damaging substances like drugs, smoke, or pollution.

As handy as glutathione is, you want to keep as much of it in your body as possible, right? Unfortunately, glutathione levels tend to fall as you get older. However, a recent study found that although glutathione levels were generally lower in people ages 60 to 79, the 80 to 99 age group actually had levels similar to younger people. Researchers think that people who maintain a high level of glutathione in their bodies may be healthier and, therefore, live longer. The same study found that people with a high glutathione level had lower blood pressure and cholesterol levels and maintained a more sensible body weight than people with low levels of glutathione. These glutathione-rich people also rated their own health higher when asked, even though they didn't know they had more of this health-building handyman in their bodies.

5 WAYS GLUTATHIONE FIGHTS AGING

Prevents pollution damage. You will probably live longer than your great-grandparents did. You have modern advances in medicine and technology to thank for those extra years of health. However, modern living does present some dangers to your health that weren't a problem to your forefathers. Your environment is becoming more and more hazardous, and you may be exposed to chemicals that didn't even exist in your grandfather's day. And while modern drugs have helped millions of people live longer, taking too many drugs, or the wrong kind of drugs, can be deadly. Luckily, glutathione can neutralize many of these modern hazards, making them less harmful.

Destroys free radicals. Free radical damage may be the main culprit in the aging process. Glutathione wipes out these pesky cell-damaging particles like an exterminator wipes out termites.

Boosts immunity. Your body has a marvelous built-in immune system that protects you against disease, but this immune system begins to break down as you age. For one thing, you begin to produce fewer T cells — white blood cells that direct attacks against foreign substances like bacteria and viruses, and the T cells you do produce become less effective. One reason for this deterioration is that the cells of your immune system are particularly enticing to free radicals because they have a high fat content. Free radicals love to oxidize fat. After years of free radical damage, your immune system cells simply can't do the job as well as before. Glutathione, in its role as an antioxidant, helps minimize free radical damage. Studies also show that glutathione helps your body make more disease-fighting T cells, and it helps these cells to be more effective.

Saves your sight. Glutathione levels are especially high in your eyes, and this helps protect your precious vision. Studies show that an adequate level of glutathione in your eyes can protect against cataracts, even when substances known to cause cataracts are present.

Cuts down cancer. Glutathione's main anti-aging role is its ability to neutralize toxic substances before they can harm your body. This role makes glutathione an effective cancer preventive. It binds with cancer-causing substances and makes them harmless. In one study, when rats with liver tumors were treated with glutathione, their tumors became smaller.

YOUR ACTION PLAN

HOW TO GET MORE GLUTATHIONE NATURALLY

Watch your weight. Do you need yet another reason to pass over the cheesecake for dessert at lunch? How about staying younger and living longer? The more fat you eat the more free radicals you create. That's because fats are oxidized very easily. Glutathione levels become depleted quickly in overweight people, probably because so much of it goes to fighting free radicals that are created by too much fat.

Experiments have also shown that caloric restriction boosts glutathione levels.

Eat fresh foods. Although your body manufactures glutathione, you can also get it from your diet. Fresh fruits and vegetables are the richest source of glutathione. More highly processed foods, like canned vegetables, contain less glutathione than fresh foods.

For example, a 100 gram serving of fresh peaches contains 7.4 milligrams (mg) of glutathione, but the same amount of canned peaches contains only 1.9 mg. Fresh meat also contains more glutathione than smoked or processed meat. Fats and oils don't contain any glutathione.

Get plenty of vitamin C. Citrus fruits can provide you with glutathione, but the vitamin C they contain may also help your body produce more glutathione. Studies show that glutathione levels rise with vitamin C consumption.

Do you need supplements?

If you eat plenty of fresh fruits and vegetables, you are probably getting an adequate amount of glutathione. However, if you eat a lot of canned and processed food, you may want to take supplements.

One of the best ways to boost your level of glutathione is to take glutamine supplements. Glutamine is the most abundant amino acid in the human body. Interestingly, when taken as a supplement, glutamine is converted into glutathione in your body. This seems to work better than taking glutathione directly.

Glutathione-rich foods

Food	Mg of glutathione per 100 grams
Asparagus, fresh, cooked	28.3
Avocado, raw	27.7
Broccoli spears, fresh, cooked	9.1
Cantaloupe	6.9
Cauliflower, fresh, cooked	9.1
Oranges	7.3
Peaches, unsweetened, raw	7.4
Potatoes, fried	14.3
Spinach, raw	12.2
Squash, winter, baked	11.0
Strawberries, fresh	7.1
Tomatoes, raw	9.0

GLORIOUS GLUTAMINE

Considering all that glutathione can do to keep you young and healthy, any substance that will help you produce more of it is a valuable substance indeed. Glutamine does just that. Glutamine is an amino acid that is one of the building blocks of glutathione, but glutamine is more than just a stepping stone to higher glutathione levels. It has some benefits in its own right.

Glutamine is classified as a nonessential amino acid because your body can manufacture it. Researchers, however, are now calling it a "conditionally essential" amino acid. Why? Because when you are ill, your need for glutamine increases. One of the things that makes glutamine so valuable is its ability to help you recover from illness more quickly.

For example, in a study of people hospitalized for bone marrow transplants, researchers found that those who received glutamine supplements reduced the time they spent in the hospital when compared with those not receiving glutamine. One reason for the shorter stays was that the glutamine-supplemented people were less likely to get infections during their hospital stays. The average cost of the hospital stays was $26,000 less for the lucky glutamine recipients. Now that's a valuable benefit!

It's a decision every woman must face. Should you or shouldn't you use hormone replacement therapy during and after menopause?

HORMONE REPLACEMENT THERAPY — NATURALLY

Researchers recently stopped a large hormone replacement therapy (HRT) study because they were concerned about health risks. Five years into the study, they were startled to see a significant increase in invasive breast cancer as well as other health problems. Their research showed:

- a 26 percent rise in breast cancer

- 22 percent more cardiovascular disease

- a 29 percent increase in heart attacks

- a 41 percent jump in stroke

- twice the rate of blood clots

That translates into seven to eight more cancer or heart disease cases per 10,000 HRT users each year. That may not seem like a lot, but when you look at the population as a whole, it could mean thousands more health problems over time. In addition, hormones impact your health in other ways.

Hinder your breathing. HRT can make airway inflammation or spasms worse. That will increase your risk of developing asthma — by as much as 80 percent, according to the well-known Nurses' Health Study. Your risk grows according to how much and how long you take estrogen.

Endure break-through bleeding. As you probably know, HRT can cause occasional, light uterine bleeding. Although unpredictable and a nuisance, it's not considered a medical problem.

Complicate mammograms. It's not permanent, but while you're on HRT, your breast tissue will probably change — becoming more compact or dense. This makes it hard for radiologists to read your mammograms and can affect how accurately you're screened for breast cancer. Once you stop using HRT, your breasts should return to normal.

Realize a cancer risk. If you take estrogen for ten years or more after menopause, your chances of getting — and dying from — ovarian cancer increase. No one can explain exactly why. Experts do know, however, taking estrogen for less than ten years won't significantly raise your risk. There's also no information on the risk for women taking estrogen combined with progestin.

Another, more rare, type of cancer is on the rise in women over 50. Lobular carcinoma affects the small spaces in your breasts that contain milk-producing glands. While some experts believe HRT is associated with this cancer, there's not yet enough hard evidence.

Go up against gallstones. Women taking estrogen replacement therapy are at higher risk for developing gallstones. One study found those with heart disease taking HRT were 40 percent more likely to develop gallbladder disease.

Because of the scope and danger of these side effects, the Food and Drug Administration (FDA) now advises doctors to prescribe HRT only when benefits clearly outweigh health risks. The FDA says doctors should prescribe HRT just long enough for successful treatment — and at the lowest effective dose. What's more, women should consider non-HRT treatments for vaginal dryness and osteoporosis.

Reversing the long-held notion that HRT protects against heart disease, both the FDA and American Heart Association now warn against using hormone therapy to reduce the chances of heart problems.

So what can you do to balance your body chemistry during menopause?

DOUBLE YOUR DEFENSE WITH DIET

Some experts suggest a natural eating plan may help you survive menopause and control the related risks of heart disease, osteoporosis, and cancer. That means you should make a nutritious diet your first line of defense. Lifestyle changes — such as a high-fiber, low-fat diet rich in antioxidants — may help lower menopause risks and symptoms, suggests the American Academy of Family Physicians.

Generally, focus on foods that come from plants. Many contain substances that may help regulate hormones. And you'll be less likely to add weight at the waist — a common complaint with menopause. Pick foods that are fresh, unrefined, and unprocessed. For instance, replace refined white and brown sugar with raw honey and real maple syrup. Emphasize fruits and vegetables. Try locally grown produce for just-picked freshness, and eat organic foods often. Avoid those with additives, colorings, or preservatives. Replace table salt with herbs and spices.

These expert tips will help you fill your body with vital nutrients that ease menopausal symptoms and fight serious disease.

Choose whole grains. Rich in hormone-regulators and nutrition, whole grains include oats, whole wheat, rye, millet, barley, and corn. Read nutrition labels on breads and cereals to make the healthiest purchase.

Add vitamin A. During menopause, vitamin A can help counteract dry skin and fight bothersome yeast infections. Also a powerful antioxidant, it helps prevent cancer. Most women over 50 need 2,300 IU (international units) or 700 RAE (retinol activity equivalents) of vitamin A every day. You get it naturally in the form of beta carotene in foods. Dark green and yellow-orange vegetables are good sources.

Count on calcium. Even though one study suggests bone loss can reach 1 percent per year during menopause, getting more calcium may fight this. Remember, you also need vitamin D because it plays an important role in how much calcium your bones actually absorb. Pour some low-fat or nonfat milk on vitamin-D-fortified cereal for a double dose of protection. What's more, some nutritionists say that calcium might help hot flashes, too. So, a glass of skim milk might keep you feeling cool long after you drink it.

While dairy is a great source of calcium, many dairy foods are full of fat. For some low-calorie high-calcium alternatives, eat spinach, beans, seeds, and almonds. For instance, you'll get up to 249 milligrams (mg) of calcium from one cup of turnip greens for just 29 calories. Try kale or Chinese cabbage (bok choy) for more calorie-scrimping calcium. But what if you crave something sweet? Check the labels of fortified orange juices for high calcium, a "no added sugar" claim, and low calories. One study found that drinking a cup of orange juice 30 minutes before a meal could help you feel more full and eat fewer calories — perhaps 300 fewer.

Depend on E. Vitamin E can reduce hot flashes and keep your skin soft and younger looking. If you drink lots of water while loading up on E, you might ease vaginal dryness, too. This nutrient also works like an antioxidant to keep cholesterol from damaging your arteries. Add E to your diet with nuts, seeds, avocados, canola oil, and low-fat creamy salad dressings. Boil a cup of frozen broccoli for a little over 3 mg of vitamin E — about 20 percent of the recommended daily allowance. Low-calorie turnip greens and mustard greens also pack in vitamin E. For a rare high-calorie treat, try almonds or sunflower seeds.

Build up your Bs. Vitamins B2, B6, and B12 are water-soluble vitamins your body flushes out daily. That means you need to replace them often. They help you turn food into energy; fight migraines, osteoporosis, and depression; and keep your heart healthy. Eat liver, mushrooms, whole grains, bananas, nuts, seeds, eggs, fish, and cauliflower.

Fill your glass wisely. Drink plenty of water, but filter it or use natural spring water. Unfiltered tap water is often contaminated with chemicals and bacteria. Don't drink diet soda and soft drinks. They are high in phosphorous, which can leech minerals from your bones. Plus, the sugar and synthetic sweeteners they contain have their own negative effects. Give up caffeine as soon as possible. Look for more natural ways to boost your energy. Limit alcohol to small amounts, and don't drink often.

Opt for healthy oils. Include extra-virgin olive oil in your diet. Snub hydrogenated oils, partially hydrogenated oils, and trans fatty acids, such as those in margarine. If a food includes a partially or fully hydrogenated oil in its label, try to find a substitute.

Pick the proper protein. Eat cold-water fish rich in omega-3 fatty acids for a super healthy protein punch. Salmon, mackerel, and albacore tuna are good examples. Add more protein-rich beans and peas to your diet for their hormone-regulators. Try chickpeas, lima beans, and kidney beans. Don't be afraid to eat eggs, but do limit them to four a week. Eat meat sparingly. To start cutting back, serve up smaller portions of beef, poultry, and pork. One serving should be about the size of a deck of cards.

With this healthy arsenal of nutrition, you can minimize menopause symptoms now while building a healthier body for the years to come. Remember, every time you add nutritional superstars to your diet or reject those that are bad for you, you rev up your body's defenses. A stronger body will go a long way toward protecting you against health risks and unpleasant menopausal symptoms.

HERBS HEAL MENOPAUSAL SYMPTOMS

If you and your doctor have decided hormone therapy is simply wrong for you — physically or emotionally — then explore these alternative therapies that are, after all, the source of many traditional medications.

Cool down with cohosh. If hot flashes and mood swings are bothering you, black cohosh could be just the thing you need. Once called squaw root, Native Americans used this plant for thousands of years to treat female problems. The German equivalent of the Food and Drug Administration approved black cohosh for menopause symptoms years ago. Today, doctors in Germany often prescribe black cohosh to treat PMS symptoms as well as anxiety, mild depression, and sweating in menopausal women. The plant has an estrogen-like effect, and reduces levels of a hormone that causes hot flashes — although relief could take four to six weeks. What's more, a recent German study found that black cohosh taken twice a day may improve physical and emotional menopause symptoms.

Hot flashes are a problem for breast cancer survivors, too, especially those on tamoxifen. A recent study discovered that two months of daily black cohosh may not help hot flashes in breast cancer survivors, but it might ease sweating.

Keep in mind that black cohosh may give some women a mild upset stomach. Large doses may even cause nausea and dizziness. Until long-term safety studies can be done, don't take black cohosh for more than six months.

You'll find it in capsules where supplements are sold. Try taking 40 milligrams (mg) a day, but not for longer than six months.

Vanquish insomnia with valerian. A recent German study found that valerian extract may relieve mild insomnia. In earlier studies, valerian users reported that they got to sleep faster and slept better.

In the U.S., capsules containing 400 to 530 milligrams (mg) of whole ground valerian root are generally taken 30 to 60 minutes before bedtime. You may also find capsules of a root extract, liquid extracts, and tinctures. If you prefer a tea, use one teaspoon of dried root per cup.

While pregnancy probably is not a concern if you're menopausal, remember that valerian is sometimes used to treat uterine contractions.

Stay dry with evening primrose oil. Studies have found that evening primrose oil might reduce night sweats although it does not seem to control hot flashes. No one knows whether it is safe to use for long periods, so if you try this herb, just take it for a short time to see if it helps. Never take evening primrose oil with nonsteroidal anti-inflammatory drugs (NSAIDs) or anticonvulsant drugs.

Rely on St. John. Hippocrates, of ancient Greece, recommended the popular herb St. John's wort for menstrual problems. Over two thousand years later, menopausal women still use it to feel better physically and sexually. Best of all, it comes with very few side effects. Although you may have to stay out of strong sun to avoid a rash, people rarely show allergic reactions.

Be sure the supplement you buy is a reputable brand and contains 0.3 percent hypericin, the active ingredient. The usual dosage is 300 mg, three times daily. Talk to your doctor about using St. John's wort for longer than a few weeks.

Don't single out dong quai. Dong quai is an ancient Chinese remedy for feminine complaints. Yet a six-month study found that dong quai alone may not help hot flashes or night sweats. Chinese herbalists argue that dong quai is not supposed to work alone. They say it must be part of a combination of herbs that must work together to be effective. Although herbal combinations are on the market, none have been tested.

Dong quai may cause bleeding in some people, especially those taking warfarin. It also makes your skin sensitive, so anyone using this herb should stay out of the sun.

Review red clover. A small Dutch study reported over 40 percent fewer hot flashes with a daily red clover supplement containing 80 mg of isoflavones. On the other hand, two small clinical trials in Australia found no benefit from red clover. But red clover may affect more than just menopause symptoms.

Some experts think red clover may lower the higher cardiovascular risk that follows menopause. Although studies suggest

HORMONE REPLACEMENT THERAPY FOR MEN

The male sex hormone doesn't take a plunge at mid-life like estrogen does. For men, testosterone gradually drops 30 to 40 percent starting around the late 40s. Some recent studies suggest that men can stay happier, stronger, and leaner by taking testosterone supplements to make up for their naturally declining hormone levels.

Men taking testosterone definitely report a stronger sex drive and an overall better mood. The supplements also lowered their cholesterol levels, and urine tests showed that the men lost less bone mass.

What's the down side? The men's prostate specific antigen (PSA) levels rose, and that's a red flag for prostate cancer.

Large studies on the safety and effectiveness of taking testosterone are underway. For now, talk to your doctor if you believe your sex drive and your quality of life are waning. If tests show you have low testosterone levels, you may be able to experiment with supplements as long as you keep a close watch on your PSA levels.

red clover does not lower cholesterol, it may help your blood vessels stretch more easily. No one knows whether that means a lower risk of death from heart disease, but more flexible arteries may shrink the risk of heart trouble.

Red clover contains several isoflavones including genistein and daidzein. Initial research studies suggest that genistein could be connected to breast cancer tumor growth, senility, brain aging, and slowed thyroid activity. More research is needed to confirm or disprove these findings.

The University of Pittsburgh Cancer Institute recently discovered that red clover may also have high estrogenic activity — a possible risk for breast cancer. If your family history or personal history includes breast cancer, don't try red clover.

Make sure you ask your doctor before trying herbs. You'll enjoy herbal benefits even more when you know they're safe to take.

STUDY THE SOY ISSUE

When menopause steals your estrogen, replace it with plant sources. Also called phytoestrogens, these can give you some of the protective benefits of natural estrogen. Good sources include oats, wheat, corn, apples, almonds, cashews, and peanuts.

A specific kind of phytoestrogen, called isoflavones, is found mostly in soy-based foods like soybeans, tofu, miso, and soy nuts. Asian women eat about one type of soy food every day and report very few hot flashes and mood swings during menopause. This could mean they're getting some estrogen from their diet.

Unfortunately, experts have concerns. Although some research shows soy helps your heart and prevents osteoporosis, other studies suggest it makes your brain age faster. The latest buzz is the more soy you eat, the greater your risk of developing senility.

Talk to your doctor about eating soy during menopause.

You can find out more about living an all-natural menopause by consulting a naturopathic physician (ND). These doctors specialize in alternative treatments — no drugs or surgeries. To find an ND near you, go to the Worldwide Directory of Naturopathic Practitioners, Colleges, and Organizations on the Internet at <www.naturopathics.com >. Or contact:

The American Association of Naturopathic Physicians
3201 New Mexico Ave NW
Suite 350
Washington D.C. 20016
866-538-2267
202-895-1392

HEART DISEASE RISK FACTORS

Age 55 or older
20 to 30 percent overweight
Excess weight around waist (apple-shaped)
Family history (especially a parent who had a heart attack at an
early age)
A high-stress lifestyle
Cigarette smoking
High blood cholesterol
High blood pressure
Diabetes
Physical inactivity

OSTEOPOROSIS RISK FACTORS

Being a Caucasian or Asian woman
Fair, pale skin color
Female relatives with osteoporosis
Menopause before age 40
Short and thin
Having no children
Drinking lots of alcohol or caffeine
Cigarette smoking
Low-calcium diet
High-salt or high-protein diet

BREAST CANCER RISK FACTORS

Strong family history (mother or sister with breast cancer)
High-fat diet
High-alcohol intake
Early puberty (before 13)
Late menopause (after 50)
Not having breast-fed any children

Melatonin is the master of your body's internal clock. The hormone produced in your brain only during the dark regulates your circadian rhythms, telling your body when to sleep and when to wake. Melatonin is a powerful antioxidant, too. That means it may keep your body's clock ticking a little longer so like the Eveready bunny, you can keep going and going.

MELATONIN

In 1985, a team of researchers led by Dr. Georges Maestroni began a ground-breaking study that produced strong evidence for melatonin's power to lengthen the life span. Maestroni and company took 20 middle-aged mice and plopped them into a tightly controlled lab environment. All the mice received exactly equal treatment — except for one thing. Half of them drank water laced with melatonin.

After five months (that's 15 years in a human life), the no-melatonin mice were looking old. They were frail and hump-backed, with dry, patchy hair. They also moved a lot slower.

But the other group resembled the characters in the movie *Cocoon*. They appeared to have found the fountain of youth. They were running around their cages, full of energy.

Even more astonishing was their longevity. The mice that were given melatonin lived an average of 20 percent longer than the other mice.

This important breakthrough opened the door for more research into melatonin as an anti-aging hormone. Other scientists since then have shown that low melatonin levels speed up aging. Researchers have even removed the pineal glands in the brains of rats. That's the gland that makes melatonin. Young rats without a pineal gland will start to show signs of aging within days.

You can't always assume that human bodies react the same way that rats do, but scientists do know that just like rats, humans produce less and less melatonin as they get older.

7 WAYS MELATONIN FIGHTS AGING

Did you know that the free-radical-fighting antioxidants you find in your fruits, vegetables, and vitamin supplements are also produced naturally by your body? Melatonin is one of the strongest antioxidants known to man, and it's produced by the pineal gland, deep inside your brain. That's one thing that makes melatonin so potent, experts say. It's created and released in the brain — right where free radicals do their worst damage.

Natural sleeping pill. Melatonin regulates your body's internal clock, or circadian system. Light stops your pineal gland from working, so melatonin is only made in darkness.

That's why people who work at night often have difficulty keeping on a sleep schedule. It's also why jet lag is such a problem for people who fly across several time zones. Some airports are considering installing full-spectrum lights to simulate the sun. The lights would stop melatonin production and help weary travelers reset their internal clocks for the day.

Everyone has difficulty falling asleep now and then, and it usually has nothing to do with melatonin. But for some regular insomniacs, the problem could well be that their bodies don't produce enough melatonin. Without that substance, your body doesn't realize it's time to sleep. Melatonin supplements may be a natural sleeping pill for these people.

Protects the brain? Free radicals are produced when your body uses oxygen. Since the brain is one of the biggest consumers of oxygen in the body, there's a natural pipeline of free radicals to the brain. Like bad neighbors moving into the house next door, these free radicals move into the brain and decide they like the area.

Brain tissue is full of unsaturated fatty acids and is rich in iron. Both of these substances act like free-radical magnets, attracting large quantities to the brain. Then, you can't get the free-radical rabble to leave, and they lower the property value.

Free radicals kill brain cells, and once the damage is done, there is no way for your body to repair the cells or make new ones. The kinds of cells targeted by free radicals control every mental function of your body, and free-radical damage is now believed to play a role in most brain disorders. You may not be surprised to learn that higher melatonin levels have been linked to a lower risk of developing Alzheimer's disease.

Another aspect of melatonin that makes it so valuable is its ability to cross the blood-brain barrier. Because the brain is so important, the body has developed this natural defense against foreign substances. While it doesn't keep out everything (such as free radicals), it does a good job of keeping many harmful substances away from the brain.

It also does a good job of keeping most antioxidants away. But melatonin crosses the blood-brain barrier with ease. Melatonin goes right from the pineal gland into blood vessels in the brain where it spreads to the entire body.

Tranquilizes your ticker? Melatonin may protect you from heart attacks. During the night, when the hormone is at its highest levels, your heart beats slower, blood pressure falls, and the level of cholesterol in your bloodstream dips. Fewer heart attacks happen during these hours.

And it's not just because you're asleep. Even people who stay awake during the night have these heart-healthy changes when darkness comes and melatonin levels increase.

But as your body prepares for the day and melatonin levels drop, usually around 6 a.m., your blood pressure picks back up, and your heart begins to beat a little faster. Getting revved up for the day puts you at greater risk for a heart attack. In fact, some doctors call the hours between 6 a.m. and noon the "heart attack zone."

The researchers think that melatonin may help your heart by affecting the part of your brain that controls blood pressure and heart rate.

Keeps clogged arteries open? Like all the antioxidants, melatonin may help keep cholesterol levels low and arteries clear. Studies show that people with clogged arteries have lower levels of melatonin in their blood.

Other research shows that melatonin keeps your platelets from clumping together to form deadly clots. During the day, when melatonin levels are lowest and your body is more likely to need platelets to stop blood flow from an injury, platelets are stickier and clump easier. At night, when melatonin is flowing freely, platelets get slicker and less clumpy.

Eases arrhythmia? About 40,000 people die in the United States each year because their heartbeats are so irregular that their hearts can't pump enough blood to their bodies. Doctors call this arrhythmia, and it is caused by a disruption of the electrical signals from the brain to the heart. One study determined that melatonin made the heart less likely to fall into arrhythmia. Arrhythmia is more likely to occur during the day, when melatonin levels are low.

A new cancer weapon? No medical miracles yet, but melatonin looks promising in cancer research labs.

Ten years ago, two researchers sprinkled melatonin into test tubes filled with human breast cancer cells. The melatonin blocked the cell's growth by 75 percent.

The scientists were astonished to find that huge amounts of melatonin didn't stop the cancer — only small amounts. You would think that the more, the better — but just the opposite is true. The best dose seems to be what the body normally produces in younger people (you produce less as you age). And melatonin seems to work even better when the dose is increased and decreased on a 24-hour cycle just like the circadian rhythm produces in your body.

While it's too early to say that taking melatonin supplements will prevent breast cancer, some doctors say it may make the breast cancer drug tamoxifen more effective.

For men, melatonin offers some hope in the battle against prostate cancer. Prostate cancer is similar to breast cancer.

WHAT THE SKEPTICS SAY

Some sleep specialists have called people taking melatonin "unwitting subjects in a large-scale uncontrolled experiment." Most medical experts are skeptical about the new "wonder drug."

Why? Because many of the studies have been in animals rather than humans, and we don't always react to drugs the same way animals do. Plus, different studies have had different results. Scientists have urged the National Institutes of Health to begin a trial to determine if melatonin is safe and effective.

One concern is that people may take melatonin instead of going to the doctor right away when they have insomnia. Insomnia can be a symptom of some other illness, so always see your doctor when you have trouble sleeping.

Also, no studies reveal how melatonin interacts with other drugs. That might be a problem for people taking prescription or over-the-counter medicines.

In some studies, melatonin seems to be linked with constriction of the blood vessels to the heart and brain. That could decrease blood flow — a serious problem.

So if the medical community isn't completely sold on melatonin, why is it available? Because it is marketed as a food supplement rather than a drug. Food supplements aren't subjected to strenuous testing by the Food and Drug Administration. As long as the product makers don't advertise any health claims, they are free to distribute the product.

The bottom line: Melatonin is most likely to help you fight circadian rhythm disturbances, such as jet lag or sleep problems if you work the night shift. Some researchers have high hopes for other benefits, but they are unproven.

Both are associated with hormones — breast cancer with estrogen and prolactin, and prostate cancer with testosterone. Some studies show that people with either form of cancer have unusually low levels of melatonin. Melatonin has also helped some people with cancer relax, sleep better, and gain weight.

Improves your mood? Many people who take melatonin report that it lightens their moods or produces euphoria. These reports have spurred researchers to take a close look at the role of melatonin in depression.

The first piece of evidence is that many depressed people have low melatonin levels. Researchers have also studied the level of melatonin in the pineal glands of suicide victims. Compared with people who died suddenly or violently through murder or accident, suicide victims had significantly lower levels of melatonin. The difference was greatest when death occurred at night, when levels of melatonin should be at their highest.

While this is only indirect evidence, it becomes more significant when you consider that many of today's antidepressant drugs stimulate the production of melatonin.

One note of caution: If you have the winter blues, a melatonin supplement may make your depression worse. Many people get sleepy, hungry, tired, and edgy during the winter. It's called Seasonal Affective Disorder, or SAD, and it appears to be linked to the decrease in daylight hours during winter. People who have the disorder respond well to light therapy, perhaps because light stops the body's production of melatonin.

If you suffer from panic disorder or schizophrenia, you might also want to stay away from melatonin. People with these diseases tend to have high levels of the hormone.

YOUR ACTION PLAN

There are two ways to increase the level of melatonin in your body — eat certain foods and take supplements.

HOW TO GET MORE MELATONIN NATURALLY

You can increase your melatonin naturally by changing what you eat, say melatonin experts. Start eating more whole grains, legumes, nuts, milk, meat, fish, poultry, and eggs. These foods don't contain melatonin, but they contain the amino acid tryptophan. The body converts tryptophan into serotonin and finally to melatonin. Eating any of these foods about an hour before bedtime may increase your melatonin and help you sleep better.

Some foods that contain melatonin are oats, sweet corn, rice, ginger, tomatoes, bananas, and barley.

Whole grains and milk might be your best bet for better sleep, since they are more easily digested.

Other ways to increase your melatonin levels naturally are:

- ❦ Keep your bedroom very dark.
- ❦ Get eight hours of sleep every night.
- ❦ Get plenty of sunshine during the day.

DO YOU NEED SUPPLEMENTS?

Most experts don't think you should take melatonin supplements, but others believe the possible health benefits outweigh the potential risks. Supplements are easy to find. Check your local health food store or buy through mail order. You can even find melatonin at discount stores. You don't need a prescription.

Some doctors recommend up to 20 milligrams (mg) a day to stimulate your immune system and up to 50 mg to help you sleep. Other experts say doses higher than 3 mg may be harmful.

Melatonin expert Dr. Russel J. Reiter, Professor of Neuroendocrinology at the University of Texas Health Sciences Center at San Antonio, takes a 1 mg tablet before going to bed. Most doctors who prescribe melatonin advise taking a very small dose — 0.1 to 1 mg at bedtime. You may need to divide your tablets to get a dose under 1 mg.

For jet lag, take up to 5 mg on the first day you arrive. Take the dose an hour before bedtime, local time.

THE WISE MELATONIN CONSUMER

It may surprise you to learn that synthetic melatonin is recommended over the natural product. They are chemically identical, but natural melatonin is extracted from the pineal glands of animals. There is no way to know what other brain substances are contained in the pills. Synthetic melatonin is safer.

You can buy several different kinds of melatonin pills. Some are slow release, some are fast release, and some dissolve under your tongue. One kind may help you sleep better than the others, so you may want to experiment. The kind that dissolves under your tongue should get into your bloodstream faster, and the slow-release kind should stay at a more even level throughout the night.

MELATONIN CAUTIONS

Remember: Don't take melatonin during the day. It could make you drowsy, and it doesn't make sense to take melatonin at a time your body doesn't naturally produce it.

If you feel tired when you wake up, you may be taking too much. Everyone metabolizes melatonin differently, so what your friend takes could be too much for you.

Only mild side effects have been reported — mainly occasional stomach cramping and sleepiness. No toxicity has been noted, even at high doses. Melatonin is not addictive.

Though melatonin is generally safe, it is a powerful hormone that can cause changes in several body systems. Because of that, several groups of people shouldn't take melatonin supplements:

❦ Women who are pregnant, breast-feeding, or trying to become pregnant.

❦ People taking cortisone medications.

❦ People with kidney disease.

❦ People with any autoimmune disease like lupus or rheumatoid arthritis.

You probably won't find pine bark and grape seeds in the produce section of your local grocery but maybe you should. These plant products pack a potent punch against aging and disease. They can boost circulation, knock out free radicals, protect you from heart disease, and give you younger-looking skin. Part of a family of semi-essential nutrients called bioflavonoids, pine bark and grape seed extract belong to a small group originally known as pycnogenols and now called proanthocyanidins or procyanidolic oligomers — PCO for short. Researchers began studying PCO in the 1950s after a trip back in time tipped them off to its value.

Pycnogenol
(Grape Seed Extract)

In December 1534, French explorer Jacques Cartier and his crew traveled up the St. Lawrence River in Canada and became trapped by ice. With only salted meat and biscuits to eat, they soon began to experience symptoms of scurvy — a severe vitamin C deficiency. Nearly a quarter of the men died and more than half were seriously affected by this debilitating illness before a Quebec Indian told them about a tea made from tree bark.

The debilitated crew rapidly recovered after drinking the tea and using poultices made from it. Why? The bark contained vitamin C plus PCO, which helps the nutrient work faster and better.

Some 400 years later, a French researcher, Jacques Masquelier, read Cartier's account and started studying pine bark. He discovered that the maritime pine, or Bordeaux pine, in southern France was a rich source of this substance. In 1951, Masquelier patented a method of extracting PCO from pine bark.

What's in a name? The term Pycnogenol is now a registered trademark of a Swiss company that sells PCO supplements. It specifically refers to pine bark extract from maritime pine from Quebec and southern coastal France. But you can find PCO in lemon tree bark, peanuts, cranberries, and citrus peels, and in smaller amounts in foods like apples, onions, tea, and blueberries, as well as in grape seeds.

In fact, PCO from grape seeds, or grape seed extract, is cheaper and even more potent than that from pine bark. Plus, most research on PCO has been done on grape seed extract.

Regardless of the source, PCO may prove a mighty ally in battling conditions common to aging including hardening of the arteries, stroke, heart disease, varicose veins, and diabetic circulation problems. As a bonus, PCO may keep you looking younger because it acts as an antioxidant to protect your skin from the sun and other environmental assaults. And it helps rebuild your skin, too.

5 WAYS PCO FIGHTS AGING

Antioxidant armor. PCO helps two other antioxidant nutrients, vitamins C and E, block free radicals. And, as you know, free radicals may be the culprits in some 60 diseases that doctors can't pin on germs, including heart disease, cataracts, arthritis, allergies, diabetes, liver disease, and perhaps even cancer.

By helping your body better use vitamin C, PCO protects this essential vitamin and, indirectly, aids vitamin E also. PCO stops free radicals from shutting down vitamin C and even converts injured vitamin C back to normal. In turn, vitamin C renews vitamin E that's surrendered to free radicals and protects vitamin E from further harm.

PCO acts on its own, as well, to disarm free radicals. In laboratory experiments, Japanese researchers found the nutrient was 20 times more powerful than vitamin E and 50 times more

Pycnogenol is the trade name of pine bark extract from the Bordeaux, or maritime, pine that grows along the southern coast of France. The extract contains PCO, which acts as an antioxidant in your body to help prevent several common diseases of aging.

BORDEAUX, OR MARITIME, PINE

powerful than vitamin C at trapping free radicals. In fact, some researchers believe the PCO found in grapes should get credit for the way wine seems to protect you from heart disease.

Circulation superstar. Acting as an antioxidant isn't PCO's only role in health. Europeans have been using it for more than two decades to promote healthy blood vessels and treat circulation disorders. Here's why:

First, PCO strengthens collagen, the basic building block of our skin, tendons, ligaments, and cartilage, as well as a major part of the "intercellular cement" that fills the space between every cell in our body. Strong collagen is especially important for blood vessels — and critical in the tiniest of blood vessels called capillaries.

Capillaries carry oxygen and nutrients to the cells and take away waste. Without them, cells would starve or drown in their own waste. Only one cell thick, capillaries are reinforced with collagen and depend on it to keep them strong enough to do their work.

PCO not only supports vitamin C, needed to make collagen, but it also sticks to collagen, making it even stronger. Think of it as steel reinforcement for your circulatory system. This is important because if a capillary develops a hole it's a prime target for a free radical attack. And leaky capillaries also mean cells don't get the nourishment they need to be healthy.

By strengthening weak blood vessels, PCO helps prevent bruising and improves circulation in the legs to prevent swelling, pain, and varicose veins.

Reinforcing artery walls also helps prevent injuries to the walls that may cause hardening of the arteries. Once arteries are damaged they tend to collect fat and cholesterol deposits, which narrow the passage, making it more difficult for blood to get through.

Plus, PCO also seems to stop blood from getting sticky and clotting — another way it can help you ward off heart attack or stroke. Finally, the blood-vessel-building power of PCO can help prevent the type of stroke caused when arteries burst or leak.

Protects vision, especially for diabetics. For a lot of people, when they get older, the capillaries supplying blood to the eyes weaken and rupture. That's one of the main reasons you lose your eyesight as you age. People with diabetes are very likely to have this problem. It's called diabetic retinopathy.

Since PCO strengthens the capillaries, it can decrease this bleeding considerably.

Even people with normal eyesight apparently benefit from PCO. Night vision and after-glare vision improved considerably in a group of healthy volunteers who took PCO.

Younger-looking skin. As you age, your skin becomes thinner. The layer under the surface loses fat, causing the outer layer to sag. The skin fibers, once elastic, lose the ability to bounce back. In short, you get wrinkles.

Skin counts on collagen for strength, elasticity, and smoothness. The older you get, the more free radicals have battered the collagen in your skin. To make things worse, you somehow let your natural defenses slip against two enzymes that damage collagen even further. To the rescue: PCO, which not only halts free radical damage but binds to the collagen to prevent deterioration by enzymes. Plus, it can even return collagen fibers to their youthful, undamaged state. It's like a cosmetic you put *in* instead of *on*.

This free-radical fighter can also protect your skin from further damage from the ultra-violet radiation of the sun. One laboratory study in Finland showed that 35 percent more skin cells survived sunlight exposure when protected by PCO.

Europeans can already buy "anti-aging" creams containing PCO. Look for a burst of PCO skin care products over here once the American cosmetics industry discovers the benefits of this bioflavonoid. Many companies are already touting products with antioxidants, but PCO's chemical structure makes it penetrate your skin more easily. This may make PCO products more effective than those containing vitamins C and E.

Keeps swelling down. PCO may be helpful in inflammatory diseases such as arthritis, lupus, colitis, and hepatitis, but no one knows this for sure because researchers haven't studied PCO's effect on these illnesses.

Many people believe it helps reduce swelling caused by allergies — especially hay fever. PCO cuts down on the amount of histamine you make. That's the stuff responsible for your swelling nasal passages and watery eyes. In Finland, PCO is a very popular allergy remedy.

Combine the power to stop swelling with the power to repair connective tissue and you come up with a mighty good way to prevent inflammation and swelling from a soft-tissue injury like a sprained ankle or knee. That's why some sports doctors recommend athletes take PCO regularly.

YOUR ACTION PLAN

Most Europeans buy PCO in the form of grape seed extract. Here in the United States, mainly because of aggressive marketing, pine bark extract called Pycnogenol is more popular. Both contain PCO but grape seeds are a more potent source. Plus, the process for getting PCO out of grape seeds is cheaper. That makes grape seed extract much less expensive than that from pine bark.

HOW MUCH IS ENOUGH?

If you decide to take PCO for a specific ailment such as heart disease or allergies, experts say you should start by taking 100 to 150 milligrams (mg) daily for one to several weeks. Then switch to a maintenance dose of 50 mg a day.

People who want to add more antioxidants to their diet should take 50 mg a day. Take it daily because you don't store it in your body.

PCO appears to be completely safe even in very large doses, as long as you're not allergic to pine.

How to get more PCO naturally

You can also eat PCO-containing foods such as citrus fruits, tea, onions, apples, blueberries, peanuts, and cranberries for a lot less money than buying a supplement.

Do you need supplements?

If you want to be sure of the amount of PCO you're getting, you can buy capsules or tablets containing 20 to 100 mg of the substance at your local health food store.

The wise PCO consumer

Check to see that the PCO supplement contains a standardized amount of proanthocyanidins from either pine bark or grape seeds. Supplements called Pycnogenol will contain only pine bark extract. Others will be labeled "grape seed extract" or a trade name like Grapenol from the Solaray company. Some products, like one from Source Natural, contain both pine bark and grape seed extracts.

Expect to pay about $20 for 30 capsules containing 50 mg of Pycnogenol. A comparable bottle of grape seed extract tablets or capsules will cost you about $9.

PCO cautions

Unfortunately, some companies overzealously market PCO and make dubious claims about its benefits. Salespeople may promote it for diseases like AIDS, Alzheimer's, arthritis, and cancer. Because no research has been published to prove PCO's benefit in treating these serious diseases, the National Council Against Health Fraud warns consumers not to be swayed by advertising claims, saying that the value and safety of specific antioxidants, such as PCO, are still in question.

SUPER LIFE EXTENDERS

To lengthen thy life, lessen thy meals.
Benjamin Franklin

Benjamin Franklin may have known 200 years ago what scientists are now confirming. Restricting your calories may not only make you slimmer and more attractive, it may help you live longer. Though the weight debate continues in the scientific community, evidence is mounting that subtracting calories may add years to your life.

CALORIC RESTRICTION

Scientists have long compared different populations and cultures for clues to longevity. The people of Japan have a strong reputation for longevity, so they are often studied by aging experts. In Okinawa, 40 times as many people live to be over 100 as in the rest of Japan. Okinawans are also about one-half to two-thirds less likely to suffer from cancer, stroke, heart disease, and other chronic diseases than other Japanese people. Scientists looked at the eating habits of Okinawans for an explanation and found that they eat, on average, about 20 percent fewer calories than their fellow countrymen. This is one argument for caloric restriction as a life-prolonging strategy.

Numerous studies have shown that caloric restriction can extend the life spans of laboratory animals. For example, in one study, mice were fed 40 percent less than they normally would eat. This caloric restriction extended their life spans by 30 to 40 percent. That would mean an extra 22 to 30 years for people!

The only caloric restriction experiment on humans so far occurred accidentally in the Biosphere 2 experiment, in which eight people were sealed in a closed ecological environment for two years. Their food-producing efforts weren't as fruitful as they had planned, so they were forced to live on a limited number of calories until their two years were up. Luckily, the doctor for the team was Roy L. Walford of the University of California at Los Angeles, a prominent aging and caloric restriction expert. He helped his team members maintain proper nutrition while consuming fewer calories. The results — eight members lost a substantial amount of weight (not too surprising), but they also lowered their cholesterol levels, blood pressures, glucose levels, and white blood cell counts. These results were exactly the same seen in rodents involved in caloric restriction experiments. The life-extending results found in rats on calorie-restricted diets may indeed affect humans the same way.

No one knows for sure why caloric restriction slows the aging process, but there are several theories. One theory is that caloric restriction slows the rate of cell division in tissues. Since some scientists think that aging is controlled by a preset number of cell divisions, this would lead to a longer life.

Another theory is that caloric restriction slows aging by lowering glucose (sugar) levels. This would slow the damage to proteins in your body caused by glucose and allow you to live longer.

The leading theory, however, goes along with the leading theory on the cause of aging — free radicals. When your body breaks down food to be used for energy, more free radicals are created. This can cause damage to cells that will eventually lead to more rapid aging.

Caloric restriction as an anti-aging strategy in people may not be practical. For one thing, people are not known for their ability to resist tempting calorie-laden foods. For another, caloric restriction will only work if adequate levels of nutrition are met, making it an even more difficult plan to follow.

Studies on caloric restriction continue. Perhaps in the future, it will become an accepted method of delaying the aging process.

4 WAYS CALORIC RESTRICTION FIGHTS AGING

You may have heard that a little extra weight in your golden years can be beneficial, but most studies find that being overweight can shorten your life substantially. Maintaining a healthy weight protects you from many conditions that could shorten your life, and limiting your calories will help keep your weight under control.

Lowers the boom on high blood pressure. Can you picture what 2.5 billion pounds looks like? That's approximately how much excess weight people in the United States are lugging around. High blood pressure is the most common chronic disease in the United States. Coincidence? No weigh. Next to a blood pressure cuff, your weight is the strongest indicator of what your blood pressure is. But if so many people are living with high blood pressure, it can't be a very serious problem, right? Wrong. High blood pressure is a major contributor to such life-threatening conditions as heart disease, stroke, and kidney failure. Many people with high blood pressure must take medicine every day to help keep it under control. Up to half of these people could stop taking these drugs if they would just drop some weight. Studies have found that even people who lose a modest amount of weight can lower their blood pressures.

Trims down cancer risk. Carrying excess weight on your body may make you more likely to fall prey to cancer. One study found that an extra 10 pounds can increase a woman's risk of breast cancer by almost 25 percent, and an extra 20 pounds more than doubles the risk. Men aren't exempt from the cancer-causing dangers of excess weight either. Overweight men are 50 to 70 percent more likely to develop prostate cancer and colorectal cancer than other men.

Eases risk of heart disease. Lighten the weight on your body, and you lighten the load on your heart. Excess weight contributes to heart disease and makes many of the other factors that contribute to heart disease worse, like high blood pressure and high cholesterol. According to one study, each 10 percent decrease in a man's body weight resulted in a 20 percent reduction in his risk of heart disease.

Helps you dodge diabetes. If you are carrying around excess pounds, you may be just asking to develop type 2 (noninsulin-dependent) diabetes. Extra weight and diabetes seem to go hand-in-hand. In fact, the more overweight you are, the greater your risk. If you are only mildly overweight, you are twice as likely to get diabetes as someone who maintains a healthy weight. If you are moderately overweight, you are five times as likely to develop diabetes, and if you are severely overweight, you are 10 times more likely to develop this serious disease.

YOUR ACTION PLAN

One expert says that a reasonable caloric restriction plan for humans would be to take in about one gram of protein and no more than half a gram of fat for each kilogram (2.2 pounds) of your body weight. Sound too complicated for you? How about eating fresh, nutritious foods; limiting your fat and calories; and getting plenty of exercise? If you do that, you should eventually reach a healthy, slim, life-extending weight.

CALORIC RESTRICTION CAUTIONS

Because of the danger of malnutrition, caloric restriction is not recommended without a doctor's guidance. If you do choose to try caloric restriction as an anti-aging strategy, remember these guidelines:

❦ Cut back on calories slowly, particularly if you are older.

❦ Don't make your caloric restriction so severe that you fall below 25 percent of your set point (the natural amount your body tends to weigh).

❦ Make sure you get all the nutrients you need. Calories should be the only thing you cut.

❦ No one under the age of 20 should engage in caloric restriction. It could result in growth abnormalities.

❦ About 1,800 to 2,000 calories a day is probably what the average-size person on a calorie-restricted diet should take in.

❦ A multivitamin and mineral supplement may be necessary to maintain proper nutrient levels.

"The closest thing to an anti-aging pill that exists."
Drs. Ronald Klatz and Robert Goldman, Stopping the Clock

When you're young, exercise is an option. After age 40, though, it's essential if you want to avoid the slow decline into old age. But it's never too late to start. In fact, researchers say that older people's bodies respond even better to exercise than young people's. Much of what people call aging is actually lack of use, according to Richard Sprott, associate director of the Biology of Aging Program at the National Institute on Aging (NIA). Regular exercise, no matter when you begin, increases your body's oxygen use and can reverse 20 years of aging!

EXERCISE

There's no such thing as a typical mature adult. One 75-year-old can barely walk a quarter of a mile while another runs seven miles a day and enters marathons for fun. You will get older (if you're lucky), but most of what you consider "aging" is a matter of lifestyle choices.

The Smiths are a couple who made a choice to stay young through exercise. In 1989, when an invitation to his 50th high school reunion came, S. David Smith and his wife, Mabel Dunkirk Smith, decided to make the nearly 2,500-mile trip by bike. Both retired music teachers, he was 68, she was 62. They rode 30 days, averaging about 80 miles a day on the 40-day trip, stopping to camp and visit friends along the way.

"We got the prize for coming the longest way," recalls Smith.

The couple, who live in Morristown, Tenn., began bicycling in graduate school nearly 20 years earlier. They also rode bikes when they toured Europe, but the reunion trip was their first really long ride. Since then, they've completed a long ride every year, biking across Tennessee several times, down the East Coast, and from Canada to Mexico.

Today, at the ages of 70 and 76, the Smiths keep in shape walking and swimming, as well as biking 12 miles to the closest town on errands. Mabel takes aerobics classes, too. "Sometimes when it's nippy we go and walk in the malls," she adds. "If you don't use it, you lose it."

If you find the Smith's example more daunting than inspiring, you're not alone. Most older people are more like Mrs. Mendez, a 73-year-old who, although in good overall health, is overweight and relatively immobile. Result? She has such poor balance that she relies on her son to do her grocery shopping out of the fear she'll fall.

Starting an exercise program is really a challenge for someone like Mrs. Mendez — but it's not impossible. Anyone with strength enough to pick up this book and the mental power to understand these words can stage a physical comeback. The action plan outlined below is just for you.

Even people as old as 96 can increase muscle strength and size by 200 percent in just eight weeks, research shows. And the worse shape you're in, the more you can improve.

NIA's Sprott offers this encouragement: "Most people can do a lot more than they think they can," he says. "Believing you can do something is often more than half of what it takes to get there."

INCREASE YOUR HEALTH SPAN

Increasing your life span and your health span are the two goals of any good anti-aging program. Like most of the other methods you'll find in this book, exercise does both. But it excels at increasing your health span — helping you to feel good every day and improving your quality of life. Exercise can bring back a satisfying sex life, a good night's rest, less tiring days, a happier feeling about life, fewer visits to your doctor, and less fear of the diseases of age — heart disease, arthritis, stroke, emphysema, osteoporosis, diabetes, and even cancer.

But it all depends on what you do right now — this week — not what you did 20 years ago. Exercising when you're young has very little effect on the way you feel as you age because you don't store exercise benefits. In fact, one study showed it was better to have been inactive at college but active in old age rather than the reverse.

And what you eat or what supplements you take can do absolutely nothing to make you physically stronger and younger if you don't exercise, too, according to a 1994 study on exercise and nutritional supplementation.

INCREASE YOUR LIFE SPAN

Apart from its disease-fighting powers, vigorous exercise can also increase your life span. A recent study at the Cooper Institute for Aerobics Research in Dallas showed that men who ran, walked briskly, swam, jogged, or played tennis lowered their risks of dying early by 64 percent.

Even men who had not exercised before but became fit during the five-year study reduced their risks of dying by 44 percent compared with men who didn't exercise.

10 WAYS EXERCISE FIGHTS AGING

Many elderly people aren't suffering from any serious illness but, nevertheless, are dependent on others, needing assistance simply to stand or walk to the bathroom. They've lost their muscle tone and seem to have "rusted out" like old pieces of machinery. Some researchers have named this common problem "sarcopenia" in hopes of getting more attention for it.

"Sarco" is Greek for body flesh and "penia" means reduced amount. Together they refer to the overall weakening of the body as muscle is replaced by fat over a course of decades. Beginning at age 40, if you're not physically active, you lose 6 percent of muscle, nearly 7 percent of heart function, and 8 percent of lung function every 10 years. These losses take a toll on your ability to live independently.

Plus, like a car that hasn't been maintained, you're likely to break down. A host of chronic diseases from heart disease to osteoporosis to high blood pressure are frequently blamed on old age but, in fact, are more often the result of misuse and abuse of the body.

But this extremely common condition in the elderly is not inevitable. Physical activity — muscle-building and aerobic exercise — is the remedy. It will help keep you self-reliant and able to perform everyday tasks for yourself in your own home. And it can ward off or improve the following discomforts and diseases associated with aging.

Tell arthritis pain to take a hike. "The weakest and oldest among us can be some kind of athlete; only the strongest survive as spectators; only the hardiest withstand the perils of inertia, inactivity, and immobility," writes Dr. John Bland, professor of medicine-rheumatology, emeritus at the University of Vermont.

Bland, along with many other doctors, says walking, bicycling, swimming, water exercises, weight training, and cross-country skiing are all excellent for people with arthritis. The exercises will increase your mobility and decrease your pain and stiffness. You should start slowly, take care to warm up, and rest joints that are red and inflamed.

Nearly all doctors agree that mild exercise is good for arthritis, but vigorous exercise has been more controversial. Now, however, new studies show that most people with arthritis can jog or do aerobic dance without further damaging their joints.

Of course, like almost every disease known to man, arthritis is complicated, so prescribing exercise is tricky. Not only are there different forms of arthritis, but people react differently to various medications, treatments, and exercise. That's why you need to talk to your doctor and tailor an exercise program to your individual body and your needs.

Warm up to exercise and cool down your cancer risk. Exercise may be a good defense against breast, uterine, and colon cancers, according to researchers. Why?

❦ **It reduces fat, a cancer risk factor.** Colon cancer risk, especially, seems to be boosted by too much weight and is lowered by exercise, according to one study. A weekly game of tennis or a couple of hours of brisk walking can drop your risk of developing colon cancer by 30 percent, according to the Harvard researchers who published the study. And those who exercised even more — running more than four hours a week or walking more than 12 — cut their risk by more than 50 percent!

❦ **It boosts your immune system.** Exercise stimulates white blood cells in your immune system called macrophages. These cells are your first line of defense against invaders like viruses and bacteria. Because exercise slightly damages soft tissue, macrophages are routinely called upon to repair the tissue. This may keep them in shape for fighting tumor cells, according to researchers.

❦ **It lowers the amount of estrogen in a woman's body — a culprit in breast and uterine cancers.** One recent study suggests that moderate, regular physical activity can cut a woman's risk of developing breast cancer by as much as 60 percent. The greatest benefit came from exercising four hours a week, but even two or three hours of exercise weekly appears to help.

❦ **It lowers your insulin levels.** Inactive people may be more likely to develop colon cancer because they have higher insulin levels than exercisers, say doctors who study the disease. Insulin, a hormone your body uses to help metabolize sugar, encourages tumors to grow in animal studies and perhaps in humans. Exercise reduces the amount of insulin your body needs because it makes you more sensitive to the hormone.

Bypass surgery, without doctors or hospitals. Do your legs ache and cramp when you exercise? One out of 10 people over 70 have claudication pain, and the cure is — exercise, or dangerous, expensive surgery to bypass those clogged arteries in your legs.

When you have claudication, you feel leg cramps and tingling and numbness in your feet when you walk because clogged arteries are cutting off the circulation to your lower legs.

Fortunately, you can heal yourself if you're willing to work at it. The prescription is walking, or using a treadmill or stair stepping machine. These exercises encourage your body to gradually build lesser-used "collateral" arteries to bypass the clogged ones. But you have to be committed to the program. Building the arteries takes a year, and they shrink again unless you keep exercising.

Studies show that walking works. Among exercisers with claudication, pain-free walking time increased a striking 134 percent! Here's the program:

- ❦ Walk or step until you're in pain.
- ❦ Rest until the pain stops.
- ❦ Resume exercise until you've walked or stepped for 30 minutes to an hour.

Huff and puff to raise HDL. Simply put, the more you exercise, the more of the good kind of cholesterol, called HDL, you'll have. This lowers your risk of having a heart attack. Men and women who run have higher levels of HDL. And the more they run, the more HDL they have.

So how much do you have to exercise to gain this benefit? One study concludes jogging seven to 14 miles a week at a pace of 10 to 11 minutes per mile gets you there. Another indicates women who run nine or more miles a week have significantly higher HDL levels. While brisk walking increases fitness, you need to do more than that to really build up the good-guy HDL.

Slow and steady will win diabetes race. Diabetes is the fastest growing chronic disease in the United States. Why? We are an aging and overweight society.

Fortunately, people with both insulin-dependent and noninsulin-dependent diabetes will benefit from exercise because physical activity helps the body use insulin more efficiently.

In fact, a 1996 study on Finnish men indicates that just 40 minutes a week of moderate exercise — not a day, but a week — can reduce your risk of developing type 2 diabetes. That level of exercise reduced the men's diabetes risk by 50 percent compared with nonexercisers. Men who exercised more than 40 minutes a week reduced their chances of developing diabetes by 64 percent.

Moderate exercise means slightly out of breath and some sweating, according to the report. Recommended exercises include brisk walking; slow swimming; light bicycling; easy aerobic dance; tennis; basketball; and exercise on treadmills or skiing, rowing, or stepping machines.

Because diabetes frequently causes eye and foot problems, ask your doctor's advice about setting up an exercise program if you are diabetic.

Hard muscles keep bones thick and strong. It's exercise, not just milk, that builds strong bones in older folks. Researchers from Tufts University's Center on Aging found that doing 45 minutes of weight-lifting exercises twice a week improves strength, bone density, and balance. Result? Fewer falls and fewer fractures.

Researchers say bones are like muscle — if you don't use them, you lose them. That means you need to work muscles that support your bones against a resistant force such as gravity. The stress builds up your bones. But you have to keep up the good work because as soon as the stress is gone, your bones start to break down.

Weight lifting is especially effective because it stresses muscles more than walking, jogging, or swimming. To build bone, you need to work hard. You should repeat each weight-lifting exercise eight to 12 times, take a brief rest, then do another set. If you can do more without a rest, then you're not working hard enough. You need to increase the amount of weight you're using.

Boost your mood and your creativity. You know it's smart to exercise, but did you know people who exercise are smarter? Physical exercise helps your brain function better. Research shows it can encourage creativity, speed your thinking, and even help you beat the blues.

By flooding the brain with more blood, aerobic exercise fuels brain cells with oxygen and nutrients. The blood flow even increases the number of connections between nerve cells in the brain. That may be why exercise can boost your reaction time and improve the speed at which you process information.

Exercise also increases certain brain chemicals that, in turn, stimulate the growth of new brain nerve cells.

Combining mental exercise with physical exercise may be the best way to stimulate the brain, experiments suggest. Learning a new aerobic dance step is a great example.

It can even improve your mood if you exercise hard enough, long enough. How much do you need? Thirty to 60 minutes of aerobic exercise increases the amount of a brain chemical called serotonin. And the more serotonin you have, the better your mood, according to researchers.

In fact, one study found aerobic exercise just as effective as psychotherapy in helping mild depression. Several studies have shown it to be one of the most effective strategies for getting people out of bad moods.

Plus, if you exercise longer than 60 minutes, it suppresses your sensitivity to pain. You get the "runner's high" that comes from another set of brain chemicals called endorphins.

Lower high blood pressure without pills. Walking, not running, may be the better exercise for lowering blood pressure, according to some studies. But jogging, bicycling, swimming, rowing, stair climbing, aerobic dancing, and even weight lifting are helpful to people whose blood pressure is slightly above normal.

Keep the following points in mind:

❦ Check with your doctor before beginning an exercise program if you have a blood pressure problem.

❦ Exercise boosts blood pressure so people with more than mild high blood pressure may need to control it with medication first.

❦ Never drink coffee and then exercise — caffeine raises your blood pressure, too.

❦ In weight training, lift lighter weights many times rather than heavier weights fewer times. Weights that are too heavy could raise your blood pressure dangerously high.

❦ Avoid isometric exercises where you tighten your muscles without moving a joint, such as pushing against a wall.

❦ Stick with it — results may take a few months.

Hearts that pump harder — during regular workouts — pump longer. Do you realize that exercise is just as important as quitting smoking for heart health? In fact, you can cut your heart attack risk in half just by walking 30 to 45 minutes three times a week.

Another important point: People with a family history of heart disease benefit from exercise just as much as those whose genes dealt them a better coronary hand, recent studies show.

Without exercise, your heart gradually loses its ability to circulate blood. One group of 12 men exercised under researchers' watchful eyes for 25 years. These men, most of them old when the study ended, had 60 percent better circulatory function than the average man. Plus, they had low blood pressure and body fat, so they were truly young at heart.

People who have already had heart attacks also benefit from exercise as long as they have their doctor's OK. Even exercising just their forearms helped men with chronic heart failure open their blood vessels so more blood could flow through, according to one recent study.

But if you're not a regular exerciser and you do have heart disease, you need to be careful not to overdo it when you start. Vigorous exercise, like snow shoveling, can cause heart attacks in people with heart disease who are usually inactive; smoke; or have high blood pressure, high cholesterol, or diabetes.

Put three city blocks between you and a stroke. Good news! You don't need to run a marathon to reduce your risk of stroke. Walking just three blocks a day lowered risk 30 percent and walking a mile (about five blocks) cut risk in half for men between the ages of 50 and 60 in one recent study.

This seems to be true even if you smoke or have high blood pressure or diabetes, say researchers. Imagine how much good it can do you if you don't have those other risk factors.

YOUR ACTION PLAN

You've probably heard a lot of different advice about what you need to do to get in shape. That's because certain types of exercise carry certain health benefits. For example, huffing and puffing for 20 minutes or more will improve cardiovascular fitness, or heart and lung endurance. Weight lifting, on the other hand, is good for building muscles that can store more blood sugar — so it's great for increasing your energy and stamina.

Generally, for most people, improving overall health and preventing disease are the most important goals. And you can do that with just three 10-minute walks a day! So what are you waiting for?

How fit are you?

To begin, take one of these simple tests to determine how fit you are.

Quarter-mile walk — This is for people who haven't been exercising at all but are ready to catch up.

First, mark out a quarter-mile course. Pick a safe, flat path or find a running track. Most tracks are one-quarter mile. The distance doesn't have to be exact but always perform the test on the same course so you can compare results.

Use a watch with a second hand to time yourself, and see how long it takes to walk the course. Walk as fast as you can.

At the end of the course, stop dead in your tracks and immediately measure your pulse rate. Locate a pressure point at your wrist, temple, or throat where you can feel your artery throbbing. Gently touch the point so you can feel how many times your heart beats during a 30-second time period.

Do this every two weeks for the first four months of your exercise program so you can compare results. You'll be amazed at how much faster you'll get and how much your pulse rate will drop as you get more fit.

Step test — For people who can't get outdoors. Warning: If you haven't exercised in more than a year or have any type of heart trouble, talk with your doctor before taking this test.

Find an 8-inch-high step or sturdy stool. Then practice until you can step up and then down with each foot — two "up-down" cycles — in five seconds. Ask a partner to time you.

Next, for three minutes, step up and down with alternate feet. Wait 30 seconds and then take your pulse for 30 seconds. Check the following table to rate yourself.

Ages	20-29	30-39	40-49	50+
Men	**Number of beats/30 seconds**			
Excellent	34-36	35-38	37-39	37-40
Good	37-40	39-41	40-42	41-43
Average	41-42	42-43	43-44	44-45
Fair	43-47	44-47	45-49	46-49
Poor	48-59	48-59	50-60	50-62

Ages	20-29	30-39	40-49	50+
Women	**Number of beats/30 seconds**			
Excellent	39-42	39-42	41-43	41-44
Good	43-44	43-45	44-45	45-47
Average	45-46	46-47	46-47	48-49
Fair	47-52	48-53	48-54	50-55
Poor	53-66	54-66	55-67	56-66

1.5 mile run/walk test — For those already exercising who want to improve.

Mark out a 1.5 mile course or use a running track (six laps around the average quarter-mile track). Time yourself with a watch that has a second hand to see how long it takes you to cover the course.

If you can't run it, start off walking and then break into a run near the finish. You should feel physically tired toward the end of the course, not weak or nauseous.

Hint: Don't eat for two hours before the test and do a few minutes of walking to warm up. Afterward, cool down with slow walking for five minutes or so to avoid soreness.

The 12-minute test — For exercisers who are already in good condition and want to measure the success of their fitness program. This test gives you a good estimate of your aerobic capacity.

All you have to do is see how many miles you can walk or run in 12 minutes. Then find your fitness level on the following chart.

Be sure to fully warm up and cool down, and take the test on a level surface.

Women		**Men**	
30s		**30s**	
1.30 to 1.39	Excellent	1.57 to 1.69	Excellent
1.19 to 1.29	Good	1.46 to 1.56	Good
1.06 to 1.18	Fair	1.31 to 1.45	Fair
.95 to 1.05	Poor	1.18 to 1.30	Poor

Women			**Men**	
40s			**40s**	
1.25 to 1.34	Excellent		1.54 to 1.65	Excellent
1.12 to 1.24	Good		1.40 to 1.53	Good
.99 to 1.11	Fair		1.25 to 1.39	Fair
.88 to .98	Poor		1.14 to 1.24	Poor
50s			**50s**	
1.19 to 1.30	Excellent		1.45 to 1.58	Excellent
1.06 to 1.18	Good		1.31 to 1.44	Good
.94 to 1.05	Fair		1.17 to 1.30	Fair
.84 to .93	Poor		1.03 to 1.16	Poor
60s plus			**60s plus**	
1.10 to 1.18	Excellent		1.33 to 1.55	Excellent
.99 to 1.09	Good		1.21 to 1.32	Good
.87 to .98	Fair		1.03 to 1.20	Fair
.78 to .86	Poor		.87 to 1.02	Poor

How to get started

Now that you know where you stand — or sit — here's what to do:

Get going! The point is to accumulate 30 minutes a day of exercise over your normal daily activities. It doesn't even have to be consecutive or vigorous. Just regular.

The Journal of the American Medical Association suggests:

❦ brisk walking
❦ bicycling
❦ swimming
❦ calisthenics
❦ racket sports
❦ golf (if you pull your cart or carry your clubs)
❦ housecleaning
❦ raking leaves

All of these are moderate-intensity physical activities that will help you live longer.

How about trying something new?

You can do it indoors or out, alone or in a group, and its gentle movements make it ideal for those who want a workout but whose bones can't take the jarring that comes with many forms of exercise.

Tai chi is an ancient form of exercise that originated in China. It involves a series of slow, concentrated movements designed to take you through a wide range of motion over a prolonged period of time — 10 to 60 minutes.

Be sure to find a knowledgeable teacher to learn tai chi correctly. It's usually taught in martial arts schools and often in community centers, adult education classes, many fitness centers, or YMCAs. Also, the Arthritis Foundation has an exercise program based on tai chi called ROM (range of motion) dance.

Yoga is another form of exercise ideal for the older body because it gets you moving without jarring and panting. Instead, by stretching, relaxing, and breathing deeply in various postures, you gain flexibility and balance, as well as strength and stamina.

Forget the idea that you have to turn your body into a pretzel. You can do yoga postures sitting in a chair, lying in bed, or just standing still. Intrigued? Try this simple yoga exercise to help you reach overhead, carry things, and perform other daily living tasks more easily.

Arm circles — for shoulder flexibility and for shoulder, arm, and back strength. Begin by taking a few deep breaths through your nose. Stretch your arms out to your sides until they're level with your shoulders. Turn palms outward with fingers together and wrists bent up like you want to stop traffic.

Next, slowly move your arms in large circles toward the front five times. If your shoulders hurt, make smaller circles.

Now relax your arms at your sides for a few moments and then repeat the entire sequence, only this time make backward circles.

You can easily find yoga classes at local YWCAs or YMCAs, fitness centers, adult education and community centers, and junior colleges. You can even get videotapes from your local library or video store.

READY FOR MORE ACTION?

Once you're exercising regularly, add to your program. For maximum fitness, you need to exercise hard and steadily for 20 minutes or more at least three times a week. This means fast walking, jogging, bicycling, swimming laps, and the like.

To strengthen your heart and lungs, you should exercise at 60 to 70 percent of your maximum heart rate. Determine your target heart rate range by subtracting your age from 220, then multiplying that number by 0.6 or 0.7.

During exercise, stop and find your pulse just as you did in the exercise tests described earlier. Note how many times your heart beats in 10 seconds. Multiply that by six to see how hard you're working. The number should be in the target range you calculated above. If not, adjust your exercise accordingly.

If you're just beginning to do aerobic exercise, you may need to start with 10 minutes of exercise at 50 percent of your maximum heart rate (220 minus your age, times 0.5)

Hint: Warm up by walking around for five to 10 minutes and then stretching for five minutes before you begin exercising hard. It will lower the stress on your heart as well as your muscles. At the end of your session, cool down with slow walking and stretching for five minutes or until your breathing and pulse have returned to normal. This will help keep you pain-free and flexible.

TIME TO ADD STRENGTH TRAINING

The next step·is strength training. You may be tempted to skip this part of the program, but don't. It's not as hard as it sounds. The four exercises listed here are all you need to do.

Complete three sets of each exercise. In each set, do eight to 12 repetitions, or whatever you can manage.

❦ Easy push-ups — Lie face down on the floor with your feet together and the palms of your hands flat on the floor on either side of your chest, as in the drawing. Support your upper body weight on your arms as you raise your body, keeping your back flat but allowing your knees to bend.

Inhale as you go up, exhale as you go down. Try to establish a rhythm. This exercise builds your arms, shoulders, chest, and back. Eventually, you'll have enough strength to do the harder, straight-knee version.

❧ Upper-arm (triceps) exercise — You'll need weights for this one. Try using plastic milk containers, with easy-to-grip handles, filled with water or sand. You can add more weight to the jugs as you get stronger.

Sit in a straight-backed chair. Hold a weight in each hand and raise both arms over your head. Bend one elbow as you lower that hand behind your head. Raise it back overhead and repeat with the other arm. Keep alternating.

❧ Knee extension and flexion — Sit in a chair. Extend your leg straight out in front of you. Lower your leg to starting position. Rest no more than one second before repeating the same lift. Then do the exercise with your other leg. When that becomes easy, strap or tie weights onto your ankle. You can fashion weights out of plastic bags filled with sand or dirt.

❧ Hip and knee extension — Stand up straight, plant your feet firmly with toes pointing out. From this position, bend your knees slightly to get your body weight over your toes. Keep your heels on the floor. Do not do a deep knee bend — just a slight dip. Return to your starting position and repeat. Use a chair back or counter top for balance if you need to.

DON'T LET YOURSELF RUN DRY

Fluid acts as your cooling system and just like a car's, it spells trouble if you run dry. Older people need to drink between one and two quarts of fluid a day (32 to 64 ounces). Exercise increases your need for fluid, so be sure to drink enough water to replace any fluid you lose through sweat.

How do you know how much is enough? Make a habit of weighing yourself before and after exercise. Drink back the amount of weight you lost in nonalcoholic, noncaffeinated beverages. Water or water mixed with fruit juice is best.

For example, if you dropped a pound and a half, you lost a little more than a half-quart of water. You need to replenish your fluid by drinking more than a half-quart (16 ounces) of water.

Don't rely on thirst to tell you what you need — it's an unreliable measure in most people and even more so in older people. Another way to tell if you're drinking enough fluid is by your urine. It should be clear, not dark. Dark urine means you're dehydrated.

Other exercise and diet tips:

❦ Avoid alcohol, caffeine, and sugar prior to exercise.

❦ To help you build muscle damaged by exercise, take 400 IU of vitamin E daily and consider taking extra vitamin C.

❦ Get between 1,200 and 1,500 milligrams (mg) a day of calcium to help you build bone and compensate for what you lose in sweat.

ENJOY YOURSELF

Willpower is great, but a little enjoyment goes a long way. For more fun when you exercise:

❦ Choose an activity you like.

❦ Give yourself feedback and rewards. For example, wear a pedometer to measure how far you walk and chart your progress. Reward yourself for your effort.

❦ Exercise to music. People tend to keep going 25 to 29 percent longer when listening to tunes.

❦ Find an exercise buddy.

❦ Challenge yourself. When walking becomes easy, add distance, speed, or buy a weight belt.

THE TV WORKOUT

Sitting in front of the television brings on the urge to snack. Instead of exercising your jaws, consider bringing your exercise bicycle, treadmill, rowing machine, or stair stepper out of your basement and into your living room. That way, instead of passively watching, you can be active and entertained at the same time.

No equipment? Try walking or jogging in place or get a low and sturdy stool to step up on. Use barbells or "milk jug" weights to do strength training while you watch.

All you need is a towel and a dishpan to do this exercise, which strengthens and improves flexibility in fingers, wrists, and forearms. Put a little water in a plastic dishpan, put it on your lap, dip a towel in the water, and then wring it out. Alternate inward and outward rotations.

Couch potatoes don't have to look lumpy!

JUST DO SOMETHING

Having trouble getting with the program? Remember — for basic disease prevention, all you need to do is add 30 minutes of activity to your day.

Why not make today "Just Do Something" Day? Here's one way to start:

❦ Walk the dog (or just yourself) for 14 minutes in the morning. Time your walk — seven minutes out, seven minutes back. You'll be surprised at how much ground you cover.

❦ After lunch, take an eight-minute walk instead of reading a book — very coordinated people can do both at once.

❦ Before or after dinner, take another eight-minute walk.

It's that simple. Mix and match activities — you might like to swim, bike, dance, or garden instead of walking. The point is ... just be active.

GROW A GARDEN EXERCISE PROGRAM

Gardening may be in the category of "I can't believe it's exercise" for those who love it. But, in fact, tasks like digging, raking, and planting are the equivalent of brisk walking, playing volleyball, or snorkeling.

The toughest gardening workout comes from mowing the lawn with a push mower, chopping wood, shoveling, and tilling. These activities are on par with doubles tennis, fencing, downhill skiing, and playing softball.

Here are some tips for "fitness gardening":

❦ Warm up first with some stretches and walking around.

❦ Alternate your grip when raking, digging, or hoeing. Example: If you're right-handed, rake first with a right-hand grip, and then switch to your left hand.

❦ Bend at the knees, not the waist, to pick things up.

❦ Break down your gardening sessions into two- or three-hour periods rather than all-day marathons. Garden at least 30 minutes a few times a week — ideally, every other day.

❦ Combine light gardening with stretching activities, such as the "lunge and weed." Lunge forward with one leg (be sure to keep your knee over your ankle and not beyond your toes), weed for about 20 seconds, then stand up and alternate legs.

❦ Breathe in and out in a steady rhythm as you work.

❦ Use your legs, not your back.

❦ Cool down afterward by walking around and surveying the results of your labor.

You are what you eat. When it comes to fat, that statement is right on the mark. Eating fat makes you fat. It also puts you at risk for heart disease, cancer, diabetes, and other life-threatening diseases. Choosing a healthy lifestyle and low-fat diet can protect you from a horde of ailments that can make you old before your time.

LOW-FAT LIVING

We didn't always worry about the fat in our diets. Remember how we used to enjoy a breakfast of fried eggs, bacon, sausage, and biscuits without a twinge of guilt? As far as we knew, fat was good for us. It gave us energy and kept our bodies going when times were lean and food was scarce.

In fact, we do need fat to survive. It protects our organs and insulates our bodies. It carries critical nutrients and fat-soluble vitmins. And it makes foods taste good! It gives them a tenderness and enticing aroma we find hard to resist, which stimulates our appetites. Fat also slows our digestion, making us feel fuller longer.

But thanks to medical research, we're now aware that fat does bad things to our bodies as well. In 1908, researchers first found that rabbits on diets of meat, whole milk, and eggs developed fat deposits on their artery walls. These fat deposits narrowed the artery openings and made it harder for blood to pass through.

It was five years before they identified the sticky substance that caused those fat deposits. Can you guess what it was? Today "cholesterol" is a household word, but in the early 1900s, scientists were still putting pieces of the cholesterol puzzle together.

In 1916, Dr. Cornelius de Langen found another link between cholesterol and diet. He researched the eating habits of Indonesian natives and found those who ate a plant-based diet had much lower rates of heart disease. The natives who ate meat and dairy products like the Dutch had higher cholesterol levels and heart disease.

De Langen was the first to suggest that diet, cholesterol levels, and heart disease were related. Unfortunately, his theory was mostly ignored for close to 40 years.

LEARNING FROM OTHER CULTURES

How would you like to live on the beautiful Greek island of Crete? Or would the crisp, cold air of Alaska or Greenland be more to your liking? Either way, you'd be doing your heart a favor.

We take for granted that high-fat diets and heart disease go hand-in-hand, but it's not true in all areas of the world. If you lived on Crete, you'd eat lots of olive oil, which has been found to do great things for your cholesterol levels.

If you roughed it with the Eskimos of Alaska and Greenland, your diet would be filled with salmon, mackerel, and other fish rich in omega-3 fatty acids. These fish oils lower the bad cholesterol levels in your blood, and the lower your cholesterol, the happier your heart.

5 WAYS A LOW-FAT DIET FIGHTS AGING

As you get older, your past eating habits catch up with you. If you've watched your diet, ate lots of fruits and vegetables, and cut back on meat and dairy products, chances are your body will carry you through your golden years in fine shape. But if you've overloaded your body with harmful fats and sugars, you may be in trouble.

Notice yourself moving a little slower these days? As you get older, your metabolism slows down and you tend to exercise less, so it's easier to put on the pounds. A high-fat diet helps the pounds pile up even faster.

As you get more overweight, your body has a harder time controlling your sugar levels. Your cells actually refuse to accept the insulin your pancreas produces, so your sugar levels skyrocket. Adult-onset diabetes is the result.

As the rabbit study showed, a high-fat diet builds up "plaque" in your arteries, which leads to atherosclerosis or hardening of the arteries. This can cause high blood pressure, stroke, blood clots, and heart attacks.

Eating too much fat may even increase your risk for some types of cancer.

Dr. Denham Harmon, creator of the Free Radical Theory of Aging, calls atherosclerosis and cancer "the two major degenerative diseases" of life. Eating right helps protect your body from free radicals, which can cause these diseases.

You have the power to control what you eat. Following a healthy, low-fat diet will lessen the effects of aging and help you live a longer, healthier, more satisfying life.

Obliterates obesity. If you limit the fat in your diet, you will be guaranteed a slimmer, healthier body. There's no doubt about it. Eating fat actually makes you fatter.

One reason is because each fat gram carries more than twice as many calories as carbohydrates and proteins — 9 compared to 4. That means 5 grams of fat have 45 calories, while 5 grams of carbohydrate have only 20 calories.

Your body also finds it easier to turn food fat into body fat. That makes sense, because they're basically the same substance. Carbohydrates are more complex, so it takes your body a lot longer to turn them into fat.

Your fat cells are always happy to welcome a few more fat calories. In fact, they keep expanding to let in all the fat calories you eat, which is why you gain weight and look fatter. And once they're in, those stubborn fat calories don't want to move, so they're much harder to burn off than carbohydrate or protein calories.

Not a pretty picture, is it?

If you control your fat intake, you'll not only keep yourself fit, you may also prevent diseases and illnesses that obesity can cause.

For example, high blood pressure and stroke are twice as likely to occur in obese people. Coronary heart disease is more common, particularly in obese men younger than 40.

You're five times more likely to get diabetes if you're obese. The risk gets higher the more weight you have and the longer you keep it on.

If you're severely overweight and suffer from heartburn, you're a prime candidate for cancer of the esophagus.

Obese men may be at higher risk for cancers of the colon, rectum, and prostate. You also may have problems with urinary obstructions. The extra fat in your abdominal area can press against your prostate gland, obstructing urinary flow.

With increasing weight, women are more at risk for breast, uterine, and cervical cancers. Obesity also may aggravate osteoarthritis because extra weight places more strain on your joints.

Controls your cholesterol. Everyone has heard of cholesterol, but do you know what it is exactly? Think of it as sort of a "cousin" to fat. Both belong to the same family of chemical compounds called lipids. Triglycerides are another lipid you may be familiar with. These ugly, yellow globules appear in your bloodstream about an hour after you eat a high-fat meal.

Your body needs fat and cholesterol to function. Fat cells store energy for your body to use, while cholesterol builds cell membranes and tissues in your brain and nerves. It also helps regulate some of your body processes. In fact, cholesterol is a part of every cell in your body.

So why is it so bad for you? To start with, your liver makes enough cholesterol for your body's needs. That's why you don't want to include more in your diet. When you eat a lot of animal products, such as meat and eggs, your body can't get rid of all the extra cholesterol. The soft, waxy substance builds up in your blood and sticks to your artery walls, forming fat deposits or "plaques." This leads to atherosclerosis, which can cause heart disease and stroke.

Fats and cholesterol travel around in your body on lipoproteins. Low-density lipoproteins (LDL) carry more fats, while high-density lipoproteins (HDL) are loaded with more protein.

HDL is known as the good guy because it helps move the fat-laden LDL out of your body and protects you from heart disease.

So all you have to do is watch the amount of cholesterol you eat, and you're home free, right? Not necessarily. The fats you eat actually raise your blood cholesterol level more than the cholesterol in your food. Saturated fat is your biggest enemy because your body makes cholesterol from it. The best way to control your cholesterol level is to eat less saturated fat.

Lowers your risk of heart disease. Is your cholesterol level high (above 240 mg/dl)? Then you have a good chance of suffering heart disease. Love fried foods and creamy desserts? Consider yourself in double trouble.

Heart disease is the number one killer of adults in the United States. Studies have shown that fat and cholesterol are major contributors to heart disease.

If you eat large amounts of saturated fat and cholesterol, you can overwhelm the "receptors" that help remove cholesterol from your blood. You'll also lower the number of receptors you have. That makes it harder for your body to get rid of cholesterol it doesn't need.

Cholesterol builds up in your arteries when it has nowhere else to go. Your body also uses the sticky stuff to help repair blood vessel walls, which can be damaged by high blood pressure.

Imagine blood pounding through your arteries like a flood through a narrow mountain pass. Eventually, it can wear down or even tear an artery wall. Your body puts cholesterol and other things over the injury as a "bandaid" to protect the area. But this bandaid catches other cholesterol floating by and gets larger and larger.

The pile of plaque eventually hardens, making the artery wall narrow and less flexible. Your blood pushes harder to get through, your pressure rises even more, and your heart goes into overdrive. Blood clots, aneurysms (balloon-like weaknesses in the artery walls), heart attack, and stroke may be the unfortunate result.

Unless you've been a strict vegetarian all your life, you'll probably have well-developed plaques by the time you're 30 years old. So the question is, what can you do to slow down the damage or even reverse it?

Limit the fats in your diet — particularly saturated fats — and you'll be on your way to cleaner, freer-flowing arteries. Add regular aerobic exercise, and you'll help keep them — and you — as young and vibrant as ever.

Protects your eyes. A diet high in saturated fat and cholesterol can affect your eyes as you grow older. Studies have shown it may put you at a higher risk for a type of vision loss known as age-related maculopathy. Eat more grains and vegetables and you may save your sight.

Fights cancer. No one is really sure what causes cancer, but researchers know diet plays an important part, both in developing cancer and preventing it. It's possible that up to 40 percent of the cancers in men, and 60 percent in women, are caused by the high-fat, low-fiber foods we eat.

A high-fat diet seems to put you more at risk for certain cancers. Although fat does not actually cause the disease, it helps certain cancers develop faster and earlier. One way it does this is by changing your cell membranes so they're not strong enough to resist cancer-causing invaders.

Researchers call fats "promoters" of cancer. If carcinogens, or things that cause cancer, get a foothold in your body, promoters help them enter the cells and multiply.

How important is diet to cancer? Studies don't always agree. For example, some breast cancer researchers believe a high-fat diet increases your chances of getting the disease. Others have found that saturated fat doesn't affect your chances of developing cancer, while unsaturated fats — particularly olive oil — seem to protect you against breast cancer.

But if you already have breast cancer or are in remission, a low-fat diet may help keep the tumor from growing or coming back.

❦ **Ovarian cancer.** According to a Johns Hopkins study, you're three times more likely to develop ovarian cancer if you have cholesterol levels above 200 mg/dl. But researchers aren't sure about this connection either. While some studies agree with these results, others find no relationship between a high-fat diet, cholesterol, and ovarian cancer.

❦ **Non-Hodgkin's lymphoma.** Love big, juicy burgers and chargrilled steaks? If you eat a lot of red meat and other animal fats, you may get non-Hodgkin's lymphoma, a cancer of the immune system. A seven-year study discovered that women who ate more animal protein, especially red meat, had a higher risk of developing this disease. Eating hamburgers might account for most of the increased risk. Researchers think cancer-causing substances or unknown contaminants are spread when the meat is ground.

🐦 **Skin cancer.** Everyone knows sunbathing can give you a bad case of sunburn and maybe even skin cancer. But now it seems the cheese dog and fries you eat at the beach may be just as bad for your skin. Studies show a high-fat diet may contribute to nonmelanoma skin cancer. Apparently, fat acts as a promoter to help the cancer grow after the sun damages your skin cells.

🐦 **Prostate cancer.** Men who have prostate cancer also may benefit from eating low-fat foods. Studies with mice show a low-fat diet keeps prostate tumors from growing as quickly.

SUBSTITUTES FOR HIGH-FAT INGREDIENTS

Whole milk products	Nonfat milk products
Cream	Evaporated nonfat (skim) milk, canned
Sour cream	Yogurt or fat-free sour cream
Butter	Reduced calorie margarine, butter replacers, wine, lemon juice, broth, fruit butters
Whole milk ricotta	Part-skim/fat-free ricotta; low-fat or fat-free cottage cheese
Regular cheese	Part-skim, low-fat, or fat-free cheese
Regular mayonnaise/ salad dressing	Low-fat or fat-free mayonnaise/salad dressing
Oil-packed fish and meat	Water-packed canned fish and meat
Ground beef	Lean ground meat and grain mixture
Ice cream	Low-fat frozen yogurt or sherbet
Butter, bacon fat	Herbs, lemons, spices, fruits, liquid smoke flavoring, oil-free dressings

❦ **Colon cancer.** If you eat a lot of saturated fats and omega-6 fatty acids, you'll have a higher risk of colon cancer. Omega-6 fats are found in vegetable oils, seeds, nuts, and whole-grains. Omega-3 fats, like those found in fish oils, apparently reduce the size and number of colon tumors. Fish oil also lowers the amount of cancer-causing agents your body excretes, which may reduce your risk of colon cancer.

YOUR ACTION PLAN

HOW MUCH TO CUT BACK?

It's certainly not necessary to eat nothing but fruits, vegetables, and grains to live a low-fat lifestyle. Today, many calcium-rich dairy products are fat free, and some meats are low in fat.

A sense of balance is important in choosing a healthy diet. If most of your meals include whole, fresh foods, then an occasional candy bar or snack food won't hurt you.

It's a good idea to limit red meat and other animal products to once or twice a week. Always choose the leanest meats possible, and make sure you trim those edges. You can cut almost 100 calories from a pork chop just by cutting off the fat.

Enjoy a fish dinner at least twice a week, and try to include fish rich in omega-3 fatty acids, such as salmon, sardines, tuna, mackerel, and herring.

Use low-fat or skim milk dairy foods. Substitute olive or canola oil for other vegetable fats, and use chicken broth, lemon juice, and herbs and spices to add flavor to your food.

Eat more plant foods, such as fruits, vegetables, and grains, and your body will sparkle from the extra vitamins, minerals, fiber, antioxidants, and other cancer-fighting substances you take in. These nutrients are your best protection against age-related diseases and the ravages of the environment — from dandruff, bad breath, and wrinkling to cataracts, cancer, diabetes, and heart disease.

THE WISE LOW-FAT CONSUMER

You wouldn't want to come home one day and find your house had been robbed. So why stand by and let your body be robbed of what it needs to stay healthy? "Stressor" foods do just that — they rob your body of essential nutrients rather than nourish it.

A good diet is low in stressor foods, such as refined sugars, flours, and pastas; cola; processed fats, such as cheeses; and hydrogenated fats like margarine and deep fried foods.

LOW-FAT DIET CAUTIONS

Do you usually buy snack foods labeled "fat free," "low-fat," "light," or "reduced calorie"? If so, you're on the right track to healthy, low-fat living. These definitions must meet strict government standards, so if they appear on a label, you can trust what they say.

But that doesn't mean you can gorge yourself with all the low-fat cookies you want. Sometimes fat-free or low-fat versions of snack foods contain extra sugar or salt to make up for the flavor that's lost when fat is taken out. You can still put on the pounds from all the calories, so exercise some restraint when munching fat-free goodies.

And watch out for foods labeled "cholesterol free." They're often loaded with saturated fat, which raises your cholesterol even more than eating cholesterol.

What about fat substitutes? You may think you've finally reached fat-free heaven, but don't start counting your cookies. Most substitutes haven't been researched thoroughly yet, so it's too soon to tell what the long-term effects might be.

Olestra (trade name Olean) is made of sugar and vegetable oil, but it's put together in such a way that the body can't absorb it. The Food and Drug Administration (FDA) approved it as a replacement for fat, but only in snack foods like chips and crackers.

How safe is it? Studies have found that olestra can cause abdominal cramping and loose stools. It also keeps your body from absorbing some nutrients like beta carotene, an important antioxidant. In fact, the FDA requires food companies to add vitamins A, D, E, and K to any foods containing olestra to help replace the lost nutrients.

It's too soon to tell how olestra will affect your general health. It's up to you to decide whether the benefits of fat-free snack foods outweigh possible risks later on.

The FDA approved another fat substitute called Simplesse for use in frozen desserts, mayonnaise, and salad dressings. Simplesse is made from proteins that form creamy particles. It's actually digested and absorbed by your body rather than passed through like olestra. If you're on a protein-restricted diet, you may not be able to eat foods containing Simplesse.

A fat substitute called Z-trim may be more promising. Developed by the U.S. Department of Agriculture, it's made from agricultural byproducts, such as the hulls of oats, soybeans, peas, and rice, or the bran from corn or wheat. Since it's made from natural fibers, it won't upset your digestive system if you eat normal amounts. As usual, the key is — don't overdo it.

LOW-FAT STRATEGIES

Are you a cheese lover? If so, you're not alone. A recent study found that cheese is the largest single source of saturated fat in the diets of American women. If you can't do without it, try the low-fat or fat-free varieties, which are also lower in calories.

Eat less meat, and you'll also cut back on saturated fats. Try using beans and tofu instead of meat in casseroles, soups, and stews.

Lower your total fat intake to 30 percent or less of your total calories. That means if you eat 1,500 calories a day, you should have no more than 50 grams of fat. Keep saturated fat to 10 percent or 16 grams. Try not to eat more than 300 milligrams of cholesterol.

Learn about saturated, polyunsaturated, and monounsaturated fats. The more solid a fat is at room temperature, the more saturated it is. Butter and lard are good examples.

Vegetable oils are usually polyunsaturated, but beware of coconut and palm oils, which are highly saturated. These often are used in nondairy whipped toppings and packaged desserts, so read your labels carefully.

Monounsaturated oils, such as olive and canola, are considered the healthiest type. But keep in mind that, calorie-wise, they're just like any other fat, with more than 100 calories per tablespoon. You're better off using a nonstick skillet and cooking spray whenever possible.

Don't be afraid to try a variety of foods. Include fruits, vegetables, and high-fiber grains. If you do that and eat less fat, you can be confident that you're on your way to a healthier life.

Why not try these other tips for healthy, low-fat living:

❦ Use low-fat or nonfat dairy foods to replace cream in sauces.

❦ Steam, poach, broil, grill, microwave, or bake foods rather than sauté or pan-fry them. Cook meat on a rack so the fat drains off.

❦ Skim the fat off soups or stews. If possible, cook the broth in advance, chill, then remove the hardened layer of fat.

❦ Season vegetables with herbs and spices instead of high-fat butter and sauces. Experiment with new seasonings.

❦ Perk up flavors with balsamic vinegar, sun-dried tomatoes, Dijon mustard, Tabasco sauce, salsa, catsup, green chilies, or small amounts of sesame or hot chili oils.

❦ Make your own reduced-fat dressing by using more vinegar and less oil. Use lemon juice and Italian herbs for fat-free flavor.

❦ Cut back the fat in your favorite recipes by a third and replace the fat in baked recipes with applesauce or pureed prunes.

❦ Take advantage of healthful cookware, such as microwave ovens, vegetable steamers, pressure cookers, and nonstick pots and pans. These help foods keep their nutrients and make cooking them a little easier as well.

BEWARE OF PHANTOM FATS

By now, you're probably an expert on the different kinds of fats and how they affect your body. But there's a phantom fat you may never have heard of — trans-fatty acids. These are created when vegetable oil is hardened through a process called hydrogenation.

Many foods made with partially hydrogenated oil or shortening seem to be healthy because they have no cholesterol or saturated fat. But the trans fats in them are just as bad, because they raise your "bad" cholesterol levels as much as saturated fat does, and they lower your good cholesterol.

Most of the trans-fatty acids in your diet are from hydrogenated shortenings used to make cookies, french fries, and donuts. They're almost invisible because they're not listed on any food package labels. Fast-food restaurants don't mention them either. If they did, they'd have to admit their french fries are just as artery-clogging as when they were deep fried in lard.

Chicken nuggets, fried chicken and fish sandwiches, margarine, baked goods — all these have hidden trans fats that can more or less double the damage to your blood vessels.

So how can you avoid these artery-clogging demons?

❦ Buy foods made without vegetable shortening or partially hydrogenated oil.

❦ Avoid deep-fried foods. The less fat, the less trans-fatty acids, so look for lower-fat margarines, chips, crackers, and other processed foods.

❦ Use olive or canola oils instead of butter, margarine, or shortening whenever possible. Canola oil is lowest in saturated fat and highest in omega-3 fatty acids.

❦ Use tub margarine rather than stick, and buy light, low-fat, or fat-free brands. The American Heart Association recommends margarine with no more than 2 grams of saturated fat per tablespoon. The softer it is, the less trans fat it has.

❦ Beware of foods labeled "cholesterol-free," "low-cholesterol," "low-saturated fat," or "made with vegetable oil." These aren't necessarily low in trans fat. Look for "saturated-fat-free" foods.

Good fats? Sounds fishy to me

Believe it or not, some fats are actually your friends. Omega-3 and omega-6 fatty acids are essential to your health, and you can only get them from the foods you eat.

Omega-6 plays a critical role in your cell membranes. If you eat vegetable oils, seeds, nuts, and whole-grain products, you probably get enough of this fat to meet your body's needs. Omega-3 is the problem for most people. Because it's found mainly in fish, most people don't eat enough to reap the benefits.

Remember how your mother always told you fish was "brain food?" She may have been right. Studies have found that two omega-3 fats, EPA and DHA, are important for brain development. They're also critical for keeping your eyes sharp. Some researchers think your eyes deteriorate as you age because you don't maintain enough omega-3 fatty acids in your retinas.

Omega-3 also helps thin your blood, making it a great weapon against heart and artery disease.

Your fat tissue can store omega-3 fatty acids, but only if you take in more than your body needs. Most people get too much omega-6 instead, which can raise your bad cholesterol levels and lead to heart disease.

If you eat fish two or three times a week, as well as small amounts of vegetable oils, you'll get the right balance of omega-3 and omega-6 fatty acids

Some new studies have shaken up old notions about the dangers of too much salt. Sodium chloride may no longer be Public Enemy No. 1, but there are still plenty of reasons for healthy adults to go easy on the salt.

LOW-SALT DIET

A salty, mineral-rich fluid constantly bathes the cells of our bodies. Scientist Claude Bernard made that discovery in the mid-1800s, and he realized the fluid must contain the right amounts of sodium, chloride, and potassium to allow our cells to grow, work, and survive.

One hundred years later, researcher Homer Smith theorized that the cell-bathing fluid contains minerals similar to the salty seas that bathed and nourished the earliest one-celled organisms.

In order to keep that cell-bathing fluid in balance, what goes in must come out. You take in sodium and chloride in your diet, and, unless you sweat a lot or have diarrhea, more than 98 percent comes out in your urine. All creatures, including humans, have kidneys that strictly regulate the mineral and water balance in the body.

Eating too much salt isn't as dangerous as it might seem. That's because most people's kidneys are capable of providing an exit for all the sodium and chloride their mouths take in — even 10 times the average daily amount. Even so, eating too many salty foods can cause some problems:

❦ Your kidneys will have to work extra hard.
❦ You may excrete other important minerals along with the extra sodium and chloride in your urine.
❦ You will need more water in your body to help balance the extra sodium.

A few people (about 60 percent of those with high blood pressure) have kidneys that don't work very well. When your kidneys can't get rid of the excess salt you take in and you have extra sodium, chloride, and water in your body, the compartments that hold the cell-bathing fluid have to expand.

This could cause high blood pressure, swelling, and fluid in your lungs — all dangerous and damaging conditions. Retaining fluid is a factor in congestive heart failure and kidney disease. People who have these problems are considered salt-sensitive.

2 WAYS A LOW-SALT DIET FIGHTS AGING

The older you are, the more sensitive you are to salt. That may be because your kidneys don't work as well as you age, and your kidneys are responsible for getting rid of salt.

In all but the most remote populations around the world, blood pressure rises from young adulthood into middle and older ages. Between the ages of 25 and 55, your blood pressure will go up an average of 10 to 11 mg Hg. Over your entire lifetime, your blood pressure tends to increase about 40 to 50 mm Hg.

Some doctors speculate that most of that jump in blood pressure is due to years of exposure to salt. Your kidneys just can't handle it anymore.

Lowers blood pressure, if you're salt-sensitive. Most people can eat as much salt as they like. They have efficient kidneys that excrete the salt almost as fast as they take it in.

About 60 percent of the people with high blood pressure are salt-sensitive. (That's less than 10 percent of the entire population if you include people without high blood pressure.) They are sensitive to salt for a variety of reasons — their kidneys don't work very well, for instance. The more salt these salt-sensitive people eat, the higher their blood pressures. Restricting salt lowers their blood pressures.

What's the big controversy over salt that keeps this lowly mineral in the news? It's whether or not you should cut salt out of your diet even if you don't have high blood pressure.

Some doctors think cutting way back on salt can cause health problems. They say getting almost no salt in your diet would actually make your blood pressure rise. Their reasoning: You have less sodium in your body, so you retain less water. This could cause your blood volume to drop. If this happens, your blood vessels become narrower, and your blood pressure goes up.

Some researchers say salt restriction causes other problems, too — like more heart attacks, higher LDL "bad" cholesterol levels, sleep disturbances, and a reduced ability to absorb other nutrients.

However, you can rest assured that just about no one in the United States is going to have problems because they get too little salt.

Controversy aside, what should you do about eating salt? Most experts agree with the FDA's recommendation to limit sodium to 2,400 milligrams (mg) a day (just over one teaspoon of salt). Limiting salt may be a good idea. It could affect your blood pressure someday, and it may affect other parts of your body, like your bones. But don't make a huge effort to cut back to less than the recommended limit unless you have high blood pressure.

People with high blood pressure should try to restrict sodium to 2,000 mg a day (about one teaspoon of salt). If your blood pressure goes down when you cut back on salt, that's a good sign you're salt-sensitive, and you will benefit from a low-salt diet.

Reduces risk of osteoporosis. When water, waste products, and important nutrients pass through your kidneys to be made into urine, your kidneys pull out, or reabsorb, what your body needs. Sodium chloride competes with calcium for reabsorption by your kidneys.

This means you are going to get rid of more calcium in your urine when your kidneys are busy absorbing extra sodium chloride. The amount of calcium you excrete in your urine goes up a small amount for every teaspoonful of salt you eat. Unless you make up for that by eating more calcium, that loss could dissolve 1 percent of your skeleton every year — that's 10 percent of your skeleton gone in 10 years.

In studies, women with osteoporosis do tend to have higher than normal amounts of salt in their urine.

YOUR ACTION PLAN

HOW MUCH IS ENOUGH?

There's no Recommended Dietary Allowance (RDA) for salt, but we need only 500 mg of sodium a day to survive. That's about 1/4 teaspoon of salt.

HOW TO LOWER YOUR SALT INTAKE

It's sodium and chloride together, also known as salt, that affect blood pressure. Sodium alone doesn't seem to raise blood pressure, so you don't have to avoid products such as baking soda (sodium bicarbonate) and other sodium salts.

When you cut back on salt, the salty food you once enjoyed will start tasting too salty. Try these tips to dampen your salt craving.

🍀 **Avoid processed foods and fast foods.** Most salt comes from these sources, not from the salt shaker. Remember, foods don't have to taste salty to be salty. Look for low-sodium products.

🍀 **Cook without salt.** Add your salt later at the table. You can add less salt at the last minute and get a more salty flavor than by adding it earlier. Also cook with salt-free spices and sour flavors, like lemon.

❧ **Use salt substitutes.** Try some of the new reduced-sodium salt alternatives. One new product, sold only in pharmacies, is supplemented with potassium and magnesium.

Caution: Using a salt substitute high in potassium can put you at risk for potassium overload, especially if you have kidney problems.

❧ **Increase your potassium and calcium intakes.** These minerals help you excrete more salt in your urine.

❧ **Eat less sugar if you're salt-sensitive.** Rats who are salt-sensitive get even higher blood pressures when they add sugar to their diets.

HOW IT ALL SHAKES DOWN

Here's the bottom line. Our average daily intake of salt is 3,900 mg, and some people get a lot more than that. If you have normal blood pressure, you should try to limit your sodium intake to 2,400 mg (just over one teaspoon of salt) a day. The possible benefits to eating less salt:

ቘ   No rise in blood pressure with age
ቘ   Healthier bones
ቘ   Less fluid retention

If you have high blood pressure, experiment with a low-salt diet around 2,000 mg or less (less than one teaspoon) a day. If you are salt-sensitive, it could help you lower your blood pressure naturally.

And, of course, no one should try to cut out salt completely. That would be dangerous, too.

Sex can be lots of fun, and it can keep you young, too — physically and mentally. Here are just five healthy reasons to have sex: It banishes pain, relieves stress, improves incontinence, helps insomnia, and boosts self-esteem.

SEXUAL LIVING

Your best years are not behind you. Your children may be shocked, and even you may find it hard to believe, but sex, like good wine, improves with age. "Textbooks teach us that men reach their sexual peak in adolescence; women supposedly reach theirs shortly thereafter," remarks sex therapist David Schnarch. "But," he continues, "if you want intimacy with your sexuality — which has a huge [mental and physical] impact — then there isn't a 17-year-old alive who can keep up with a healthy 50-year-old."

You do hit your genital prime when you're a teen-ager, but most people who reach their full sexual potential do it during their 50s. There's no doubt that genital response, especially men's, slows with age.

But other things compensate for a man's increased diffi-culty in having an erection. Meaningful, intense sex is "often experienced for the first time when spouses are well over 45," says Schnarch.

Why does sex improve? Mature women have learned to accept themselves, especially their sexual selves. They also are more assertive. Men learn to be more intimate and more loving.

For example, when you get older and better at sex, you're more likely to have "eyes-open sex." You can look your partner in the eyes, without fantasizing, and truly connect with each other.

If you've decided you're too old for sex, think again. Studies show that people are able to lead satisfying sex lives into their 80s and 90s. After all, gentle, easy sex only takes about as much energy as walking up two flights of stairs. If for no other reason, consider keeping the sexual fires burning for your health's sake.

5 WAYS SEX FIGHTS AGING

Banishes pain. Like most any exercise, sex releases a rush of endorphins, the body's natural painkillers. And sex can relax all your muscles, taking the tension off your joints and skele-ton. That will naturally improve your arthritis symptoms.

Relieves stress. Since just about every health problem can be linked to stress — from colds and flu to heart disease, cancer, and osteoporosis — sex could have amazing healing powers. Sex relieves stress because it completely relaxes your muscles and eases the tension in your body, the same principle behind most relaxation techniques. And it will take your mind off your problems for a while.

Boosts healthy hormone levels. According to Joel D. Block, Ph.D., author of *Secrets of Better Sex,* frequent sex boosts estrogen production, and that can be healthy for your bones and your heart.

Well-respected Dr. Susan Lark, author of *The Estrogen Decision,* says sex doesn't change your estrogen level, but it does increase your ovaries' output of androgens. Androgens are male hormones that are responsible for sexual desire for both men and women. So the more you have sex, the more your body will want it.

Burns calories. Active sex will use up approximately 300 calories, says Dr. Whitehead, director of the Association for Male Sexual Dysfunction. Since one pound is approximately 3,000 calories, you can shed a pound a month if you have sex about 10 times.

Improves urinary incontinence. Sex is a natural Kegel exercise, says Myrna Lewis of the Mount Sinai School of Medicine. Women who have regular sex are less likely to leak urine when they sneeze, laugh, or exercise.

YOUR ACTION PLAN

SOLUTIONS FOR WOMEN

A woman's body changes during and after menopause. The vaginal lining becomes thin, the vagina lubricates less and more slowly, the shape of the vagina can change, and uterine contractions because of orgasms can be painful. These changes don't have to sap the enjoyment out of sex. Here are some solutions:

❧ **Stay sexually active.** You've heard it before ... The more you have sex, the easier it is. Frequent sex will slow some of the vaginal changes that menopause brings. Sex increases hormone levels and blood flow to the genital area, and it also exercises this area.

❧ **Do your Kegels.** Kegel exercises contract and relax your pelvic-floor muscles. Strong muscles will help you hold your urine better, and they may also make sex more pleasurable.

❧ **Use an over-the-counter vaginal lubricant.** Some women never produce much lubrication, no matter what their age. And at certain times of the month, they produce less than usual. More than half the women over 40 will have some problems with dryness. A water-based lubricant you can buy at a pharmacy may be all you need to put the pleasure back in sex. Don't use oil-based lubricants. They can bring on a vaginal infection.

❦ **Eat soy for better sex.** Soy milk, soy flour, tofu, tempeh, and other soy products contain phytoestrogens, a very weak natural estrogen. Studies show that soy products can help the hot flashes that come with menopause, and they may be able to strengthen vaginal walls and improve lubrication.

❦ **Ask about androgens.** If you have a very low sex drive, ask your doctor about taking testosterone. This male hormone, a type of androgen, is responsible for maintaining your sex drive. The ovaries produce almost half of a woman's androgen supply, but the uterus produces some, too. Women who have had a hysterectomy may have a very low supply of testosterone.

❦ **Don't believe it's over after surgery.** Some women feel less feminine after a hysterectomy or a mastectomy, even though their bodies are as sexual as ever. If you are having this problem, you may just need someone to talk with. You can get in touch with women who are happy to share their experiences through the American Cancer Society's Reach to Recovery program. They also offer counseling. Look in your phone book to find a program near your home.

SOLUTIONS FOR MEN

Men have a lot more to worry about than women when it comes to sexual performance as they get older. The changes a man faces will be very obvious. It may take longer to get an erection, or the erection may not be as firm. The warning time when you know ejaculation is about to happen may be shorter. You'll probably lose the erection faster after ejaculation, and have less seminal fluid and lower ejaculatory pressure.

Erectile dysfunction — the new, improved name for impotence — becomes a big problem for many older men. Until recently, everyone thought that when a man was unable to perform, the problem was all in his head. Now experts have figured out that psychological problems like stress and anxiety are the culprit only about 10 percent of the time. The other nine out of 10 men have a physical problem causing their dysfunctions, like diabetes, heart disease, high blood pressure, drugs, and prostate surgery.

❦ **Go see your doctor.** Anytime you're having a sexual performance problem, you need to see your doctor. About half of the men having problems wait one to two years before seeking treatment. That's bad for your sex life and bad for your health. Erectile dysfunction may be your first warning sign of a dangerous disease.

You have an erection when the arteries leading to your penis relax and blood rushes into the spongy, fibrous tissue. Problems with an erection could signal any disease that affects your arteries and blood flow. Diabetes damages your nerves and blood vessels, and about 15 percent of diabetic men have difficulty with erections by age 35. By age 60, most of them will have difficulty. If you do have a serious disease, you need treatment.

❦ **Don't blame your partner.** In fact, you need to reassure her. She's probably going to feel somehow at fault. Accept the change, maybe even laugh about it, and take the opportunity to touch more and be romantic. If you feel like your partner is pressuring you, you need to discuss it.

❦ **Explore options with confidence.** Communicate your sexual desires to your partner and ask her what you can do to please her.

❦ **Eat a healthy diet and exercise.** A healthy lifestyle will help keep your arteries clean, and that will keep blood flowing properly to your penis. Stay away from fatty foods, alcohol, and smoking.

❦ **Consider testosterone replacement therapy.** Testosterone levels decrease with age, and testosterone is responsible for your sex drive. If you've lost sexual desire, talk with your doctor about your options.

❦ **Improve performance with creams and shots.** Medical treatment for erectile dysfunction has come a long way. In a new research study, almost 300 men gave themselves shots of alprostadil into the opening at the tip of the penis five or 10 minutes before sex. Most men were very happy with the results, and few had side effects. The Food and Drug Administration has approved this use of alprostadil.

Researchers are also getting great results from a cream that you rub on before intercourse. In a recent study in Egypt, almost six out of every 10 men reported full erections and satisfactory intercourse using the cream.

The old medical standbys for impotence are a vacuum device or a penile implant. A vacuum device is a plastic tube that fits around the penis. You pump air out of the tube, and the vacuum draws blood into the penis. The blood is trapped by a ring you roll to the base of the penis. The erection lasts for 20 to 30 minutes, and the seminal fluid is released when you remove the ring.

COFFEE DRINKERS HAVE BETTER SEX?

Drinking a cup of coffee a day is linked with more sex for older women and more potency for older men — if you can believe the results of a questionnaire sent to Michigan residents age 60 and older.

Men who didn't drink coffee were more likely to be impotent, and women who didn't enjoy a morning cup just weren't as sexually active.

Why? Your guess is as good as that of the pollsters'. Caffeine is a powerful central nervous system stimulant, and it relaxes the smooth muscles. Scientists know it enhances your senses and speeds up your reflexes.

But, the link could just mean that people with health problems avoid coffee and sex.

With the penile implant, you squeeze a pump implanted in the scrotum to inflate a liquid-filled cylinder in the penis. Another type of implant is a bendable rod that is rigid enough for sex and flexible enough not to be noticed under your clothes. Any of these devices can allow satisfying and romantic sex if both partners are committed to making it work.

HEART DISEASE, ARTHRITIS, AND SEX

A stroke or a heart attack does not signal the end to your sex life. Sex only increases your heart attack risk by one chance in a million, and you can lower this tiny risk even further by getting regular exercise. From four to 16 weeks after a heart attack, your sex life should be getting back to normal.

Arthritis pain and stiffness can take the appeal out of sex. Some solutions are:

- ❦ pillows, especially to cushion painful hips,
- ❦ pain medicine taken before sex,
- ❦ a warm bath or shower beforehand, and
- ❦ early morning sex, when you are less tired and joints are less inflamed.

DRUGS THAT PUT A DAMPER ON SEX

When you've lost your physical desire for your spouse, check your medicine cabinet before writing it off as just getting older. More than 200 medicines can cause sexual problems, and combining two or more drugs could be deadly for your sex drive. Blood pressure medicine is a major culprit, as well as steroid drugs you may take for arthritis.

You don't have to just accept the sexual side effects of drugs as inevitable. Several drugs may be available to treat your health problem, and some of them may not cause sexual problems as a side effect. Or you may be able to take a lower dose of your medicine.

One option for people on blood pressure medicine is to try intercourse first thing in the morning, before you've taken the medicine.

Here are a few of the drugs that can cause low sexual desire or problems with erection or ejaculation:

❦ Antianxiety drugs — BuSpar, Valium, Xanax, Libritabs

❦ Antidepressants — Desyrel, Elavil, Norpramin, Paxil, Prozac, Sinequan, Tofranil, Zoloft, Asendin

❦ High blood pressure drugs — Aldomet, Catapres, Esimil, Inderal, Lopressor, Minipress, Tenormin

❦ Diuretics — Aldactone, Diamox, Dyazide, HydroDIURIL, Lozol, Maxzide

❦ H2-receptor antagonists (ulcer drugs) — Pepcid, Tagamet, Zantac

❦ Digoxin (heart drug) — Lanoxin

The secret to staying young could simply be a good night's sleep. Sleep rejuvenates and revitalizes your body. Human growth hormone (HGH) is produced only during deep sleep. The amount of deep sleep you get, and the amount of growth hormone you make, decreases with age. If you could get more deep sleep and, therefore, produce more HGH, you might be able to slow down the aging process.

SLEEP

As you drift into sleep, late evening thoughts and dreamy images begin to fade. Blood flow to your brain drops as it flows out to meet the needs of your muscles and internal organs. Like a house settling down for the night, your central nervous system rests so you aren't bothered by sounds, smells, and other distractions of the senses. Your body temperature drops. You just let it all go as respiration, blood pressure, metabolism, and heart rate slow.

Then, like the thermostat in your house, deepest sleep kicks on the mechanisms in your pituitary gland to release human growth hormone (HGH) in precise amounts. Deep sleep, with the aid of HGH, enables your body to repair skin, organs, and bones. It replenishes blood cells needed to ward off disease and infection. And it builds and repairs muscles. According to Dr. Michael Thorpy of the Sleep-Wake Disorder

Center in New York, muscle tissue regenerates only when you sleep. Therefore, deep sleep may be the real fountain of youth, and HGH, the revitalizing spring.

Sleep consists of two types — rapid eye movement (REM) sleep and non-REM sleep. When you settle down for the night, you move through the four non-REM stages. They last 80 to 100 minutes altogether. Stage 1 sleep is the lightest. In the slightly deeper stage 2 sleep, brain activity slows. Finally, you enter stages 3 and 4, marked by slow brain waves known as delta waves. This is deep sleep.

Afterwards, brain activity kicks back on as you enter REM sleep. Here, you dream. Your eyes race back and forth under closed lids. Your muscles go limp to prevent you from acting out your dreams. After approximately 30 minutes of REM sleep, you begin again. You cycle through non-REM and REM sleep four or five times a night. Each time, deep sleep grows shorter and REM lengthens.

Without REM sleep, you may suffer behavioral or psychiatric disorders or have trouble learning and remembering. But without deep sleep, your body weakens.

5 WAYS SLEEP FIGHTS AGING

As you get older, your sleep patterns change. Your needs do not. At age 20, you get close to two hours of deep sleep a night. By age 65, you get 30 minutes. You wake up easier at night. And though you may nap in the daytime, it does not compensate for your deep sleep needs.

Reasons for changing sleep patterns vary. Your sleep can be disrupted by medical conditions, a slower metabolism, depression, lack of exercise, shift changes, or medicine you take.

Researchers are finding that some older people don't produce enough of the hormone melatonin that's needed for sleep. They still don't know for sure what comes first — too little melatonin or breakdowns in your body clock that make it harder for you to produce melatonin.

However, if you can find out what problems or factors are disturbing your sleep, you can change them. Deep sleep can be increased, giving you greater rejuvenating power.

Stroke. Are you a heavy snorer, or have you ever woken up at night gasping for air? Has your spouse ever shaken you awake because you stopped breathing in your sleep? You may have sleep apnea. Sleep apnea refers to shallow or disrupted breathing during sleep. This thief in the night robs you of oxygen, upsetting your heart rhythm and causing surges in your blood pressure. Ultimately, these changes might increase your risk of stroke. Knowledge is power, however. And apnea can be treated.

Heart disease. That snorting and gasping in the middle of the night may make you more likely to suffer heart disease, too. When blood oxygen levels drop because you aren't breathing in enough air, your heart muscle can weaken. Arteries can become strained. Your heart rhythm can run off kilter, forcing your heart to jump-start itself. This can be particularly tough on people who already have heart disease, accelerating the disease and increasing their risks of heart attack in the morning.

Memory and learning. Getting enough sleep improves your ability to learn and remember. REM sleep helps you learn mental tasks like solving math problems and word puzzles or operating that new computer program. According to Dr. Carlyle Smith of Trent University in Ontario — lose REM sleep on the first and third day after learning a task, and you lose information.

Remember the words of British writer Martin Farquhar Tupper, "It is well to lie fallow for a while." Like soil that loses its nutrients when it's overused, your brain needs time to rest and rejuvenate in order to produce. Stage 2 sleep may be crucial to learning motor tasks like skiing, riding a bicycle, or performing an appendectomy. You may be stumbling along the first day, but after a good night's sleep, you may demonstrate a 20 to 25 percent improvement in your skills.

It's not only how much sleep you get, but the timing as well. If you go to sleep later than usual, you lose information, even if you get a full eight hours sleep. So during learning periods, stay in step with your body clock.

Immune system. When you are sick, your doctor tells you to get plenty of rest, but what about when you are well? Not only does sleep speed up your recovery from illness or injury, it also bolsters your immune system for the needs of tomorrow. In sleep, your body replenishes the cells needed to fend off infections and diseases. One study showed that losing just one night of sleep lowers the action of tumor-fighting blood cells by as much as 30 percent.

Accident prevention. The best accident prevention strategy could be a good night's sleep. Sleepiness is thought to contribute to nearly half of all accident-related deaths in the United States. A congressional commission report listed fatigue as a contributing factor in the Challenger space shuttle explosion, the Exxon Valdez grounding, and the collision of two Conrail freight trains.

Did you know that most accidents occur from 2 to 7 in the morning and from 2 to 5 in the afternoon? That's when most people are least alert. Poor sleeping habits aggravate the situation. Just a couple of hours less sleep a night than usual can leave you nodding at the wheel.

Even the simple change from standard to daylight savings time can jeopardize your performance. So sleep well and keep to a schedule.

YOUR ACTION PLAN

Almost everyone experiences insomnia at some time. Three types of insomnia include transient insomnia, short-term insomnia, and long-term or chronic insomnia.

Transient insomnia is brief. It's what happens during temporary excitement or stress, like when your work shift changes or you just got a promotion and are thinking of what to do with the extra money. This type passes within three days.

Short-term insomnia is caused by illness, pain, grief, or ongoing personal problems — like if your 30-year-old son moves back in with you or you're agonizing about another corporate takeover. Or maybe you just went on a diet and can't sleep because you feel like you're starving to death. This type of insomnia lasts from three days to three weeks.

Long-term or chronic insomnia lasts more than three weeks and could be caused by chronic physical problems, alcohol or drug abuse, or psychological problems such as depression.

Natural methods are the best treatment for most cases of insomnia. Fortunately, self-help suggestions are available.

HOW TO GET MORE SLEEP NATURALLY

First, determine if you have a problem. How well do you feel during the day? Are you energetic and alert? If so, you're probably fine. If you feel tired and irritable in the daytime or feel the need to nap frequently, you may have a sleep problem. Most people are not aware of how often or why they awaken in the night. People who are aware that their sleep is disturbed are rarely able to name the real reason. That's why most sleep problems go untreated.

Keep a sleep journal. Look at how you feel during the day. Take note of when you go to sleep, how long before you fall asleep, and when you wake up. Look at your eating habits. What and when do you eat or drink during the day? Try to count how many times you awaken in the night. List sleeping pills or stimulants you take. Record times you take medication.

Ask yourself if you have more trouble falling asleep, staying asleep, or waking too early. If you have trouble falling asleep, the problem might be in your lifestyle habits like eating or drinking. It could also be from stress, worry, or shift changes.

If you have trouble staying asleep, look at underlying medical conditions, sleep apnea, restless leg syndrome, or psychological problems like depression.

Set a regular schedule for sleeping and waking. We sleep according to an internal body clock known as circadian rhythms. Even the smallest changes in light, body temperature, mealtimes, and daytime activities can throw your internal sleep/wake clock out of whack.

You might be one of those rare birds who have never been able to sleep to anyone's clock but your own. While everyone else is sleeping, you just lie in bed staring at the ceiling until 3 a.m. And then you can't wake up and get to work before noon. Your body clock is offbeat. It's called delayed sleep-phase syndrome.

It's not hopeless. Researchers have found that bright light, much brighter than normal, can kick your body clock into step. So if this has been a lifelong problem for you, consider bright light therapy with a professional. Light exposure therapy can also help if you have jet lag or you have to keep changing your work shift.

Exercise in the afternoon at least three times a week. One study found that 45 minutes of aerobic exercise three times a week increased deep sleep and HGH. Those who only did stretching exercises showed no change in HGH. Afternoon exercise raises body temperature in the daytime, which can increase deep sleep at night. Take care not to exercise too close to bedtime. That will keep you awake.

Take a hot bath. One study found that women over 60 who took a hot bath (105 degrees F) one hour before bedtime increased deep sleep.

Watch your naps. Avoid oversleeping in the morning and don't take late afternoon or evening naps. If you have to nap, the best hours are between 12 and 2 p.m. You can still get some deep sleep time during those hours.

Don't smoke for three to five hours before bed. If you smoke and have insomnia, it may be the smoking that keeps you awake. Studies show that people who smoke often have trouble sleeping. It makes sense. Nicotine acts as a stimulant. This not only robs you of restorative sleep, but also stimulates REM sleep, which may be why you have those bizarre dreams.

Improve your sleep environment. Keep your bedroom quiet, dark, and cool. Also, your bedroom should only be used for sleeping and sex. Make sure that the mattress and sheets are comfortable. Hide the clock so you're not clock watching. Use a humidifier or dehumidifier as your room requires. White noise from a fan or white noise generator might be helpful (not from your television).

Try adjusting the light. Researchers have found that even normal levels of indoor artificial lighting can affect your internal clock. So in the evening, dim the lights before winding down. Make your bedroom dark, and keep curtains open so sunlight can enter in the morning.

Get out of bed if you're not sleepy. If you're far too alert to sleep, don't lie there and agonize. Get up and do something for a while before attempting to sleep again.

Try relaxation methods. Did you wake up this morning feeling like you had been run over by a train? Had you been up half the night worrying? Maybe deep sleep's magic fingers didn't have time to perform any healing miracles. Studies show that stress is a deep sleep spoiler. It's a vicious cycle. Stress disrupts your sleep, which makes you dragged out and irritable. This ruins your daytime performance, which leads to more stress. This ruins your sleep, and on it goes. So try relaxation techniques, such as meditation, to get your mind off your worries before bed. Trained professionals could help you with biofeedback, relaxation training, guided imagery, and hypnosis.

Avoid spicy or heavy foods and large quantities of liquids in the evening. You might find yourself waking to urinate frequently, or waking to discomforts of stomach acid.

However, many people just think they wake up frequently because they need to urinate. Nearly 80 percent of people in a 1996 sleep study awakened from sleep because of sleep apnea, snoring, or periodic leg movements. Only 5 percent correctly reported the reason.

Make sure you're getting enough air. Heavy snoring; nighttime gasping, choking, or snorting; excess upper body weight; and daytime fatigue and sleepiness provide clues to sleep apnea. Sleep laboratories or sleep monitoring equipment can help determine if you have a problem. You may just need an oral appliance that helps keep your airways open during sleep.

Lose extra weight. If snoring or sleep apnea is your problem, you may need to lose some extra weight. One study found that losing weight — even as little as 10 pounds — can cure snoring completely. One man who snored over 300 times an hour almost completely quit when he lost 12 pounds.

Sleep on your side instead of your back. Again, this suggestion is for snorers or people having trouble breathing. A tennis ball sewed into the back of your pajamas can torture you into the right position.

Limit alcohol and caffeine. Caffeine is a stimulant, so avoid drinking caffeine-containing coffee or soft drinks after 12 noon. Don't drink alcohol three to five hours before bedtime. Not only does alcohol disrupt your sleep, but it plays havoc on REM sleep. Remember, you need REM sleep to stay sane.

Alcohol, sedatives, and tranquilizers make sleep apnea and snoring worse, too.

Get treatment for restless leg syndrome. Do you wake suddenly at night without knowing the reason why? Some people are unaware of the periodic leg movements that wake them. Restless leg syndrome means you periodically extend your big toe and flex your knee every 20 to 30 seconds without meaning to. You're on automatic pilot. For some people, it could go on for hours, which can be quite a workout. However, you can still improve your sleep by following the self-help suggestions for insomnia. If all else fails, see your doctor about possible medications used to treat this condition.

Do you need sleeping pills?

Most sleeping pills produce only a light sleep. Prescribed sleeping pills actually decrease the deep sleep you need to rejuvenate your body, and they may have serious side effects. Not only can you get addicted to sleeping pills, but when you stop taking them, your insomnia may be worse than ever. And finally, you become more sensitive to side effects as you get older.

If prescribed, sleeping pills should only be used for transient, short-term insomnia. Sedatives prescribed in the United States include five benzodiazepines: flurazepam, quazepam, estazolam, temazepam, and triazolam. A new drug, Zolpidem, may have fewer side effects without affecting sleep stages. If you are taking sleeping pills, don't quit without seeing your doctor. Withdrawal symptoms can be fatal.

Most over-the-counter medications contain the antihistamines diphenhydramine or doxylamine. Read the label carefully, and don't use them if you have breathing problems, glaucoma, or an enlarged prostate gland. Also, don't mix with alcohol or other sedating/tranquilizing drugs. Diphenhydramine can cause constipation, urinary retention, confusion, poor memory, disorientation, and hallucinations.

> Sleep that knits up the raveled sleave of care,
> The death of each day's life, sore labor's bath,
> Balm of hurt minds, great nature's second course,
> Chief nourisher in life's feast.
> *Shakespeare s MacBeth, Act II, Scene ii*

WHAT ABOUT HERBAL SLEEP POTIONS?

Melatonin. The verdict is still out on melatonin. Melatonin is a hormone produced in the pineal gland, signaling sleep-wake rhythms. It works by fine-tuning your body's temperature and internal clock. Researchers have found that some older people have a melatonin deficiency. Melatonin replacement therapy did improve their sleep quality. Also, it has been found to be useful in treating visually impaired people with sleep disturbances, people with delayed sleep-phase syndrome, and people with jet lag.

However, correct dosage and timing is critical, and researchers are still trying to figure these out. One study found that the maximum effective dosage with the least adverse effects seems to be .3 to 1 mg. Most over-the-counter preparations are well over this amount.

According to Richard Wurtman of the Massachusetts Institute of Technology's Clinical Research Center, no one should take melatonin outside of controlled research facilities. First, melatonin is not FDA regulated, which leaves room for contamination in commercial preparations. Second, over-the-counter dosages are far higher than that normally found in the body. And finally, possible drug interactions and long-term effects haven't been determined yet.

Taken by mouth, melatonin has mild sleep-inducing effects, but this is light sleep. Like prescribed sleeping pills, it seems to diminish deep sleep. Also, melatonin may deepen depression and constrict arteries. We still don't know about the effects on pregnancy or puberty. And finally, despite claims of cancer-fighting abilities, one study found melatonin to increase melanoma cancer in hamsters.

For more information about melatonin, see the *Melatonin* chapter.

Valerian. Recent tests of the herbal sleep aid, valerian, found it to have a mild tranquilizing effect in older people with disturbed sleep. Valerian improved the quality of sleep by increasing slow wave delta sleep and reducing stage 1 sleep. Researchers found no change in young people with normal sleep. Valerian can be purchased for under $10 at most health food stores.

Lavender. The sweet aroma of lavender may help people with insomnia. In one study, elderly people enjoyed a more restful sleep after being exposed to the smell of lavender oil.

WHAT DREAMS SAY ABOUT YOUR HEALTH

The ancient Greeks believed that dreams could warn us about potential illness. They may have been right, says tentative research reported in the *British Medical Journal*.

For example, if you're a man and you dream about death and dying, you could have a heart problem. If you're a woman, a heart problem might surface in dreams of separation.

Dreams of losing items you need could mean you're losing brain function.

When you dream that you can't remember things or when your dreams have little visual content, something could be going wrong with your central nervous system.

If you often get angry in your dreams, you're at risk for high blood pressure.

And finally, with severe disease, you may not be able to dream at all.

"Flight or fight." That basic, instinctive reaction to danger primed our bodies for battle or hasty retreat in prehistoric times. But today, when our hormones surge in response to stress, it's all too often inappropriate and even harmful. Traffic jams, workplace wars, family squabbles, and depression leave our bodies worn out every day. Those powerful stress hormones can eventually weaken our immune systems and our health in general.

STRESS-FREE LIVING

Suppose you are in a car accident, or someone is attacking you. Your body releases chemicals that prepare you to cope with the stress or run from it. Scientists call this the "fight or flight response." Here's what the chemicals adrenalin and cortisol do:

❦ Your muscles contract to provide a stronger protection from bodily injury.

❦ Your metabolism speeds up to provide strength and energy.

❦ Your heart beats faster.

❦ Your digestive system speeds up to give your muscles extra nutrients.

❦ You breathe rapidly to provide more oxygen to your body.

❦ Your pupils dilate to aid vision, and your hearing becomes more acute.

❦ Blood clots more quickly and arteries constrict. That keeps you from losing as much blood if you are cut. Ever notice that your hands and feet get colder when you are under stress? It's because your arteries have tightened up and reduced blood flow.

Nature has provided all these helpful responses for emergency situations. Unfortunately, your body responds in just about the same way to chronic stress. That's the long-term kind of stress you experience daily because your life is too fast-paced or your negative emotions are out of control.

QUICK STRESS BUSTERS

On some days, it's tough to squeeze out even 20 minutes to practice stress reduction. Here are some quick, simple things you can fit into even the busiest day to reduce your stress and lighten your mood.

❦ Listen to music.
❦ Do 10 jumping jacks.
❦ Squeeze a stress ball.
❦ Sing.
❦ Watch fish in a aquarium.
❦ Do a crossword puzzle.
❦ Read a magazine or newspaper article.
❦ Savor a glass of water with a lemon twist.
❦ Rub a pet.
❦ Look at the sky for one minute.
❦ Ask a friend to tell you a joke.

Do these sound silly? Try them. They work.

8 WAYS STRESS-FREE LIVING FIGHTS AGING

Makes bones stronger. Studies show that exposure to the stress hormone cortisol causes the bones to lose mass and become brittle. People who are depressed, with bloodstreams constantly full of circulating cortisol, are more likely to have osteoporosis.

You may know that cortisol is also made in laboratories as a drug to treat problems like rheumatoid arthritis and asthma. Doctors have known for years that long-term use of these steroid drugs can cause health problems like thinning bones. It's not so surprising that you can face similar health problems if your body produces too much cortisol in response to long periods of stress.

Slims and trims your waistline. Both cortisol and adrenaline cause your body to redistribute excess fat to your tummy where it's less healthy. Of course, eating too much food and not exercising enough can play a role in your increasing waistline as well.

Keeps your brain young. Learning to relax will help you maintain your brain power into old age. The chemicals released during stress destroy brain cells, especially in the area that controls learning and memory.

This same brain area is in charge of releasing stress hormones. Damage to this area causes more hormones to be released, which only harms that same area of the brain even more. The effects of this vicious cycle are even stronger in older people subjected to stress.

Boosts immune function. A relaxed person is a healthier person. Even the ancient Greeks realized that stress was connected to illness. Recent studies prove that stress slows the body's production of natural bacteria and virus fighters. Without the right level of these germ-busters in your body, you go to war against disease without any guns.

Wounds heal faster. In one study, older people with stubborn ulcers of the feet and legs were taught relaxation techniques with biofeedback. After six months, these people experienced

10 times greater healing of the ulcers than people who didn't use the relaxation techniques.

In another study, researchers carefully wounded 26 women with an instrument. Half the women were caring for a relative with Alzheimer's disease. The wounds of these caregivers took significantly longer to heal than normal. Researchers linked the slower healing with the extreme psychological stress the women were under.

Life is happier and more hopeful. Stress in itself is bad enough, but life under pressure can eventually turn into depression — a much worse state of affairs. Sometimes, stress as far back as childhood can change the way you deal with life, leading to more stress and depression as you get older.

For example, if you grew up in a family that argued often, you may try to avoid controversy now. You may be less likely to speak up when people treat you badly, just to keep the peace. Dealing with stress this way is a prescription for depression.

Some studies indicate that stress plays a role in depression by causing the brain to produce a chemical called norepinephrine. That chemical can make you anxious, disrupt sleeping patterns, lower your appetite and sex drive, and cause feelings of helplessness. All of these are warning signs of depression.

Less stress, healthier heart. Work life, environmental catastrophes, anger, and anxiety are all stresses that, for some people, can trigger a heart attack.

Work. Working long hours in a high-pressure job causes an increase in cortisol and adrenaline. That speeds the heart and increases blood pressure, which can cause heart attacks, one study found. Some of the highest risk jobs are bus driving, railway work, and nursing. What do they have in common?

- ❦ Long hours
- ❦ A fast pace
- ❦ Lots of responsibility
- ❦ Few social contacts

People in these kinds of jobs tend to overeat and smoke to help them deal with the stress, which makes them even more likely to have a heart attack.

Of course, work doesn't necessarily stress you out. It can give you a feeling of productivity and social support that may actually lower stress. Work has been proven to help some people with heart disease.

Environmental catastrophes. California residents may not want to hear this, but natural disasters such as earthquakes can stress your body enough to cause a heart attack.

On the day of the 1994 Northridge earthquake that shook the Los Angeles area, 24 people died from a sudden heart attack. Hospitals in the area reported a 35 percent increase in admissions for heart attacks in the week following the earthquake, too.

Anger and anxiety. Your mental state appears to play as much of a role in triggering heart attacks as heavy physical activity. Anger and anxiety can decrease the flow of blood to the heart, which can cause a heart attack.

Calm outlook cuts cancer risk. Need another reason to get rid of raging emotions and day-to-day pressures? They boost your risk of cancers of the breast, colon, and rectum, researchers say. Unfortunately, events that are out of your control, like a death or illness in the family, seem to be the most harmful. But if you can learn to find peace during bad situations, you will be protecting your body as well as your sanity.

You may be interested in how Japanese researchers determined the link between stress and cancer in the body. (Animal lovers may want to skip this paragraph.) The researchers gave electric shocks to one group of rats and made another group watch, listen, and smell this cruelty. The watching rats experienced dramatic changes in their genetic material, their DNA. The same changes have been found in DNA when animals are exposed to high levels of free radicals.

So here's what the researchers theorized: The stress hormone cortisol shifts blood from the internal organs to the brain and muscles so we'll be prepared for emergencies. Once the stressful event is over, blood flow returns to normal. In fact, the blood rushes back to the internal organs, which by this time are starved for nutrients and oxygen. That burst of oxygen-rich blood increases the production of free radicals (oxygen causes free radicals, remember), and the free radicals damage your DNA.

Your body normally may be able to kill most of those damaged, precancerous cells, but stress has also weakened your immune system. You're out of luck.

YOUR ACTION PLAN

Help! Can you feel the rush of cortisol in your bloodstream? The stress of reading all this information about the dangers of stress is probably killing you. It's not like you can control the bad traffic, pushy boss, irritable spouse, ill loved one, or unhappy children in your life.

No, you can't control those stressors. But anyone who has read Stephen Covey's *The 7 Habits of Highly Effective People* knows that you can choose how you will respond to the events and people in your life. As far as *you* are concerned, there's a lot you can control.

Understand yourself. Do you feel guilty because things that are stressful for you seem to be the spice of life for your best friend? Your friend may have life more under control, but the two of you probably just have different personalities. Use this quiz developed by the True Colors, a personality consulting firm, to better understand yourself. That's a good start to putting some peace in your life.

Gold personalities are very organized. They plan ahead, uphold tradition, are practical, dependable and have a clear sense of right and wrong. You are happiest at work when you have clear procedures to follow every day. Your major stressors:

❦ constant change
❦ disorganization

Blue personalities are very caring, affectionate and do anything to avoid conflict. (Don't worry about the label; it doesn't mean you live a sad life!) The feelings of others are important to you, and you constantly strive to improve yourself. Your major stressors:

❦   rivalry and competition

Green personalities are the thinkers. They like to see the big picture, and they look at things in a logical way. They are often demanding, especially of themselves. Routine bothers Greens, and they constantly try to improve things. If you are a perfectionist, you are probably a Green. Your major stressors:

❦   repetitive tasks
❦   people who want to play rather than work

Orange personalities live for the moment and like a lot of activity. They are easily bored and enjoy doing things on the spur of the moment. They are spontaneous and hate to wait for anything. Disorder is their best friend. Major stressors:

❦   working in a structured environment or
      living with a spouse who makes lists for everything
❦   any activity that keeps them from moving ahead

Get it in perspective. Once you've pinpointed exactly what is stressing you, try to cut the situation down to size by asking yourself questions like these:

❦   What's the worst that could happen?
❦   How likely is that to happen?
❦   Have I done all I can to keep that from happening?
❦   Will it change my life, or will I not even remember
      it years from now?
❦   What would I tell a friend in a similar situation?

Once you gain perspective, refocus those wildly spinning thoughts. Think deeply about your goals in life. Think about a relaxing situation. Take a shower or a walk around the block. Or just realize that you are human and doing the best you can.

Relax your body. Proven stressbusters are yoga, deep breathing, or any form of exercise — different things work best for different people.

If you don't already have a favorite relaxation technique, try this one. Sit in a comfortable position in a quiet area. Loosen your clothing. Close your eyes tightly and begin to tighten the muscles all over your body from head to toe. Once your whole body is tight, begin to relax your muscle groups. As you relax, focus on breathing deeply until your entire body is relaxed.

Next, imagine you are in a place you find especially safe, relaxing, and comfortable. Let your thoughts wander like butterflies. Don't hold anything back. Stay in this place in your mind for five or 10 minutes, then slowly bring yourself back to reality. Gently open your eyes to find yourself refreshed and relaxed.

Cry when you need to. It's true that teary temper tantrums may not make you feel any better. And tears you cry to prove how pitiful you are will probably make you feel worse. But in most situations, tears can be the best thing you can do for your body.

The Roman poet Ovid wrote, "It is a relief to weep. Grief is satisfied and carried off by tears." Stress experts today echo that sentiment: It's not only all right to cry, it's healthy.

You learn that tears are wrong from your well-meaning parents, who would do just about anything to quiet your crying. But now experts realize the bodily harm of repressed tears and withheld emotions.

Asthma and hives get better or disappear once a person begins to cry. Crying lowers blood pressure and reduces muscle tension.

Some research even suggests that tears themselves help rid the body of harmful chemicals released when you are under stress. The tears your body makes because of emotional stress are chemically different from those you shed when you have something caught in your eye.

Take control with biofeedback. Imagine having control over your brain waves, temperature, blood pressure, breathing, heart rate, and the electrical charge of your body. You would have power over your physical reaction to stress.

Biofeedback lets you learn how to recognize changes in your body and use your mental powers to control those changes. You'll need the help of a trained biofeedback specialist and the right equipment to learn to control your brain waves and your body's electrical charge. But you can learn on your own to be aware of your breathing, heart rate, and temperature.

When you are under stress, take a few minutes to focus on bringing your body back to normal.

Find relief in prayer. Twelve Gallup polls over the last 35 years have found that most Americans believe in the power of prayer to heal, and medical experts are coming to that same conclusion. Researchers actually did a scientific study to find out whether people cope with life stresses like major illness better if they have a strong faith and pray regularly. The conclusion? Yes, they do cope better.

Prayer is comforting because you can do it yourself and it's warm and kind — two things modern medicine is missing. Faith can offer meaning during difficult times and help you make sense of a situation. It can raise your self esteem, make you feel capable and give you feelings of dignity and purpose.

Some scientists believe that prayer heals because it relaxes you. That counters the effects of the stress hormone cortisol, which weakens the immune system so that you can't fight off disease properly.

No one can say (at least with scientific accuracy) whether a belief in God and miracles is enough to reduce stress and help the body heal, or whether God actually intervenes with a divine healing hand. Just how the healing occurs doesn't really matter to the many people who experience stress relief and healing from prayer.

Massage your stress away. Want to sink into a comfortable, safe environment far from car horns, children, and co-workers demanding something done yesterday? Lose yourself to long strokes across your back and the kneading of tight, tense muscles with a good massage. It will push stress and tension miles away.

If that's not enough to get you to a massage therapist, consider the findings from a National Institutes of Health study. Experts at the Touch Research Institute of the University of Miami Medical School knew massage had worked time after time to pull people out of depression. So they decided to try it on a group that really needed help — stressed and depressed mothers of new babies. When a mother stays depressed for more than six months after her baby is born, the baby shows delays in growth and development.

The mothers got a 20-minute massage twice a week. After four weeks, their depression and anxiety began to vanish, and they had lower levels of the stress hormones, including cortisol.

Peace grows with plants. Plants spruce up your sur-roundings and your health, too. In a University of Delaware study, hospital patients with a view of a landscape recovered from surgery nearly a day faster than patients who could only see a brick wall. They even needed less pain-killing medicine.

A 20-minute walk in a garden a few times a week did won-ders for women recovering from breast cancer surgery. Women who have had breast cancer surgery tend to be depressed. They are also so tired mentally that their ability to concentrate and focus is equal to that of people with brain dam-age. The garden walks helped the women get their lives back together more quickly.

Other studies show that plants in offices can clean up the air and lighten the mood.

DO YOUR OWN THING

Some stress busters will work for anyone. Who wouldn't benefit by a walk in the garden, for example? But stress expert Dr. Marcia Yudkin cautions that stress reduction is a personal matter. "You need to find out what works for you," Dr. Yudkin says. "It's going to be different from what works for the next person."

If you don't like animals, cuddling with a cat probably isn't some-thing you should do to relieve stress. And lifting weights at a gym could help one person blow off steam, but add stress to another person.

Dr. Yudkin suggests taking a quick look at the things you like to do to determine whether you are motivated by things that are visual, auditory (hearing), or kinesthetic (movement).

If you're always humming, you may be an auditory person. Listening to music or talking with a friend may relax you the most. Are you fidgety? You may be kinesthetic. Movement-oriented peo-ple can relax by squeezing a stress ball, touching their toes a few times, or exchanging back rubs with a spouse. If you are visual, reading or just looking at flowers or the sky will help calm you down.

SOURCES

"Facts About Potassium: How to meet your potassium requirements," American Heart Association, Dallas

"Guaranteed Potency Herbs," Nutrition Information Services, Inc.

"The Flavonoids" by Dr. Elliott Middleton, Jr., Clinical Professor of Pharmacy, State University of New York at Buffalo

A Profile of Older Americans. U.S. Administration on Aging. Internet WWW page <http://www.aoa.dhhs.gov/>

Across the Board (33,2:21)

Ad for Chrom'n SWEET

Age and Ageing (20:169; 22:5; and 25:285)

AIDS Weekly Plus

Alternative & Complementary Therapies (2,1:1,51,56)

Alternative Medicine: The Definitive Guide, Future Medicine Publishing, Puyallup, Wash.

Alternative Medicine: What Works, Odonian Press, Tucson, Ariz.

American Botanical Council, Botanical Series No. 302 - *Siberian Ginseng,* No. 303 - *Asian Ginseng,* No. 308 - *American Ginseng,* No. 311 - *Garlic*

American Diabetic Association Diabetes Information Service Center, 1660 Duke St., Alexandria, VA 22314

American Family Physician (46,1:250; 50,5:1067; 51,8:1977; 53,4:1245; and 54,4:1367,1374)

American Fitness (10,5:46)

American Health (15,1:67; 15,4:94; and 15,9:66)

American Heart Association News Release No. 96-4396 and No. 96-4408

American Institute for Cancer Research Newsletter (39:4,5; 47:9; 48:10; and 49:10)

American Journal of Cardiology (65,7:521 and 66,4:504)

American Journal of Chinese Medicine (IX,2:112)

American Journal of Clinical Nutrition (52,11:93; 58,4:468; 61,2:320; 62,2:392; 62,4:740; and 63,3S:423)

American Journal of Epidemiology (133,8:766; 139,12:1180; 143,3:240; and 144,3:275)

American Journal of Epidemiology Supplement

American Journal of Hypertension (4,6:557)

American Journal of Medical Science (306,1:10; 306,5:320; 310,6:242; and 311,5:205)

American Journal of Natural Medicine (2,1:6)

American Journal of Nursing (78,8:1352)

American Journal of Physiology (264,5:R992)

American Journal of Psychiatry (147,4:462)

An Introduction to the Doctrine of Signatures. Tamarra S. James. Internet WWW page <http://www.capital.net/users/tamlin/sigdoc.htm>

Annals of Internal Medicine (115,10:753; 116,5:353; 119,7:599; 120,1S:9; 124,7:673; 124,9:825; 124,12:1051; and 125,2:81)

Annals of Pharmacotherapy (29,6:625)

Annals of the New York Academy of Sciences (570:283,291; 587:196; 669:87; 676:188; and 691:148)

Annals of the Rheumatic Diseases (53,1:51)

Annual Reviews in Biochemistry (52:711)

Archives of Biochemistry and Biophysics (279,2:402 and 300,2:535)

Archives of Environmental Health (46,1:37)

Archives of Family Medicine (4,4:304; 4,8:667; 5,7:420; and 5,10:593)

Archives of Internal Medicine (150,1:197; 155,3:241; 155,4:415; 155,7:734; 155,21:2302; 156,5:537,545; 156,6:637; 156,10:1097; 156,11:1143; 156,12:1258,1293; 156,14:1506; 156,18:2073; and 156,19:2213)

Archives of Ophthalmology (112,2:222)

Arteriosclerosis and Thrombosis (13,8:1205)

Arthritis and Rheumatology (39,1:64)

Arthritis Today (1,30:4; 4,8:1; 5,5:44; 6,4:34; 9,4:9; 9,6:9; 10,1:51; 10,2:35; and 10,3:13,31,34,48)

Ask Dr. Weil. Internet WWW page <http://www.drweil.com>

"Aspirin and health: impressive new health benefits of a very old remedy," American Council on Science and Health

Aviation Medical Bulletin

Basic Life Sciences (61:17)

Better Nutrition (51,10:23)

Better Nutrition (58,1:12,34; 58,2:54; 58,3:68; 58,4:36,54,62; 58,5:28; 58,7:16,34; and 58,9:34)

Better Nutrition for Today's Living (55,2:56; 55,7:46,58; 57,4:12; 57,7:28; 57,8:28; and 57,10:12)

Biochemical and Biophysical Research Communications (192,1:241 and 204,1:98)

Biological Psychiatry (23,4:405 and 29,11:1092)

Biology: The Network of Life, HarperCollins Publishers, New York

Biomarkers: The 10 Keys to Prolonging Vitality, Fireside, New York

Biostatistical Fact Sheet. American Heart Association. Internet WWW page <http://www.amhrt.org/>

Biotechnology Therapeutics (5,3-4:117)

Boosting Immunity With Herbs. Herbal Research Foundation. Internet WWW page <http://www.herbs.org/herbs/immune/html>

Bowes and Church's Food Values of Portions Commonly Used, HarperPerennial, New York

Brain Research (447,2:269; 448,1:178; and 633,1:253)

British Journal of Cancer (73,5:687)

British Medical Journal (299,6705:934; 305,6866:1392; 306,6875:448; 306,6883:993; 306,6889:1367; 306,6890:1468; 309,6948:167; 310, 6981:693; 310,6986:1050; 310,6994:1559,1563; 311,7013:1124; 311,7017:1399; 311,7018:1486; 311,7019:1527; 312,7031:599,608; 312,7041:1237,1242,1249,1263; 312,7045:1512)

Can Hormones Reverse Aging? U.S. Department of Health and Human Services, Public Health Service, National Institutes of Health, National Institute on Aging, Gaithersburg, Md.

Can Selenium prevent cancer? Epidemiologic study expanded to investigate selenium's impact on multiple cancers. Internet WWWpage <http://www.azcc.arizona.edu/www/text_files/prev_cont/selenium.html>

Canadian Medical Association Journal (154,8:1193)

Cancer (64,11:2347)

Cancer and Nutrition, Avery Publishing Group, Garden City Park, N.Y.

Cancer Biotechnology Weekly

Cancer Detection and Prevention (18,6:415)

Cancer Research (49,14:4020 and 56,8:1724)

Cancer Researcher Weekly

Cancer Weekly

Cancer Weekly Plus

Cardiovascular Research (18,10:591)

Care and Planting of Ginseng Seed and Roots. North Carolina Cooperative Extension Service. Internet WWW page <http://gopher.ces.ncsu.edu/depts/hort/hil/hil-127. html>

CDC AIDS Weekly

Cecil Textbook of Medicine, W.B. Saunders Company, Philadelphia, Pa.

Chest (109,3:659)

Chinese Journal of Integrated Traditional and Western Medicine (4,10:578; 7,5:262; 10,10:579; and 11,8:451)

Circulation (87,3:1017; 90,3:1154; 90,4:I-665; and 94,1:14)

Comparative Medicine East and West (VI,4:277)

Complete Guide to Symptoms, Illness & Surgery, The Berkley Publishing Group, New York

Complete Guide to Vitamins, Minerals and Supplements, Fisher Books, Tucson, Ariz.

Consultant (36,1:124)

Consumer Reports (60,8:510 and 60,11:698)

Consumers Research Magazine (73:8 and 78:10)

Controlling Your Fat Tooth, Workman Publishing, New York

Country Living (19,1:42 and 20,3:23)

Current Health (22,4:26)

Delaying the Onset of Late-Life Dysfunction, Springer Publishing Co., N.Y.

Delicious! Magazine. Internet WWW page <http://www.newhope.com/public/delicious/ D!_backs/Apr_96/ginger.html>

DHEA: A Practical Guide, Avery Publishing Group, Garden City Park, N.Y.

Diabetes & the Hypoglycemic Syndrome, New Lifestyle Books, Seale, Ala.

Diabetes (40,5:583)

Diabetes Care (17,12:1498 and 18,10:1373)

Diabetes Forecast (48,9:52)

Diabetes: The Facts That Let You Regain Control of Your Life, John Wiley and Sons, New York

Dietary Fiber to Lower Cancer Risk, American Institute for Cancer Research, 1759 R. Street, N.W., Washington, D.C., 20069

Dietary Guidelines to Lower Cancer Risk, American Institute for Cancer Research, 1759 R. Street, N.W., Washington, D.C. 20069

Digestive Diseases and Sciences (35,5:630)

Discover (17,4:50)

Documenta Ophthalmologica (81,4:387)

Dr. Dean Ornish's Program for Reversing Heart Disease, Random House, New York,

Drug & Cosmetic Industry (158,1:44)

Drug Metabolism and Drug Interactions (8,3-4:313)

Drugs Under Experimental and Clinical Research (XVI,10:537)

East West Natural Health (22,1:33)

Encyclopedia of Natural Medicine, Prima Publishing, Rocklin, Calif.

Environmental Nutrition (13,3:1; 14,8:1; 16,3:1; 18,2:1; 18,12:3; 19,2:1,7; 19,5:7,8; 19,7:7; 19,9:1; and 19,10:1,7)

Essence (27,1:40)

European Journal of Cancer Prevention (3,2:101)

European Journal of Clinical Nutrition (47:97 and 49:282)

Everything You Need to Know about Diseases, Springhouse Corporation, Springhouse, Pa.

Executive Health's Good Health Report (32,4:6)

Experimental Cell Respiration (217,2:309)

Experimental Gerontology (28,4-5:473)

EXS (62:411,423)

Facts About Olestra, Nutrition Fact Sheet from the National Center for Nutrition and Dietetics

Facts and Comparisons Drug Newsletter (15,9:71)

FASEB Journal (9,3:A135 and 10,8:829)

FDA Consumer (26,5:26; 27,5:9; 28,4:15; 28,7:14; 30,2:25,31; 30,3:2,8; and 30,5:30)

Flower & Garden Magazine (37,3:28)

Food Safety Notebook (7,1:4 and 7,6:54)

Free Radicals, Aging, and Degenerative Diseases, Alan R. Liss Inc., New York

General Pharmacology (16,6:549)

Geriatrics (45,4:81; 47,11:39,45; 48,5:61; 48,10:57; 49,9:20; 50,1:20,56; 50,2:59; 50,7:14; 51,4:16,23,58; 51,5:11; 51,6:19,60; and 51,9:13)

Gerontologist (30:39A)

Ginger Ale. Cats Meow 3. Internet WWW page <http://alpha.rollanet.org:80/cm3/recs/12_09.html>

Gut (38,1:59)

Hamilton and Whitney's Nutrition Concepts and Controversies, West Publishing Co., St. Paul, Minn.

Harvard Health Letter (18,3:8; 21,6:6; and 21,11:6)

Harvard Heart Letter (6,11:1)

HeadLines (92:2)

Health (10,4:70)

Health and Stress (2:1)

Health Benefits of Soy Protein. James W. Anderson, M.D., <http://www.ag.uiuc.edu/~stratsoy/soyhealth.html>

Health Link (2,1:1)

Health News and Review (18:1)

Healthfacts (21,205:1)

HealthNews (2,5:1,3 and 2,17:3,8)

Healthy Weight Journal (8,4:73)

Heartstyle (3,3:2)

Herbal Medicine, Beaconsfield Publishers Ltd., Beaconsfield, England

Herbal Prescriptions for Better Health: Your Everyday Guide to Prevention, Treatment, and Cure, Prima Publishing, Rocklin, Calif.

Herbal Tonic Therapies, Keats Publishing, New Canaan, Conn.

HerbalGram (25:7,16,18,41; 27:22,23; 30:11; 31:16; 32:13,35; 33:13; 34:12; 36:17,62; 37:16,17,34,38,64; and 38:47)

Herbs for Health (1,3:27,31)

Herbs of Choice: The Therapeutic Use of Phytomedicinals, The Haworth Press, Binghamton, N.Y.

Home Mechanix (92,806:36)

Hope Health Letter (XVI,2:1)

Hormone replacement therapy and heart disease: the PEPI trial, National Heart,

Lung, and Blood Institute, Bethesda, Md.

How To Be Your Own Nutritionist, Avon Books, New York

Hypertension (21,6:1024; 23,4:513; 24,1:77)

Identifying Stress. David Wayne, M.D. Internet WWW page <http://www.health-net.com/idstress.htm>

Important Events in the History of Tea. Birger Nielsen. Internet WWW page <http://www.nitehawk.dk/bnielsen/teachronology.html>

In Health (4,1:37)

In Search of the Secrets of Aging, U.S. Department of Health and Human Services, Public Health Service, National Institutes of Health, NIH Publication No. 93-2756, Bethesda, Md.

International Journal for Vitamin and Nutrition Research (30S:215; 63,3:195; and 64,1:3)

International Journal of Neuroscience (52:85)

International Journal of Obesity (10,3:193 and 14,2:95)

International Journal of Tissue Reactions (12,3:155,169)

Introduction to Coenzyme Q10. Peter H. Langsjoen, M.D., Internet WWW page <http://weber.u.washington.edu/~ely/coenzq10.html>

Investigative Ophthalmology and Visual Science (37,5:923)

Japanese Journal of Antibiotics (48,3:432)

Journal of Advancement in Medicine (8,1:37)

Journal of Clinical Endocrinology and Metabolism (77,5:1215 and 80,11:3373)

Journal of Clinical Epidemiology (47,9:1021 and 48,11:1379)

Journal of Clinical Pharmacology (30,7:596)

Journal of Dairy Science (73,4:905 and 78,7:1597)

Journal of Food Science (58,6:1407)

Journal of Internal Medicine (225,2:85)

Journal of Nutritional Science and Vitaminology (39:S57)

Journal of the American College of Cardiology (27,3:585)

Journal of the American College of Nutrition (12,2:196; 12,4:442; 12,6:651; 13,1:45; 14,2:116,124; 14,4:317,336,369,387; 14,5:419,428; and 15,4:323,340,359,364)

Journal of the American Dietetic Association (93,9:1000; 93,11:1285; 93,12:1446; 94,4:425; 94,7:739; and 96,7:693)

Journal of the American Geriatrics Society (41,2:143; 41,8:829; 43,6:663; and 43,7:822)

Journal of the American Optometric Association (67,1:30)

Journal of the National Cancer Institute (83,8:541,547; 84,1:47; 84,13:996,1000; 85,18:1448; 85,19:1571; 86,1:33; 86,11:855; 86,23:1746; 88,2:67; 88,16:1105; and 88,19;137,1339)

Journal of Women's Health (5,3:213)

Journal Watch (11,7:53; 12,1:2; 15,12:95; 16,3:24; 16,6:45,46,51; 16,11:91; 16,14:115; and 16,15:121)

Kidney International (48:475)

Let's Live (62,12:17)

Life Science (55,25-26:2019 and 58,5:87)

Lilies of the Kitchen, St. Martin's Press, New York

Look Ten Years Younger, Live Ten Years Longer: A Woman's Guide, Prentice Hall, Englewood Cliffs, N.J.

Maclean's (109,20:31)

Magic and Medicine of Plants, Readers Digest Assoc., Pleasantville, N.Y.

Magnesium Research (6,4:369)

Mechanisms of Ageing and Development (83:43)

Medical Abstracts Newsletter (13,4:2; 15,7:6; 16,2:6,8; and 16,11:7)

Medical Applications of Clinical Nutrition, Keats Publishing, New Canaan, Conn.

Medical Hypotheses (43,4:253)

Medical Tribune for the Family Physician (34,22:3 and 37,7:1)

Medical Tribune for the Internist and Cardiologist (33,22:6; 34,18:9; 36,1:16,19; 36,2:17; 36,3:1; 36,4:14,17; 36,5:9,17; 36,7:19; 36,9:4; 36,11:7,14; 36,13:24; 36,14:20; 36,15:21; 36,16:2,4; 36,18:1,8,13,17; 36,19:3; 36,20:16; 36,21:17; 36,22:7; 36,23:16,18; 36,24:2,18; 37,2:2,17; 37,3:1; 37,4:1; 37,10:1,7; 37,11:2; 37,13:8; 37,16:17; and 37,20:19)

Medical Update (19,3:5; 19,6:2,3; 19,8:6; and 20,2:2)

Melatonin: The Anti-Aging Hormone, Avon Books, New York

Melatonin: Your Body's Natural Wonder Drug, Bantam Books, New York

Midland Reporter-Telegram

Mothering (62:52)

Natural Healing Newsletter (7,74:5; 7,77:3; 7,83:6; and 8,88:8)

Natural Health (24,2:44; 25,4:92; 26,2:82; and 26,4:102)

Natural Prescriptions, Crown Publishers, New York

NCAHF Newsletter (17,6:3)

NCI Cancer Weekly

NCRR Reporter (20,3:3)

Neoplasma (40,4:235)

Neurobiology of Aging (8,4:329)

New Crop. James A. Duke. Internet WWW page <http://www.hort.purdue.edu/new-crop/duke—energy/Camellia_sinesis#Uses>

New Zealand Medical Journal (103,866:120)

Newsweek

Next Generation Herbal Medicine, Keats Publishing, New Canaan, Conn.

Nursing Research (45,2:68)

Nursing Standard (10,24:42)

Nutrition 21, supplement manufacturer, Press Release, 1010 Turquoise Street, Suite 335, San Diego, Calif. 92109

Nutrition Action Health Letter (20,7:8; 23,3:6; 23,4:10; and 23,7:10)

Nutrition and Cancer (17,1:57; 22,2:101; 23,3:247; and 25,1:71)

Nutrition Forum (8,3:23 and 11,6:53)

Nutrition Reports International (33:419)

Nutrition Research Newsletter (11,2:22; 11,3:29; 12,3:25,33; 12,5:56; 14,1:9,10; 14,2:18,20,25,28; 14,3:40; 14,6:71,74; 14,7/8:86,Y89; 14,10:112; 15,1:7; 15,2:13; 15,4:46; 15,6:63; 15,7/8:82; 15,10:104)

Nutrition Reviews (52,2:S53; 54,4:S3,S37; 54,6:178,185; 54,7:213; 54,8:225)

Nutrition Today (28,1:25; 28,3:19; 28,6:34; 29,4:28; 30,2:52; and 30,3:112)

Nutrition: Incredible, Edible Soybeans. Your Health Daily. Cynthia Washam. Internet WWW page <http://nytsyn.com/live/nutrition/270_092696_172019_9605.html>

Nutritional Intervention in the Aging Process, Springer-Verlag New York, Inc.

Osteoporosis Research, Education and Health Promotion, U.S. Department of Health and Human Services, Public Health Service, National Institutes of Health, NIH Publication No. 91-3216, Bethesda, Md.

Patient Care (24:85 and 28:130)

Perspectives in Applied Nutrition (2,3:9)

Pharmacopsychiatry (27,4:147)

Pharmacy Times (61,10:73; 61,11:50; 62,1:6,77; and 62,8:67)

Photochemical Photobiology (58,2:304)

Planta Medica (52,1985:62)

Postgraduate Medical Journal (64:841)

Postgraduate Medicine (93,8:43; 98,1:175; and 98,2:185)

Present Knowledge in Nutrition, ILSI Press, Washington

Proceedings of the 55th Flax Institute of the United States

Prostaglandins, Leukotrienes, and Medicine (25:187)

Psychology Medicine (26,2:245)

Psychology Today (23,2:62; 27,4:38; and 29,3:34)

Psychosomatics (33,1:117)

Recommended Dietary Allowances, National Academy of Sciences, National Academy Press, Washington, D.C.

Redbook (182,3:42)

Relf, Paula Diane. Virginia Cooperative Extension. Internet WWW page <http://www.ext.vt.edu>

RN (59,5:31)

Science News (134,10:155; 142,5:79; 144,13:196,198; 145,12:190; 145,25:390; 147,25:391; 149,8:116; and 149,23:365)

Scientific American (267,6:130; 273,3:135; and 274,1:46)

Scientific American Medicine Bulletin (XVIII,8:4)

Secrets of Better Sex, Parker Publishing Co., West Nyack, N.Y.

Secrets of the World's Oldest Man. WWW page <http://www.all-natural.com/oldest.html>

Self-Help & Psychology. Edward A. Dreyfus, M.D. Internet WWW page <http://cybertowers.com/selfhelp/articles/health/stress2.html>

Sexuality in Later Life. National Institute on Aging Age Page. Internet WWW page <http://www.nih.gov/nia/health/pubpub/sexual.htm>

Shape Up America, News Release, C. Everett Koop Foundation

Sleep (13,4:354 and 16,2:128)

Southern Medical Journal (97,5:S54)

Spontaneous Healing, Alfred A. Knopf, New York

Stopping the Clock, Keats Publishing Inc., New Canaan, Conn.

Stroke (27,3:401)

Super Healing Foods, Parker Publishing Co., West Nyack, N.Y.

Taber's Cyclopedic Medical Dictionary, F.A. Davis Co., Philadelphia

Tai Chi, Stanley Paul & Co. Ltd, London

Tea Facts, Internet WWW page <http://www.stashtea.com/facts.htm>

The American Journal of Clinical Nutrition (39,5:756; 49,1:112; 49,4:675; 53,1:326S; 53,1S:270S; 53,3:702; 53,4S:1050S; 54,1S:193S; 54,3:438; 54,5:909,915; 54,6S:1310S; 57,4:557,566; 58,3:385; 58,5:690; 60,4:510,573,619; 60,5:419; 61,1:62; 61,2:353; 61,3S:621S,625S,638S; 61,5:1140; 62,4:740; 62,5:897,1003; 62,6S:1381S,1448S; 63,1:72; 63,3:354; and 63,6:954)

The American Journal of Medicine (95,4:377)

The American Medical Association Encyclopedia of Medicine, Random House, New York

The American Medical Association Family Medical Guide, Random House, New York

The Atlanta Journal/Constitution

The Big Book of Health Tips, FC&A Publishing, Peachtree City, Ga.

The Clinical Investigator (71:60,116,145,383)

The Columbia University College of Physicians & Surgeons Complete Home Medical Guide, Crown Publishers, Inc., New York

The Consumer's Good Chemical Guide, W.H. Freeman and Company, Ltd., New York

The Cooper Aerobics Center, 12200 Preston Road, Dallas, TX 75230

The Creative Glow newsletter, P.O. Box 1310, Boston, MA 02117

The Diabetic's Book, G.P. Putnam's Sons, New York

The Doctor's Complete Guide to Vitamins and Minerals, Bantam Doubleday Dell Publishing, New York

The Estrogen Decision, Westchester Publishing Co., Los Altos, Calif.

The FASEB Journal (9:1643)

The Good Herb, William Morrow and Co., Inc., New York

The Honest Herbal, The Haworth Press, Binghamton, N.Y.

The John Hopkins Medical Letter (5,2:8 and 5,8:4)

The Journal of Nutrition (122,2:312; 122,3S:604,766,796; 123,1:13; 123,4:626; 123,9:1623; 123,10:1649; 124,5:655; 124,8S:1406S,1418S,1426S; 125,3S:733S; 125,4:1003; and 125,10:2511)

The Journal of the American Medical Association (270,22:2693,2726; 273,3:199; 273,14:1093; 273,15:1179; 273,20:1561; 273,21:1699,1703; 273,23: 1849; 273,24:1965; 274,17:1328,1363; 274,21:1683,1718; 275,6:447, 486; 275,17:1315; 275,18:1389,1405,1447; 275,20:1590; 275,24: 1893,1929; 276,4:313; 276,12:989,1011; and 276,17:1365, 1389, 1397,1404,1430)

The Joy of Cooking, The Blakiston Company, Philadelphia

The Lancet (2,8666:757; 336,8710:261; 340,8828:1136; 341,8849:888; 342,8871:578; 342,8881:1209; 343,8889:87; 343,8901:807,816; 343,8911:1479; 345,8943:170; 345,8951:669; 345,8962:1408; 346, 8967:85; 346,8969:207; 346,8974:541; 346,8984:1194; 347,8995: 184; 347,9004:781; 347,9012:1351; 348,9021:184; 348,9025:429; and 348,9033:969,1019)

The Lawrence Review of Natural Products, Facts and Comparisons, St. Louis, Mo.

The Merck Manual, 16th edition, Merck Research Laboratories, Rahway, N.J.

The New England Journal of Medicine (315,24:1519; 323,24:1664; 327,23:1637; 328,20:1444,1450; 330,25:1769; 332,5:287; 332,24:1589; 333,5:276; 333,10:609; 334,2:99; 334,7:413; 334,12:759; 334,14:873,913; 334,18:1150,1156; and 334,20:1298)

The Nutrition Superbook: Volume I: The Antioxidants, Keats Publishing, New Canaan, Conn.

The Physician and Sportsmedicine (20,4:51; 22,8:30; 22,12:21; 23,6:13; 23,9:97; 23,11:17,109; 24,2:45,72; 24,4:18a; 24,6:101; 24,7:30; and 24,8:21)

The Real Vitamin and Mineral Book, Avery Publishing Group, Garden City Park, N.Y.

The Saturday Evening Post (267,3:40; 267,4:14,20; 267,6:22; and 268,2:16)

The Sciences (35,5:26)

The Scientific Validation of Herbal Medicine, Keats Publishing, New Canaan, Conn.

The Shuteye News (1,1:3 and 1,2:3)

The Simple Soybean and Your Health, Avery Publishing Group, Garden City Park, N.Y.

The Universal Almanac, Andrews and McMeel, Kansas City, Mo.

The USP Guide to Vitamins and Minerals, Avon Books, New York

The Wellness Encyclopedia, Houghton Mifflin Company, Boston

Time (138,24:66)

Total Health (15,1:26; 15,2:53; 16,1:42; 17,1:48; and 18,4:30,38)

Townsend Letter for Doctors

Toxicology (105,2:267)

Tufts University Diet and Nutrition Letter (13,8:4; 14,2:3; and 14,8:1)

U.S. Department of Agriculture News Release Number 0460.96

U.S. News and World Report (109:76)

U.S. Pharmacist (18:9:100; 19,9:Supplement; 21,5:19; 21,6:12,72; 21,7:18; and 21,9:Supplement)

University of California at Berkeley Wellness Letter (12,1:4 and 13,1:7)

USA Today (125,2617:7)

Vegetarian Times (145:5; 156:6; 164:62; 225:4; and 229:66)

Vibrant Life (12,5:30)

Vitamin C, the Common Cold and the Flu, Berkley Books, New York

Vitamins and Minerals: Help or Harm?, J.B. Lippincott Company, Philadelphia

Whole Foods

Women's Edge Home Page. Internet WWW page
  <http:www.prev.com/house/tea/ginger.html>

Women's Sports and Fitness (15,2:25 and 17,1:45)

Wood, Steven, et al., "B-Carotene and Selenium Supplementation Enhance Immune Response in Aged Humans." Ph.D. diss, University of Arizona

World Review of Nutrition and Diet (64,1:1)

Yogurt, Yoghurt, Youghourt: An International Cookbook, Food Products Press, Binghamton, N.Y.

Z Gerontology (19,3:206)

INDEX

A

Adaptogen, 245
Aerobic exercise
  for depression, 298–299
Aging
  antioxidants and, 7–8
  cross-linking theory of, 11
  defined, 4
  eternal youth and, 1–3
  free radical theory of, 6–8
  genetics and, 13–16
AIDS
  green tea and, 141
  mistletoe and, 28
Alcoholism
  vitamin C and, 160
Allergies
  vitamin C for, 157
Allicin, 89, 95
Alzheimer's disease
  aspirin to prevent, 209
  calcium and, 47
  DHEA (dehydroepiandrosterone) and,
    224
  estrogen to prevent, 265
  gingko to prevent, 237–238
  melatonin and, 273
  vitamin B12 and, 37
Anemia
  zinc for, 201
Angina
  vitamin C for, 158
Antacids
  chromium and, 61
Anti-aging, benefits of
  antioxidants, 8–12
  aspirin, 208–209
  B vitamins, 36–39
  calcium, 44–48
  caloric restriction, 289–290
  cartilage, 213–214
  chromium, 56–60
  CoQ10 (Coenzyme Q10), 218–219
  DHEA (dehydroepiandrosterone),
    222–224
  echinacea, 227–230
  exercise, 294–300

fiber, 65–70
fish oil, 78–80
flaxseed, 84–86
garlic, 89–92
ginger, 98–101, 103–104
gingko, 235–241
ginseng, 245, 247–248, 250–251
glutathione, 257–258
hormone replacement therapy (HRT),
  263–266
low-fat living, 311–317
low-salt diet, 324–326
magnesium, 110–112
melatonin, 272–274, 276
PCO (Pycnogenol), 280–283
potassium, 118–119
selenium, 124–127
sex, 329–330
sleep, 337–339
soy, 131–134
stress-free living, 348–351
tea, 140–142
vitamin A, 147–151
vitamin C, 156–161
vitamin D, 166–168
vitamin E, 172–175
water, 179–182
yogurt, 190–194
zinc, 199–202
Antioxidants
  anti-aging benefits of, 8–12
  in garlic, 92
  major types of, 7
  tea and, 144
Aphrodisiacs
  ginseng, 251
  oysters, 201
Apnea, sleep, 338
Appendicitis
  fiber intake and, 68
Arrhythmia
  melatonin for, 274
Arthritis
  antioxidants for, 9
  aspirin for, 209
  cartilage for, 214
  echinacea for, 227–228
  estrogen for, 265–266